Freedom Seekers

Escaping from Slavery in Restoration London

Simon P. Newman

LONDON
INSTITUTE OF HISTORICAL RESEARCH
UNIVERSITY OF LONDON PRESS

Published by

UNIVERSITY OF LONDON
SCHOOL OF ADVANCED STUDY
INSTITUTE OF HISTORICAL RESEARCH
Senate House, Malet Street, London WC1E 7HU

ISBNs
978-1-912702-93-0 (paperback)
978-1-912702-94-7 (.pdf)
978-1-914477-24-9 (.epub)

DOI: 10.14296/202202.9781912702947

Contents

List of illustrations

Table

This compelling book shows us Restoration London, but not as we know it. The book is a restoration in many senses: of dignity and of global context to the world of Samuel Pepys and the Great Fire. Simon Newman humanizes those who were dehumanized by people who saw them as their property. Amongst the pages of this compassionate, evidence-based masterpiece, readers will discover the stories of freedom-seeking enslaved people in familiar places all over London, from Aldgate, Covent Garden and Greenwich to Fleet Street, Wapping and the East End. Through painstaking archival work these lives have been impressively reconstructed and reimagined, all underpinned by archival and interpretative rigour.

—Professor Corinne Fowler, Director of Colonial
Countryside: National Trust Houses Reinterpreted

There has long been a popular assumption that English slavery was a colonial phenomenon, alien to the liberty-loving peoples residing in the British Isles. Newman turns that notion inside out. His painstaking research and luminous interpretation reveal a community of enslaved Black people in Restoration England, yearning to escape. Evocative prose and interactive illustrations enable us to imagine their flights on the streets of London, and also to perceive the arterial network of enslavers, merchants, investors, ship captains and printers, who devised a novel way to repossess them: the runaway slave advertisement. Fashioned in the cradle of the liberal ideal, this artefact of business news would become one of the most iconic and tyrannical innovations of the age of empire and enslavement – and the clearest lasting proof of the countervailing will to freedom.

—Vincent Brown, author of *Tacky's Revolt:
The Story of an Atlantic Slave War*

Brimming with revelations at every turn, Freedom Seekers reorders our understanding of the making of racial slavery, finding the early traces of British exploitation of Black people in the streets, squares, lanes and alleyways of the expanding metropolis. Restoration London may have been far from the plantation horrors of the empire in the Caribbean but it contained the same forces of human abuse. Simon Newman gives us a new way of seeing British slavery, one in which Black and Asian captives risked their lives for freedom across the Atlantic and on both sides of the Thames.

With prodigious research into decades of newspaper advertisements of 'runaways', illuminating story-telling, copious illustrations and, most of all, sensitive attention to the humans hidden in print, this book is powerful proof that racial slavery in British history has never ever been only a colonial matter.

—Matthew J. Smith, Director, Centre for the Study
of the Legacies of British Slavery, UCL

About the author

Simon P. Newman is an Emeritus Professor of History at the University of Glasgow and is currently a research fellow at the Institute for Research in the Humanities at the University of Wisconsin. He has published widely on early modern Atlantic World and American/Caribbean history. His most recent book *A New World of Labor: The Development of Plantation Slavery in the British Atlantic* (2013) investigated the English and West African origins of plantation slavery in Barbados and beyond. Over the past decade he has been investigating enslaved people who resisted by escaping, both in the Caribbean and the British Isles, resulting in articles in the *English Historical Review* and the *William and Mary Quarterly*, and a major database *Runaway Slaves in Britain: bondage, freedom and race in the eighteenth century*. He has also worked with playwrights, film-makers, creative writers, composers and others in Britain who are presenting this history to broad public audiences. In 2018 he commissioned and helped create the graphic novel *Freedom Bound: Escaping Slavery in Scotland* which is now being used in schools across Scotland. In the same year he co-authored the University of Glasgow's report into its links to slavery, and helped create the reparative justice programme that followed.

A note on language

Just four months after the fall of the Confederacy and the symbolic end of slavery in the United States, a convention of formerly enslaved people met in Alexandria, Virginia, to draft a statement in favour of equal treatment for all people regardless of race. While debating what wording to use the delegates agreed to an amendment proposed by William E. Walker of Petersburg 'where the expression in the address read[s] – "our former masters". Walker Proposed that the word "masters" be stricken out and the words "our former oppressors" be substituted therefor.' Walker and the delegates understood all too well that the word 'master' encapsulated and legitimated the aspirations and values of the class of White men who had held them in bondage, and that it did so without in any way acknowledging as immoral and inhuman the ownership and brutalization of enslaved people upon which mastery had rested. The words used to describe enslavers and enslaved mattered, and Walker and his colleagues were determined to delegitimate two centuries of language that had normalized racial slavery.[1]

It is essential that historians heed Walker's call and carefully consider the language that we use to describe slavery, the enslaved and those who enslaved them. If we reproduce the language found in sources created by early modern White men and women we risk inadvertently echoing the racist assumptions of those who created and perpetuated racial slavery while dehumanizing the people who were enslaved. Thus, for example, to refer to one person as a 'slave' and another as a 'master' may be to use the terminology found in early modern documents, but these terms potentially reinscribe and implicitly normalize the notion of a legally sanctioned social system in which some people were chattel owned by other people. In this book I shall try to avoid such language, although I will use the word 'master' because in Restoration London this word was not racialized in the way that it was in the colonies. This can be seen clearly in such sources as the Old Bailey Proceedings, which contain a detailed record of court cases in the capital during the last quarter of the seventeenth century. These records demonstrate that employers, businessmen and women, and heads of households were commonly referred

---

[1] *Liberty and Equality before the Law: Proceedings of the Convention of Colored People of VA., Held in the City of Alexandria, Aug. 2, 3, 4, 5, 1865* (Alexandria, Va., 1865), p. 10. See also 'The Afterlife of Slavery: Language & Ethics', compiled by L. S. Autry, Wakelet, July 2018 <https://wakelet.com/wake/f589cdc4-7512-43ff-a489-5ed48062179f> [accessed 17 March 2021].

to as masters and mistresses by London's tens of thousands of White servants, maids, apprentices and employees.[2] Thus both White and Black workers, whether employees or enslaved, referred to those who controlled their labour as master or mistress, and so these words were not freighted with the overtones of racial dominance implied by the term 'master' on plantations in the colonies. While London's enslaved experienced very different lives from the city's White population, the words 'master' and 'mistress' are not key to understanding those differences.

The words 'boy' and 'girl' were equally pervasive in Restoration London and were regularly used by employers and enslavers to refer to young working people regardless of their race and status. In the colonies the terms 'boy' and 'girl' could carry racist and derogatory meanings when used by enslavers to refer to enslaved children and adults. Once again, however, the Old Bailey records reveal that these terms were used by Londoners to refer to young people of all races.[3] Moreover, regardless of their race, the young males who attended ships' officers were commonly referred to as cabin boys: thus a White 'Cabin-boy' appears in the opening scene of John Dryden's play *The Tempest*, while the *Gloria Britannica* detailed the pay and conditions of Royal Navy sailors 'from a Captain to a Cabin-Boy'.[4] Newspaper advertisements seeking young White apprentices, servants and maids contained the terms 'boy' and 'girl' as frequently as did advertisements for freedom-seeking people of colour. It was not the words 'boy' or 'girl' that defined the enslaved status

[2] Thus eg these records describe 'William Bosham, a Negro' as 'a Servant to Esq, Russel' (William Bosham, Theft, 10 Dec. 1684: Ref. t16841210-22), but then contain a great many more references to White employees and employers using similar terms. Examples include 'Robert Rouse a Sailor' accused of theft from 'the Master' of the ship on which he served (Theft, 28 Feb. 1681: Ref. t16810228-4); 'one Rookewood Servant to one Mr. Rowland Lee' ('Rookewood', Theft, 15 Jan. 1675: Ref. t16750115-2); a 'young fellow' accused of 'breaking open the house of a worthy Gentleman his late Master' (Theft, 13 Dec. 1676: Ref. t16761213-7); 'A wench coming to Service by Newgate street … takes her opportunity in her Master's and Mistrisses absence to steal a silver Tankard' (Theft, 16 May 1678: Ref. t16780516-4); and 'Ann Terry, [who] was Tried for Robbing her Mistress' (Theft, 26 April 1693: Ref. t16930426-82). See The Proceedings of the Old Bailey: London's Central Criminal Court, 1674 to 1913 <https://www.oldbaileyonline.org/forms/formMain.jsp> [accessed 15 March 2021]. All dates in this book are New Style (NS).

[3] See eg a 'Boy about Twelve Years of Age, newly come to be an Apprentice at a Shop in Fleet street' ('Killing', 28 June 1676: Ref. t16760628-4); 'A boy not above eleven years old being sent by a Gentle man in his Masters house up stairs' (Killing, 11 July 1677: Ref. t16770711-6); and 'John Redhall, a Boy about 15 Years of Age' (John Redhall, Killing', 13 Oct. 1686: Ref. t16861013-9). See Proceedings of the Old Bailey.

[4] J. Dryden, *The Tempest; or, The Enchanted Island* (London, 1670), p. 1; *Gloria Britannica; or, The Boast of the Brittish Seas … with every Man's Pay, from a Captain to a Cabin-Boy* (London, 1689).

that these freedom seekers sought to escape. In seventeenth-century London words such as 'servant', 'master', 'boy' and 'girl' related more to class than to race. I shall therefore continue to use words such as 'boy', 'girl' and 'master', suitably contextualized, but I shall endeavour to illuminate the conditions in which enslaved Black Londoners lived without echoing the racist attitudes and beliefs of those who held them in bondage.

Other words and terms are altogether more problematic, and finding new and unproblematic language is challenging for it requires that we jettison words such as 'slave', 'slave-holder', 'slave-owner' and even 'planter' to refer to people owning and exploiting enslaved people. I shall use the word 'enslaver' in some cases, for it conveys the sense that a White person who sought to retain control of an enslaved person was continually and actively working to maintain the bondage of the enslaved person. When using the words 'White' or 'Black' to refer to a person's race and ethnicity I shall follow the increasingly common practice of capitalizing the terms.[5]

Of course, many words that appear problematic today were used in the seventeenth and eighteenth centuries and will inevitably appear in primary sources quoted in the text. But they carry too much racist baggage for historians to use them in their own writing today, and readers deserve a text that tries to identify the beliefs and actions of those who enslaved people of colour without echoing the words and assumptions buried within them that were foundational to racism and racial slavery.[6] I shall do my best to use language that acknowledges the freedom-seeking people of colour whom I have researched and written about as human beings, and those who held them in various forms of slavery and bondage as their oppressors.

---

[5] On the adoption of this practice in popular and academic writing see eg N. Coleman, 'Why we're capitalizing Black', *New York Times*, 5 July 2020 <https://www.nytimes.com/2020/07/05/insider/capitalized-black.html> [accessed 16 March 2021]; University of Chicago Press Editorial Staff, 'Black and White: a matter of capitalization', CMOS Shop Talk, 22 June 2020 <https://cmosshoptalk.com/2020/06/22/black-and-white-a-matter-of-capitalization> [accessed 16 March 2021].

[6] For examples of recent discussions of how best to address the language of slavery see J. M. Johnson, 'Markup bodies: Black [life] studies and slavery [death] studies at the digital crossroads', *Social Text*, xxxvi (2018), 57–79; K. Waldman, 'Slave or enslaved person? It's not just an academic debate for historians of American slavery', *Slate*, 19 May 2015 <https://slate.com/human-interest/2015/05/historians-debate-whether-to-use-the-term-slave-or-enslaved-person.html> [accessed 21 Feb. 2021]; P. G. Foreman et al., 'Writing about slavery? Teaching about slavery?' <https://naacpculpeper.org/resources/writing-about-slavery-this-might-help> [accessed 8 Sept. 2021]; B. L. Hylton, 'Why we must stop referring to enslaved people as "slaves"', Human Parts, 13 June 2020 <https://humanparts.medium.com/why-we-must-immediately-cease-and-desist-referring-to-enslaved-people-as-slaves-85b0ddfc5f7b> [accessed 8 March 2021].

Acknowledgements

Researching and writing this book felt like a homecoming. My parents were born and raised in the East End of London and during my childhood we regularly visited my grandparents in Stratford and Leytonstone. Moreover I have returned to seventeenth-century England, the subject that first drew me to the study of history. My interest was nurtured by my father and by two exceptional schoolteachers, the late Michael Thuell and John Tyson, both of St Joseph's College in Ipswich. By the time I reached Princeton my interests had shifted to seventeenth- and eighteenth-century North American history, but Lawrence Stone and John Murrin kept me interested in Stuart England, as did Richard S. Dunn at the University of Pennsylvania. The subject remained in focus during my tenure at the University of Glasgow through the great work of my colleagues in the Early Modern Work-in-Progress group, especially Alex Shepard, Don Spaeth and Lionel Glassey. Now, in the wake of my retirement from the University of Glasgow, I have come full circle and returned to the places and to the history that were so important to me nearly half a century ago.

I could not have researched and written this book without the resources and support of two remarkable institutions. The first is the Folger Institute of the Folger Shakespeare Library in Washington, D.C. I spent the 2018–19 academic year as a Mowat Mellon Fellow at the Folger and was able to complete much of the research while enjoying access to the library's magnificent collections. The research community at the Folger is wonderful and I am especially grateful to Amanda Herbert, Kathleen Lynch and Michael Witmore, as well as my cohort of fellows. While in Washington I was fortunate to be able to spend time with Alison Games, whom I first met when we were both starting our doctoral studies, and I am deeply grateful for her friendship and good cheer. I then spent the 2019–20 academic year as a Solmsen Fellow at the Institute for Research in the Humanities at the University of Wisconsin–Madison. This is a different kind of academic heaven, a group of humanities scholars all researching, writing and sharing ideas. Steve Nadler and Ann Harris have created a wonderful community, and I have been fortunate to remain in residence at the institute as an honorary fellow. The pandemic and politics threatened to derail this project but a supportive virtual writing group at the IRH helped me get through this: Andrea Harris, Laura McClure, Keren Omry, Jennifer Ratner-Rosenhagen, Cherene Sherrard and Justine Walden have all become good friends, and their support and encouragement has made a huge difference. As I was completing the rewriting and editing of this book I was fortunate to participate in a virtual coffee house (organized by the Omohundro Institute for Early American History and Culture) for writers focused on the lives of enslaved people. My co-host of our coffee-house table was Frances Bell and I am grateful to her and to the other participants for their insights, their enthusiasm and their good cheer.

I have been working on freedom-seeking enslaved people for quite a long time now, and a few scholars have added immeasurably to my knowledge and understanding of those who resisted enslavement. Foremost among these is my friend Billy G. Smith, a wonderful scholar and an even better human being, and I owe him more than I can ever repay. I am also very grateful to my colleagues on the Leverhulme Trust-funded project 'Runaway Slaves in Britain: Bondage, Freedom and Race in the Eighteenth Century'. Stephen Mullen, Nelson Mundell and Roslyn Chapman have all helped shape my thinking about runaways, and I am particularly grateful to Nelson for all of his creative work on freedom seekers.

Over recent years I have been fortunate to work with artists, writers and cultural creators on the history of freedom seekers in early modern Britain. I have learned a great deal from these wonderfully creative people who take these histories to heart and do so well in bringing them to life for non-academic audiences. The actors and filmmakers Moyo Akandé and Morayo Akandé, the playwright May Sumbwanyambe and the graphic artists Warren Pleece and Sha Nazir are among those who have helped me imagine and understand the past in new ways, and I am tremendously grateful to them. With my Glasgow colleague Peggy Brunache, my friend Kate Birch (publisher of Ink Sweat & Tears) and Ruth Harrison (director of Spread the Word), I have developed my research into London freedom seekers for use by creative writers and artists of colour in London, and again I have learned a great deal in the process. One of these poems, by Abena Essah, sets the scene for this book, and I am grateful for the opportunity to feature this remarkable poem here. Most important of all is Anthony King, my friend since we first met at the age of ten. He is a skilled graphic designer who has helped me with some of the video maps in this book, but more than that he has enabled me to see how the visualization of historical data can yield new insights.

I presented earlier versions of part of this project to the scholarly communities at the Folger Institute, the Institute for Research in the Humanities, the Early Modern Work-in-Progress group at the University of Glasgow, a virtual coffee-house writing table organized by the Omohundro Institute of Early American History and Culture, and the McNeil Center for Early American Studies at the University of Pennsylvania. Thank you to

Acknowledgements

all who have provided feedback, including the anonymous readers of this work. I am particularly grateful to Philip Carter, whose initial enthusiasm for my project has helped make this book possible. The Institute of Historical Research is at the forefront of digital historical publications and I am very grateful for all that they have done to help make this a better book, especially Jamie Bowman, Robert Davies and Lauren De'ath. I particularly appreciate the skilled copy-editing of Jacqueline Harvey.

I am grateful to the many historians of slavery whose friendship and scholarship have helped and inspired me. There are too many to mention but an abbreviated list must include Trevor Burnard and Richard Dunn, as well as Roderick McDonald, Jennifer Morgan, Vincent Brown, James Sweet, Marisa Fuentes, Lissa Bollettino, Hilary Beckles, Gloria Whiting, Christine Whyte and Peggy Brunache. Peter Elmer provided me with data from his research into London's parish records, and Laurence Ward of the London Metropolitan Archives kindly shared data from the 'Switching the Lens' dataset. Jason McElligott shared primary sources and drafts of his unpublished work on mid-seventeenth-century newsbooks. I am particularly grateful to Mr Tony Berrett for sharing his notes of advertisements I had yet to locate.

I thank all of my family members for their interest, support and encouragement, and I am especially grateful to my niece Triona Lawrence, who produced illustrations of the freedom seekers whose stories I have focused on, helping me to see the people I was writing about. And then there is Marina Moskowitz, one of the most imaginative historians I have ever met. She supports, encourages and inspires me, and I am incomplete without her love and friendship, our shared laughter, cooking and so much more. This book is for her.

Figure 1. Wenceslaus Hollar, 'London: The Long View' (1647), Folger Shakespeare Library.

Escape Route

Abena Essah

Mile End, 23rd December 1686

My Kwabena's lips are warm
his back against the brick

gold glow pulsing from the Ball
outlines the full of his bottom lip

muffled music, black folk and
swing dancing keep us company

hand tracing his neck
like that day thigh to thigh in March

teaching his hands to stretch to my native God
Olodumare; Ashe flows endless within us

our bodies, formless and fluid
limbs hot, our beards meshing

Kwabena recalled his Maame lifting and
pounding bankye and brodeε

fufuo steaming with fish and soup
his hands scouping mouthful after mouthful.

Now he pulls at my tongue with his teeth sharp
I can tell when he remembers, a hunger to his pace;

the purpling of his skin, the pounding
siblings screaming at sea, thrown overboard.

Now, I wrap my arms around the future of him
'The whole of London will be looking for you Tobi'

he is whispering, like that first day at the piers
his hand, grabbing my leg in the shadow

of the street corner; my arms are hauling
crates of Woodfine's food,

brass choking my throat.
Kwabena had known them once

the routes I dragged my body along
so he never looked away.

Here cheek to cheek we know,
we cannot give each other our Mother's back

our tongues do not fold the same syllables
but we can name each other

Goude to Oluwuatobi
Unnamed to Akan

Woodfine cannot find us here

© Abena Essah 2021. 'Escape Route' was commissioned by Spread the Word, Ink Sweat & Tears and the University of Glasgow and was published with other creative work inspired by research into London's freedom seekers in F. Al-Amoudi and K. Birch, eds., *Runaways London: For the enslaved freedom-seekers of the 17th and 18th centuries* (London, 2021), pp. 49–50.

Prologue: *Ben*

He knew the way.[1] Walking quickly but quietly along Pancras Lane, Ben passed the ruins of St Pancras, weeds growing around the tumbled stones still black from the fire that had destroyed the church years before he was born. He continued walking along Bucklers Berry. It was a bright spring day, yet Pancras Lane and Bucklers Berry were shadowy and gloomy: these streets were narrow and each ascending storey of the buildings on either side of him jutted further out over the street, blocking all but a little natural light. When he looked up, only a narrow strip of clouds and sky was visible, and sunlight illuminated the lower stories of these streets' buildings and the ground beneath his feet for only a brief period in the early morning and mid-afternoon when the sun shone down the length of the street. As he walked out of Bucklers Berry, the street broadened and became lighter and busier, and he turned left and headed northward into Stocks Market before turning east onto Lombard Street.

For more than a year Ben had served the successful merchant Theodore Johnson. He had accompanied Johnson around the city, carrying papers and delivering messages as Johnson arranged shipping, signed contracts and negotiated purchases and sales. Before he turned onto Lombard Street Ben saw crowds of people heading along Cornhill towards the Royal Exchange and he was tempted to join them. He had spent long hours attending or waiting for Johnson on the floor of the exchange and in the coffee houses

---

[1] Virtually all of the narrative of Ben and his bid for freedom is imagined, but it builds on documentary and visual records of London and its people during in this period and on records relating to Theodore Johnson and his community. We can never know Ben's life story, his experiences, his motivations or almost anything about him, yet deep and expansive historical research may enable us to imagine something of his lived experience. If we allow ourselves to imagine we may be able to see beyond the bare bones of the advertisements for London's bound and enslaved people of colour who eloped. This narrative is inspired by the work of scholars who have imaginatively sought to hear and give voice to those who are silent in the archives. See eg S. Hartman, *Lose your Mother: a Journey along the Atlantic Slave Route* (New York, 2007) and *Wayward Lives, Beautiful Experiments: Intimate Histories of Social Upheaval* (New York, 2019); M. J. Fuentes, *Dispossessed Lives: Enslaved Women, Violence, and the Archive* (Philadelphia, 2016); K. F. Hall, 'I can't love you the way you want me to: archival Blackness', *Postmedieval: a Journal of Medieval Cultural Studies*, xi (2020), 171–9; E. A. Dunbar, *Never Caught: the Washingtons' Relentless Pursuit of their Runaway Slave Ona Judge* (New York, 2017); B. G. Smith, *The 'Lower Sort': Philadelphia's Laboring People, 1750–1800* (Ithaca, NY, 1990), pp. 7–39; and C. Townsend, *Tales of Two Cities: Race and Economic Culture in Early Republican North and South America* (Austin, Tex., 2000), pp. 23–46.

nearby, all the time listening and learning. It was an exciting place, with shops filled with colourful goods and the likelihood of encountering other boys like himself. But he continued walking eastward, seeing Lloyd's coffee house on his right and Garraway's on his left, and there were small crowds of people buzzing around the other coffee shops of Exchange Alley. Johnson regularly met friends and colleagues in several of these establishments, sharing coffee and chocolate as he conducted his business. Ben increased his pace as he approached Bowman's, hoping to quickly pass by Johnson's favourite coffee house. He saw merchants and businessmen who traded with Johnson but lowered his eyes and looked downwards. This look was well practised: he hid his eyes, secreting himself and his feelings in a seemingly deferential act that protected him. Passing beyond Bowman's, Ben looked up and along Lombard Street, and glimpsed the Tower of London rising above the jumble of buildings. It was no more than a few hundred yards distant, and if the crowds thinned out he would soon walk around it, heading east towards his destination. But the streets were full of waves of people heading in different directions and his progress was slow.

The streets were as loud as they were busy. Above the constant hum of conversation, criers advertised their wares, a pieman here, a newspaperwoman there, an oyster seller across the street and so many more. Ben looked at the signs hanging from the buildings on either side of the street, bearing colourful images identifying the premises and sometimes the occupation of the inhabitants. As he passed one of them he felt his chest tighten. Hanging above the door swung a sign bearing an image of a young African, and it was known as the sign of the Black Boy. It marked the business of the banker Stephen Evance, and when Johnson visited Evance Ben had been ordered by his master to wait outside beneath the sign. On one visit Ben had been joined by another African boy, and while each of them waited for the men who claimed ownership of them they exchanged words quietly in English, for they spoke different African languages. Both were conscious of the sign of the Black Boy swinging above their heads but they acted as if it were not there, silently agreeing to ignore the image of a Black child like themselves. Both had experienced the trade in gold and people on the coast of West Africa, and for them the link between Evance's wealth and the sign above his business was personal.

As he passed by the sign Ben clutched in his hand a packet of papers secured by a ribbon. He held them tightly, making sure that everyone could see he was about Johnson's business. He held the documents as if his future depended upon them, and in a way it did: they were his passport, helping to protect him and giving him a reason to be out on the streets. Crossing Grace Church Street, he looked to his right down towards London Bridge but did not change direction, continuing along Fenchurch Street. He would keep to the north of the Tower, continuing his journey eastward.

He was not Ben.[2] He had been born among the Oyo people almost eighteen years earlier, but nobody here knew his Yoruba-language name. The slave-ship captain who had brought him up from the hold to serve as his cabin boy had named him Ben for the Bight of Benin where he had been brought aboard, and that was his name when he and the captain arrived in London from Jamaica. Ben was the person he had been forced to become. He had been in London for more than a year, most of it spent serving Johnson, who had purchased Ben from the ship captain in another of his coffee-house deals. Twice during the past year he had met other Igbo people and they had held short, whispered conversations in the language of their birth and had told one another their true names. But he spoke that language so rarely that he was now thinking in English and forgetting some of the words of his native language. He struggled to recall the faces of the people he had left behind: all that he had left from his life in Africa were fading memories and a name he kept to himself.

Ben's stilted English frustrated Johnson, yet the young man knew and spoke English better than Johnson suspected. He intended to use his knowledge of London, his smart clothing and his language skills to escape from Johnson. He had on several occasions accompanied Johnson east of the City out to Wapping and Ratcliff to meet with ship captains who were about to set sail on ships laden with goods belonging to Johnson. While Johnson spoke with these men in riverside taverns, Ben had spoken with others like himself and had learned about the small community of free Black people who lived and worked in the East End.

Johnson regularly sent Ben to deliver or collect documents and today was no different. Johnson had arranged to meet colleagues at the exchange and, Ben hoped, to follow his business there by spending hours socializing and gossiping in a coffee house. It might be evening before Johnson realized that Ben was missing, his errand unfulfilled. Although the streets were crowded, his destination was less than two miles from Johnson's home and, if fortune

---

[2] It is impossible to know precisely where Ben came from and how he came by this name. Between 1676 and 1700 we know the 'principal place of slave purchase' for 254 English ships: some 24% loaded their human cargo from the Bight of Benin, 16% from the Gold Coast, 12% from the Bight of Biafra, 11% from West Central Africa and St Helena, and 10% from Gambia, with smaller percentages from elsewhere. The Bight of Benin is therefore a more likely place of origin for Ben than any other location. It is possible that Ben was an anglicized version of an African name, but many of the recorded African names that might fit, such as Abenee, Abeney, Yarbene and Obenee, are female. See Slave Voyages: Trans-Atlantic Slave Trade – Database <https://www.slavevoyages.org/voyage/database> and Slave Voyages: African Names – Database <https://www.slavevoyages.org/resources/names-database> [accessed 12 March 2021].

favoured him, Ben could be there before anybody knew he was gone. If he could find shelter in the East End, he could be free – free of Johnson, free of the expensive uniform he wore and hoped to sell, and free of the name that was not his.

Ben began his journey to freedom late in the morning of 11 March 1686. He was absent for three days before Johnson acted, visiting Thomas Newcomb at his printing office in the Savoy. The following day the first and second pages of the *London Gazette* were filled with a proclamation by the new monarch, James II. Eight advertisements appeared on the third page of the newspaper, and Johnson's was sandwiched between one seeking the return of a mislaid white leather bag and another offering a reward for a spaniel lost near London Bridge.

> A Blackamoor Boy, call'd Ben, about 17 years old, middle sized, well set, some pockholes in his Face, having an old gray Camblet close-bodied Coat on, and a musk-coloured quilted Sattin Wastecost, and a black feather'd Cap flower'd with Gold and Silver, speaks English indifferent well, Run away from his Master Theodore Johnson Merchant, living in Pancridge Lane near Bucklers-berry, London, the 11th Instant. Whoever gives notice of him to his said Master, shall have a Guinea Reward.[3]

Newspaper advertisements like this are often the only surviving documentary evidence of the people who attempted escape, revealing little more than a few, sketchy details of freedom seekers whose interior lives are all but invisible. These fragments are inherently problematic sources, constructed by White men and women who controlled the definition of enslaved people within brief newspaper advertisements just as they asserted ownership and control over them in life. 'Runaway slave' advertisements rendered the people they described as property and as criminally fugitive: by their very nature, these advertisements became part of the process of the commodification and depersonalization of enslaved people. Historians today who collate and analyse these advertisements engage in an act of remediation that risks continuing the datafication of enslaved people.[4]

In Restoration London, enslavers and their associates are generally far easier to find in the archives, but while the enslavers come into focus the enslaved become increasingly indistinct. It is possible to build on contextual

---

[3] 'A Blackamoor Boy, call'd Ben', *The London Gazette*, 15 March 1686. All English newspapers cited in this work were published in London unless otherwise indicated. On occasion editors amended the titles of newspapers, and the first reference to a newspaper in each chapter will give the title in full as it appeared on the newspaper masthead on that publication date.

[4] J. M. Johnson, 'Markup bodies: Black [life] studies and slavery [death] studies at the digital crossroads', *Social Text*, xxxvi (2018), 57–79.

research to imagine aspects of the material circumstances of bound people in London, such as a liveried domestic servant in a wealthy merchant's household or an enslaved seafarer on an ocean-going trade ship. But how such people experienced their lives is another matter. How did they think and feel about their earlier lives in South Asia, Africa or the colonies, about the voyages that had brought them to England, about the people who now commanded their service and about London and the people who inhabited the city? And, if we cannot know the answers to these questions, to what degree can we imagine them? Can a historian imagine London's enslaved in a manner that transcends an archival record constructed by their enslavers? Perhaps the best we can do, treading carefully as we go, is to build from archival research to hint at possibilities, encouraging readers to imagine real people who remembered, who suffered, who ate, who slept, who laughed, who sang and who danced.

Early on the morning of Valentine's Day in 1661 Samuel Pepys called on Sir William Batten. Knocking on the door, Pepys jokingly enquired if it was a man or a woman who was unlocking the door to grant him entry. Presumably speaking in a deep and unmistakably male voice, Batten's enslaved servant Mingo responded with the words 'a woman', and both men laughed at a joke Pepys recorded in his diary. Mingo was an enslaved man working in the household of an elite government official, with perhaps little contact with people like himself. Yet he joked and laughed and, as Pepys recorded in other entries, sang and danced 'with a great deal of seeming skill'.[5] Runaway advertisements described and defined people in ways that denied their full humanity and agency, and it is essential that we allow ourselves to imagine the people behind the text. By imagining the full humanity of these freedom seekers, we refuse to be bound by an incomplete and biased archive that does little more than define these people by their enslaved status.[6]

In addition to locating and imagining freedom seekers in the history of Restoration London, this book will assess their significance in the larger history of racial slavery in the British Atlantic World. Historians have focused on the mid-seventeenth-century colonies, especially Barbados,

[5] *The Diary of Samuel Pepys: Daily Entries from the 17th Century London Diary*, 14 Feb. 1661; 27 March 1661 <https://www.pepysdiary.com/diary> [accessed 15 Feb. 2021]. Mingo almost certainly began as the enslaved property of Batten; at some point he was freed but was bound to continue serving Batten. By the time Batten died in 1667 Mingo was finally fully free; in his will Batten left Mingo £10 and a paid position as keeper of the Harwich Range Lighthouse, with an annual salary of £20. See Will of Sir William Batten, 22 Nov. 1667, National Archives, PROB 11/325/434.

[6] I am grateful to R. Browne, L. A. Lindsay and J. W. Sweet for this formulation in 'Rebecca's ordeal, from Africa to the Caribbean: sexual exploitation, freedom struggles, and Black Atlantic biography', a paper presented at the McNeil Center for Early American Studies, 12 Feb. 2021.

Virginia, Maryland, Jamaica and South Carolina, as the focal points for the institutionalization of racial slavery. Many scholars have assumed that White colonists enslaved West Africans and indigenous Americans beyond the oversight of an English government that was preoccupied with religious conflict, civil war and the Cromwellian Protectorate. English colonists, historians have argued, created not only a coercive labour system but also a complex legal system designed to subordinate people of colour while protecting White colonists from resistance and rebellion by the enslaved.[7]

But this interpretation has overlooked direct English involvement, on English soil, in the early development of racial slavery. From the mid seventeenth century onwards planters, merchants, military officers, ship captains and other English men and women brought enslaved people to London, many of them children. Some of these enslaved people resisted by attempting to escape, and a few of the enslavers who claimed them responded by publishing newspaper advertisements describing the freedom seekers and offering rewards to anyone who could provide information leading to the recapture of the runaway. These were some of the very first advertisements to appear in London's (and England's) earliest newspapers, appearing alongside notices offering property, goods and especially books or livestock for sale, or seeking the return of lost or stolen goods.

Seventeenth-century London's runaway slave advertisements reveal a network of merchants, ship captains, wealthy investors and others who were all to varying degrees engaged in the creation of both the transatlantic slave trade and colonial plantation slavery. As these short newspaper notices make clear, their engagement extended to a clear desire to establish and protect racial bondage within London and England, and an enthusiasm to make use of the new print media to lay claim to ownership of people of colour who resisted by escaping. As such the runaway advertisements published in seventeenth-century London functioned as an assertion by enslavers of the legitimacy of their status as legal owners of enslaved people.

---

[7] My own work is part of this historiography, and in *A New World of Labor: the Development of Plantation Slavery in the British Atlantic* (Philadelphia, 2013) I argued that plantation slavery was developed in Barbados, from the mid 17th century onwards, beyond the oversight of the English government. R. S. Dunn made a similar argument in *Sugar and Slaves: the Rise of the Planter Class in the English West Indies, 1624–1713* (Chapel Hill, N.C., 1972), suggesting that slavery developed 'Beyond the Line' (ch. 1) of English and European law and convention. See also I. Berlin, *Many Thousands Gone: the First Two Centuries of Slavery in North America* (Cambridge, Mass., 1998); D. Eltis, *The Rise of African Slavery in the Americas* (Cambridge, Mass., 2000); M. Guasco, *Slaves and Englishmen: Human Bondage in the Early Modern Atlantic World* (Philadelphia, 2014); R. R. Menard, *Sweet Negotiations: Sugar, Slavery and Plantation Agriculture in Early Barbados* (Charlottesville, Va., 2006); E. S. Morgan, *American Slavery, American Freedom: the Ordeal of Colonial Virginia* (New York, 1975).

While colonists in the Caribbean and Chesapeake were developing both plantation slavery and the legal foundations upon which it relied, enslavers in London were likewise engaged in making slavery real and in developing a system to recapture any bound people in the capital who dared challenge their status by escaping. The creation of the runaway slave advertisement in London provides telling evidence of a much deeper and more direct English engagement in the construction of racial slavery than historians have appreciated. Racial slavery was being created simultaneously in London and in the colonies, and the development of runaway slave advertisements as a response to this form of slave resistance was actually a London creation.

Yet, if London's early runaway slave advertisements display enslavers' efforts at control, and if they represent a key part of the process of objectification of the enslaved, they simultaneously and necessarily reveal the insurgency and attempts at self-determination of the bound and enslaved. By definition these advertisements reveal resistance to bondage and assertions of individuality and agency; in a very real way these short newspaper notices were the creation as much of freedom seekers as of masters and mistresses, as narratives of agency and escape.[8] Some of these advertisements offer remarkable detail, from place of origin in Africa or South Asia to physical characteristics and mannerisms, to linguistic ability and workplace skills, to the clothing worn by a freedom seeker. However, the few dozen words of each advertisement were those of an enslaver (or the head of household or employer if the person was in a liminal state between slavery and the service of employed free people) asserting legal control of the freedom seeker, defying his or her agency by defining the freedom seeker by their bound status, the clothing they were required to wear, and more often than not a single name that had been imposed upon them. These advertisements reveal the constructions and understandings of freedom seekers by those who wrote these short notices: the words, the experiences, the motivations, the hopes and dreams of the freedom seekers themselves are largely absent from the archival record, and it requires contextual research and more than a little imagination to see the freedom seekers as individuals rather than as objects.

How, then, can we reimagine these people as present and significant in Restoration London, and what kind of reconceptualization of the historical urban setting is necessary? How must we change the ways in which we see, hear and experience seventeenth-century London to become more aware of bound and free people of colour as present and as actors – as well as people

---

[8] A. T. Bly, '"Indubitable signs": reading silence as *text* in New England runaway slave advertisements', *Slavery & Abolition*, xlii (2021), 240–68.

acted upon – in the story of the creation of racial slavery in England and the colonies? And how do we build from these individuals to an understanding of what their collective presence meant for the history of racial slavery, and the history of London and England more broadly? This book represents an attempt to at least partially answer these questions. The advertisements, analysed together, offer a collective picture of those who eloped, their origins, ages and gender, and what they looked like, what they sounded like and what they wore. Together these freedom seekers may embody the many others like them who lived, worked and died in Restoration London but who did not attempt to escape or who were not the subject of advertisements. While the lived experiences of each individual remains elusive, it is possible to gain some sense of them as a community.

The first three chapters situate freedom seekers in the larger contexts of seventeenth-century London's growing population of enslaved, bound and free people of colour; the rapidly growing city and its role as the hub of a fast-growing empire encompassing trade with South Asia, the transatlantic slave trade and the development of colonial plantation slavery; the commercial venues of the City of London and the maritime and mercantile communities hugging both banks of the Thames to the east of the City; and the development of newspapers and the advertisements they contained. The bulk of the book is then devoted to twelve shorter chapters, each of which explores a certain category or characteristic of the freedom seekers as they appeared in the newspaper advertisements. Each of these chapters begins with an advertisement and explores what we can know of the individual detailed in that short newspaper notice.

Given that surviving records tell us rather more about enslavers and their community than about the enslaved, this book also seeks to illuminate how those who owned bound people of colour in Restoration London were constructing and defending racial slavery in the metropole. The chapters focused on freedom seekers thus include consideration of the community of merchants, sea captains, investors and wealthy Londoners who owned enslaved people and who acted together to protect their right to own human property by developing and deploying runaway advertisements in the city's newspapers.

The book concludes with two chapters and an epilogue exploring how during these same years racial slavery was taking shape in the Caribbean and American colonies, and how colonial assemblies designed legal mechanisms to punish resistance and escape. Half a century after the first runaway advertisement had appeared in a London newspaper, colonial presses began publishing newspapers containing runaway notices, and over the next century and a half tens of thousands of these advertisements were published in Caribbean and North American newspapers. These runaway advertisements constitute an invaluable resource for studying the most widespread and pervasive form of resistance to slavery, and have long shaped both academic research and popular understanding of the lived experience of slavery and resistance. In the late eighteenth century Thomas Clarkson used Jamaican runaway advertisements as evidence to support the abolition of the transatlantic slave trade, and Theodore Weld and Sarah and Angelina Grimké deployed thousands of American runaway advertisements as their primary source for *American Slavery as It Is: Testimony of a Thousand Witnesses*, one of the most influential abolitionist works published in the United States.[9]

Crucially, however, there were no newspapers and therefore no runaway slave advertisements in England's American and Caribbean colonies until the early eighteenth century. The oldest surviving runaway slave advertisement in a newspaper in the English Caribbean or North American colonies appeared in June 1704.[10] Half a century earlier, when London's freedom seekers challenged their bondage, they prompted the creation of a new genre vital to the history of resistance to racial slavery, the runaway slave advertisement. Thus it was in Restoration London that newspaper runaway advertisements were created and first deployed. In telling the story of London's early freedom seekers this book will shed light on the larger story of the capital's role in the institutionalization of racial slavery: the creation of runaway slave advertisements as a response to this most significant form of resistance to slavery and the direct role of these notices in the formation of languages and concepts of both racial slavery and resistance. Racial slavery existed in seventeenth-century London, and the stories of these Black Londoners are too significant to be neglected.

---

[9] T. Clarkson, *An Abstract of the Evidence delivered before a select committee of the House of Commons in the years 1790 and 1791, on the part of the petitioners for the Abolition of the Slave Trade* (London, 1791), pp. x–xiii; T. Weld, *American Slavery as It Is: Testimony of a Thousand Witnesses* (New York, 1839). For more on these early quantitative and qualitative uses of runaway advertisements see E. G. Garvey, '"facts and FACTS": abolitionists' database innovations', in *'Raw Data' Is an Oxymoron*, ed. L. Gitelman (Cambridge, Mass., 2013), pp. 89–102.

[10] 'Ran-away … Penelope', *Boston News-Letter*, 26 June 1704.

PART I

Restoration London and the enslaved

1. London

LONDON is a World by it self. We daily discover in it more new Countries and surprizing Singularities, than in all the Universe besides. There are among the Londiners so many Nations differing in Manners, Customs, and Religions, that the Inhabitants themselves don't know a quarter of them.[1]

The dramatic expansion of London took place during the seventeenth century despite significant trauma and dislocation. In January 1642 Charles I fled from London and within six months the English Civil War had begun, a conflict that soon expanded into the Wars of the Three Kingdoms which engulfed the entire British Isles. Seven years later Charles I was beheaded outside the Banqueting House in London, heralding a decade of republican government under the direction of the Lord Protector Oliver Cromwell. Several years of chaos and conflict followed Cromwell's death in 1658, paving the way for the restoration of Charles II and the monarchy in 1660.

Despite the two decades of governmental stability resulting from the Restoration, London remained subject to further chaos. A major outbreak of bubonic plague may have killed as many as a quarter of London's citizens between the spring of 1665 and the summer of 1666. No sooner had the plague receded than the Great Fire of London broke out in September 1666, gutting the heart of the City of London and destroying more than 13,000 buildings. Between 1679 and 1681 the Exclusion Crisis raged as Protestants in parliament sought to exclude Charles II's Roman Catholic brother James, then duke of York, from succession to the throne. While this effort failed, it presaged the opposition to James II when he acceded to the throne in 1685, and the new king was deposed three years later in the Glorious Revolution. The succession of James's Protestant daughter Mary and her husband, William of Orange, finally brought stability to London, although the new political order remained vulnerable to the constant threat of rebellion in Scotland and Ireland and invasion by France in support of James II and his descendants.

Despite all of this chaos, death and destruction, London grew dramatically during the second half of the seventeenth century,

---

[1] T. Brown, *Amusements Serious and Comical, Calculated for the Meridian of London. The 2d. edition, with large improvements* (London, 1702), p. 22.

becoming Europe's largest city and the metropolitan hub of England's fast-developing empire. Between 1600 and 1720 there was 'a prodigious Increase of the Inhabitants' from about 200,000 to perhaps more than 600,000, and as many as two thirds of English urban dwellers resided in the capital.[2] London was the permanent base of the king, parliament and an elite and mercantile class with money, expertise and wealth: situated on a river navigable by ocean-going vessels, the city was uniquely well positioned as a hub for empire and trade.[3] Yet it remained a deadly place, and throughout the century more people died than were born in the city. Only a constant influx of new residents from all over the British Isles and beyond made the city's growth possible.

London was chaotic, loud and vibrant. A cacophony of dozens of church bells, criers selling their wares, craftsmen and women manufacturing and selling goods, horses and carriages navigating the narrow streets, animals and birds being taken to the markets, and tens of thousands of Londoners going about their day: all of these and more overwhelmed the senses of residents and visitors. They smelled fires and all manner of foods baking, cooking or being offered for sale in the streets, the musty odour of the woven fabrics worn by Londoners, the strong stench of pitch and tar from the riverside, and the smell of wood as carpenters and builders constructed and repaired the constantly expanding city.

Demographic expansion was matched by geographic growth (Figure 2). London had two historical centres: the ancient City of London was composed of the square mile or so within and immediately outside the ancient Roman walls; and the area around Westminster, just over a mile west of the City, was the home of the royal court and parliament and of a growing number of expensive houses and shops. Over the course of the seventeenth century each of these areas expanded, with rapid urban growth uniting the City

---

[2] Gregory King estimated that by 1680 two out of every three English townspeople were in London. See G. King, 'Natural and political observations and conclusions upon the state and condition of England, 1696', in G. Chalmers, *An Estimate of the Comparative Strength of Great-Britain: and of Losses of her Trade from Every War since the Revolution ... to which is now annexed Gregory King's Celebrated State of England* (London, 1802), at p. 411. See also E. McKellar, *The Birth of Modern London: the Development and Design of the City, 1660–1720* (Manchester, 1999), p. 13; R. Porter, *London: A Social History* (Cambridge, Mass., 1994), p. 131; R. K. Batchelor, *London: the Selden Map and the Making of a Global City, 1549–1689* (Chicago, 2014), p. 7; V. Harding, 'The population of London, 1550–1700: a review of the published evidence', *London Journal: a Review of Metropolitan Society Past and Present*, xv (1990), 111–28.

[3] N. Zahedieh, *The Capital and the Colonies: London and the Atlantic Economy, 1660–1700* (Cambridge, 2010), pp. 17–21; M. Waller, *1700: Scenes from London Life* (New York and London, 2000), p. 4.

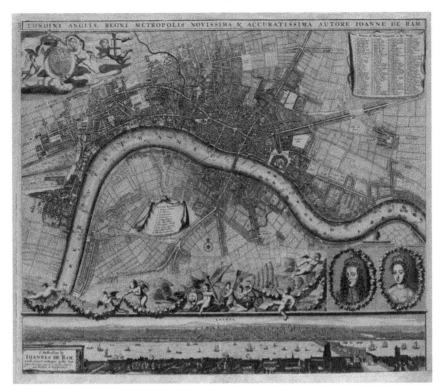

Figure 2. Joannes de Ram, *Londini Angliæ regni metropolis novissima &
accuratissima* (Amsterdam, 1690), University of Michigan, Clark Library. The
mercantile, maritime and shipbuilding communities can be seen spreading
out from the Tower of London into the East End along the northern bank
of the Thames, and spreading eastward from Southwark towards Greenwich
(off the map) south of the river. To the west the previously separate City of
London and Westminster are shown to be connected by urban growth.

and Westminster, pushing north towards Hampstead and Hackney and
south beyond Lambeth and Southwark, while new urban growth related to
international trade, shipbuilding and a host of related occupations grew up
along the river to the east of the City and south of the river from Southwark
to as far as Greenwich. In present-day London much of what remains of the
early modern city is obscured and even St Paul's cathedral, so prominent in
Claes Jansz Visscher's early seventeenth-century rendering of the cityscape
(Figure 3), has been overwhelmed by the skyscrapers and monumental
structures of modern London captured by Robin Reynolds from the same
vantage point as Visscher almost four centuries later.

Figure 3. Claes Jansz Visscher, *Londinum florentissima Britanniae urbs* (c.1625), Folger Shakespeare Library: Robin Reynolds, *Visscher Redrawn* (2016). Reproduced by permission of the artist. The two images show the City of London from the same vantage point in the early 17th and the early 21st centuries. The two images were merged by Anthony King.

London's citizenry

The people who inhabited seventeenth-century London, however, are even more elusive than the city that they inhabited. Kings, courtiers and a few of the city's more affluent citizens have left us portraits of themselves and their families, and some of the buildings they constructed and the things they owned have survived, allowing us to feel something of the tenor of their lives. Others have left diaries and documentary records or can be traced in court or ecclesiastical records. But, although a few seventeenth-century Londoners speak to us through the archives, most of their contemporaries have left little or even no trace. We can imagine their lives in only the broadest and vaguest terms and usually not as individuals but as members of a group of workers, inhabitants of a neighbourhood or parishioners of a particular church. And enslaved and bound people of colour are among the most invisible of seventeenth-century Londoners.

While the city was a vast and fast-growing physical entity, it was also a lived experience, and myriad residents and visitors faced and understood the city in often dramatically different ways.[4] London was, like England more broadly, hierarchical and stratified, a society of deep and abiding inequality. The London of a member of the monarch's household in one of the city's royal palaces was a world apart from the London of a printer and his family in Cheapside, of a merchant's family in the heart of the City, of a prostitute and her child across the river near the theatre or of a sailor and his family in Stepney.[5] Residents and visitors inhabited the city in different ways, some rarely moving beyond the communities in which they lived and worked, others ranging further afield for work or pleasure.[6] As the city expanded, many of those who could afford larger houses moved west, including courtiers, nobles, gentry, government officials and merchants. Those who lived with and served them experienced quite different lives from the servants living and working in the densely packed medieval heart of the ancient City or in the fast-growing mercantile and shipbuilding centres hugging the northern and southern banks of the Thames to the east.[7]

The upper echelons of London society consisted of the monarch and court, titled nobility, knights, esquires and the broad category of 'gentlemen'.

---

[4] P. Griffiths, *Lost Londons: Change, Crime and Control in the Capital City, 1550–1660* (Cambridge, 2008), p. xiii.

[5] K. Wrightson, *English Society, 1580–1680* (London, [1982] 2003), pp. 25–46.

[6] R. B. Shoemaker, 'Gendered spaces: patterns of mobility and perceptions of London's geography, 1600–1750', in *Imagining Early Modern London: Perceptions and Portrayals of the City from Stow to Strype, 1598–1720*, ed. J. Merritt (Cambridge, 2001), pp. 145–55.

[7] V. Harding, 'City, capital, and metropolis: the changing shape of seventeenth-century London', in *Imagining Early Modern London*, pp. 117–43, at p. 124.

Together with their immediate families, this wealthy and powerful group constituted little more than about 2 per cent of the population. Some of them inhabited apartments in the city's various royal palaces while others occupied houses in and around London and Westminster. Below them was a broad category of citizens and burgesses, including merchants, business owners and craftsmen, ranging from the very wealthy to the quite impoverished. And below these middling sorts of people was the largest category of Londoners, including workers such as day labourers, sailors and rivermen, artificers, apprentices and servants.[8]

Merchants were at the heart of London's wealth and growth, and by the mid-1670s they constituted as many as 10 per cent of householders in the City of London. The *London Directory* in 1677 recorded that 93 per cent of those engaged in overseas trade were based within the City, many of them clustered to the east of St Paul's, close to the Royal Exchange, the Customs House and the twenty-one Legal Quays between London Bridge and the Tower of London. To prevent smuggling, all dutiable goods had to be landed at these quays, which by the 1680s serviced some 2,000 ships per annum. At times ships were moored three deep, while the larger ships bringing bulkier and heavier goods from the Caribbean, North America and South Asia were too large for the quays and were serviced by lighters. Trade with the plantation colonies grew exponentially: tobacco imports grew in value from £2 million annually to £11 million in 1676 and £22.5 million in 1719, while the value of sugar imports trebled between the 1660s and 1680s alone.[9]

Servants lived and worked in virtually all of London's households, from those of wealthy elites to the more modest homes of the middling sort: one historian estimates that servants comprised well over one third of all household residents. Elite households often contained a number of domestic servants, some of them dressed in smart liveries to reflect the wealth and prestige of their masters. The larger London homes may have included business working space such as an office, workshop or shop on the ground floor; a kitchen and dining room on the floor above; and two or three floors of bedrooms, including garret rooms for servants. Wealthier households that did not contain business and work spaces could devote the ground-floor rooms to living space in which servants catered to the needs of the householder and his or her family.[10]

---

[8] Wrightson, *English Society*, pp. 27–32. As Wrightson notes, these categories were identified by contemporaries such as William Harrison and Gregory King.

[9] Zahedieh, *The Capital and the Colonies*, pp. 23, 57–8, 167–8.

[10] P. Earle, *The Making of the English Middle Class: Business, Society and Family Life in London, 1660–1730* (Berkeley, Calif., 1989), pp. 217–18, 209–10.

During the sixteenth and seventeenth centuries England shifted from a shortage to a surplus of labour, and many young people made their way to London in search of work.[11] English authorities required all people to work productively under the direction of a head of household, and most young people between their mid-teens and mid-twenties laboured as servants in husbandry in the countryside or as domestic servants in urban settings, while yet more were employed as apprentices. All told, servants constituted as much as 15 per cent of the nation's population. Parliament, the courts and local officials sought to ensure that everyone was productively situated within nuclear family households, thereby addressing the needs of the rapidly increasing English population.[12]

Apprenticeship (predominantly male but some female) gave young people a potentially superior status to servants, and after a set period an apprentice might gain the status of a skilled craftsman and a fixed status within a profession and guild. Domestic service was a more malleable and less protected form of work under the authority of heads of household.[13] Such work varied according to the size and nature of the household, ranging from well-dressed maids, footmen, butlers, pages and other servants attending to the immediate personal needs of London's wealthiest residents to those who undertook all manner of grinding household work in the homes and businesses of less affluent employers.[14] Using church court depositions, one historian has estimated that between 1660 and 1750 some 43 per cent of London's domestic servants worked in the households of knights and nobility; 20 per cent in the homes of gentry; 14 per cent in the homes and workplaces of people in the victualling trades; and 5 per cent for army or navy officers and their families. The remaining 18 per cent worked

[11] A. Kussmaul, *Servants in Husbandry in Early Modern England* (Cambridge, 1981), p. 3; Griffiths, *Lost Londons*, pp. 23–4.

[12] Kussmaul, *Servants in Husbandry*, p. 3; D. W. Galenson, *White Servitude in Colonial America: an Economic Analysis* (Cambridge, 1981), p. 7; P. Fumerton, *Unsettled: the Culture of Mobility and the Working Poor in Early Modern England* (Chicago, 2006), p. 12; K. Wrightson, *Earthly Necessities: Economic Lives in Early Modern Britain* (New Haven, Conn., 2000), pp. 30–6, 159–60. See also J. Hatcher, 'Plague, population and the English economy, 1348–1530', in *British Population History: From the Black Death to the Present Day*, ed. M. Anderson (Cambridge, 1996), pp. 9–94; E. A. Wrigley, 'The growth of population in eighteenth-century England: a conundrum resolved', *Past & Present*, xcviii (1983), 121–50, at p. 122; S. P. Newman, *A New World of Labor: the Development of Plantation Slavery in the British Atlantic* (Philadelphia, 2013), pp. 17–35; A. Balasopoulos, 'Dark light: utopia and the question of relative surplus production', *Utopian Studies*, xxvii (2016), 615–29.

[13] L. Gowing, *Domestic Dangers: Women, Words, and Sex in Early Modern London* (Oxford, 1996), pp. 15–17.

[14] For more on domestic servants see I. K. Ben-Amos, *Adolescence and Youth in Early Modern England* (New Haven, Conn., 1994); Kussmaul, *Servants in Husbandry*.

for merchants, professionals, textile and clothes producers and vendors, builders, medics, shopkeepers, transport, widows and various others.[15]

Domestic servants in seventeenth-century London were overwhelmingly female; one study of two London parishes in 1695 revealed that 81 per cent of servants were girls and young women.[16] Indeed, most seventeenth-century English women spent several years before marriage as servants.[17] In rural areas girls left their homes to enter service as early as thirteen or fourteen years of age, but those who travelled to London seeking work tended to be in their later teens.[18] For young girls domestic service could function as a kind of paid apprenticeship for marriage, for after several years in service they would have learned a great deal about running a household and saved money for a dowry or to help establish their own household once they were married. Others might have learned something of a particular business, including keeping stores, taverns or inns.[19] Some of them remained servants: when Samuel and Elisabeth Pepys occupied their first London home in 1658 they were accompanied by their fourteen-year-old servant Jane Birch, who continued to work intermittently for Pepys for the remainder of his life.[20]

Apprenticeship was the path for young boys to learn life skills and each year thousands of boys were apprenticed in London, while many more of those working in London households were simply servants who were earning and saving money rather than gaining the more marketable skills of professional craftsmen.[21] While women and girls dominated the servant workforce, male servants were rather more common in elite households, and an investigation of the occupations of employers in the late seventeenth and early eighteenth centuries found that the servants of the nobility, knights, gentlemen and the like were 42 per cent male. Male servants in elite households might identify themselves by occupational labels such as

[15] P. Earle, *A City Full of People: Men and Women of London, 1650–1750* (London, 1994), pp. 274–6.

[16] T. Meldrum, *Domestic Service and Gender, 1660–1750: Life and Work in the London Household* (New York, 2000), p. 15; Earle, *The Making of the English Middle Class*, p. 218.

[17] L. Gowing, 'The haunting of Susan Lay: servants and mistresses in seventeenth-century England', *Gender & History*, xiv (2002), 183–201, at p. 186.

[18] M. Roberts, '"Words they are women, and deeds they are men": images of work and gender in early modern England', in *Women and Work in Pre-industrial England*, ed. L. Charles and L. Duffin (London, 1985), pp. 122–80, at p. 127.

[19] L. Gowing, *Common Bodies: Women, Touch and Power in Seventeenth-Century England* (New Haven, Conn., 2003), pp. 59–60, 64.

[20] H. Summerson, 'Servants of Samuel Pepys' (2006), *Oxford Dictionary of National Biography* <https://doi.org/10.1093/ref:odnb/93850> [accessed 5 June 2020].

[21] S. R. Smith, 'The London apprentices as seventeenth-century adolescents', *Past & Present*, lxi (1973), 149–61, at p. 149.

footman, butler, groom, coachman or page, whereas young females rarely identified themselves in these terms and were more inclined to say that they 'got their living by going to service'.[22]

Well-dressed and expensively liveried male servants advertised the wealth and success of those they served and attended. Such clothing was designed to be seen and these attractively attired boys and young men worked both at home and out and about in the capital.[23] As Pepys became a wealthier and more significant government official, he and his wife employed more servants, and these included White boys such as Wayneman Birch and then Thomas Edwards: each was dressed in Pepys's livery and accompanied him about the city and ran errands on his behalf.[24] The fourteen-year-old unnamed 'Black Boy' who escaped from the shipbuilder Jonas Shish in 1683 was dressed not as the shipwrights who worked for Shish but as a liveried personal servant, in a green jacket and trousers, with a silver collar around his neck attesting to his enslaved status and Shish's wealth and standing.[25]

John Baker's diary, although recorded later in the eighteenth century, provides evidence of the kinds of work required of enslaved or bound servants attired in this fashion. When Baker returned to England from the Caribbean, he brought with him Jack Beef, an enslaved man whom he had purchased as a child. During the 1750s and early 1760s Baker's diary regularly included references to Beef and his work, from collecting and delivering correspondence, goods and horses to attending Baker's sons at their school and preparing dressed turtle for formal dinners. On one occasion Baker recorded that 'Mr. Robinson, the taylor, came and took measure of me, and of Jack Beef for a livery', the uniform that marked him as the personal servant of a wealthy man.[26]

A significant number of men and boys worked in or were connected to the building trades in Restoration London. The rapid growth of London, the rebuilding of the City in the wake of the great fire and the shift from medieval wooden to the new brick and stone buildings of the later seventeenth and eighteenth centuries all created a great deal of work for those working in or supporting the construction industry. In the aftermath of the fire the medieval guilds lost most of their control over building,

---

[22] Meldrum, *Domestic Service and Gender*, pp. 15, 22, 132.

[23] J. J. Hecht, *The Domestic Servant Class in Eighteenth-Century England* (London, 1956), pp. 119–20.

[24] Summerson, 'Servants of Samuel Pepys'.

[25] 'A Black boy', *The London Gazette*, 29 Nov. 1683; R.C. Richardson, *Household Servants in Early Modern England* (Manchester, 2010), pp. 64–7, 107.

[26] *The Diary of John Baker*, ed. P. C. Yorke (London, 1931), pp. 101, 75, 80, 107, 122, 132, 153, 165, 167.

and there were tremendous opportunities for skilled, semi-skilled and unskilled labourers. While bricklayers, carpenters and stonemasons were particularly important, a huge amount of lesser-skilled labour helped build and rebuild London. Despite the lack of evidence, boys and men of colour were probably also employed in rebuilding London, and the need for such labour may have provided work opportunities for some of those who escaped from enslavement.[27]

As the commercial hub of England's fast-growing empire, London was a centre of shipping and home to many sailors and workers in maritime and related occupations, including adolescents and men of colour. The late seventeenth and early eighteenth centuries witnessed a massive increase in England's merchant marine: in 1629 English merchant ships of more than 100 tons accounted for approximately 115,000 tons of shipping, but by 1702 London's merchant shipping alone had increased to some 140,000 tons. Over just two decades between 1664 and 1683 the annual number of ships clearing London bound for foreign ports increased from 136 to 423. Furthermore, between 1650 and 1700 the Royal Navy more than doubled in size, and between 1633 and about 1697 the number of Royal Navy sailors increased fourfold from just under 9,500 to about 42,000.[28] The rapidly increasing number and size of England's ocean-going ships created a constant need for sailors, and during this period seafaring became a regularized employment for an ever-growing group of labourers. During the 1660s London's Atlantic fleet alone accounted for approximately 3,240 seafarers, a number that had almost doubled by the mid-1680s, and many more seafarers worked on the trade routes to South Asia, the Mediterranean, Baltic and Continental Europe.[29]

These sailors were an important category of London workers, concentrated in the riverside communities of the East End and south of the Thames between Southwark and Greenwich. Seafarers, shipbuilders, dock workers and all the associated trades and communities expanded along the northern and southern banks of the Thames east of the City of London, and it was these boys and men and the ships they sailed that connected London and England with the rest of the world. Many English sailors first went to sea between the ages of about twelve and sixteen as servants or 'boys'. The Navigation Act of 1660

---

[27] McKellar, *The Birth of Modern London*, pp. 71–113.

[28] R. Davis, *The Rise of the English Shipping Industry in the Seventeenth and Eighteenth Centuries* (Liverpool, [2012] 2019), pp. 10, 14, 17, 26; N. A. M. Rodger, *The Command of the Ocean: a Naval History of Britain, 1649–1815* (New York, 2004), pp. 607–8; M. Rediker, 'Society and culture among Anglo-American deep sea sailors, 1700–1750' (unpublished University of Pennsylvania PhD thesis, 1982), p. 49.

[29] Zahedieh, *The Capital and the Colonies*, p. 159.

restricted foreigners to no more than one quarter of the positions aboard ship, an implicit recognition that ocean-going ship crews were often multinational and multiracial, sometimes including enslaved boys and men. In practice these restrictions were relaxed during wartime and when ship crews were reduced by disease in such places as South Asia, West Africa and the Caribbean.[30] It was a hard and dangerous profession, especially for those undertaking voyages of two years to South Asia or of a year or longer to West Africa and the Caribbean or to the American colonies, where many of these boys and men succumbed to tropical diseases. Seafarers were immediately recognizable, often walking with the peculiar gait of men who spent years on the rolling decks of ocean-going ships. They wore distinctive clothing well suited to their working conditions: loose and baggy breeches, shirts, heavy jackets and caps. Often their clothing was tarred or oiled to keep the wearer as warm and dry as possible. Seafarers were distinctive, marked by their clothing, their language and their shared experiences of life and work in distant places. They were a multinational group, including a significant number of adolescents and men of colour.[31]

Most of London's growing population of people of colour worked as the domestic and personal servants of elite men. Mingo was one such servant, and he and others like him knew the capital well. Mingo served Sir William Batten until the latter's death in 1667. Batten was a former naval officer who served as surveyor of the navy and who sat in the House of Commons.[32] Mingo lived with Batten in a house on Seething Lane by the Navy Office building in the eastern part of the City, immediately to the west of the Tower of London and just a few hundred yards north of the Thames. He regularly accompanied Batten to business meetings and social encounters in taverns, coffee houses and private residences across the city and in nearby maritime communities. He often strode out on his own, carrying messages, papers and goods for Batten. When Batten visited Peter Pett's shipyards, or when he enjoyed a riotous dinner at the Dolphin tavern, Mingo was there; when Batten sent messages or instructions to his associate Samuel Pepys, Mingo carried them. Mingo was walking alone through a maritime community when he was accosted by a group of sailors who stole the expensive cloak he was carrying.[33] If we imagine hundreds of people like Mingo, men,

---

[30] P. Earle, *Sailors: English Merchant Seamen, 1650–1775* (London, 1998), pp. 85, 200–4.

[31] For more on merchant seamen of this era see M. Rediker, *Between the Devil and the Deep Blue Sea: Merchant Seamen, Pirates, and the Anglo-American Maritime World* (Cambridge, 1987), pp. 7–12.

[32] C. S. Knighton, 'Sir William Batten' (2008), *ODNB* <https://doi.org/10.1093/ref:odnb/1714> [accessed 2 Feb. 2021].

[33] *The Diary of Samuel Pepys: Daily Entries from the 17th Century London Diary*, 10 April 1661; 21 Feb. 1663; 21 March 1667; 4 Nov. 1665 <https://www.pepysdiary.com/diary> [accessed 2 Feb. 2021].

women and children of colour who lived and worked in London, and who were baptized, married and buried in local churches, we can begin to sense the Black presence in Restoration London, people who were not simply present in the city but who inhabited it. While they were a minority, these people were sufficiently common to be unremarkable, making the escape of enslaved people in London a possibility.

London's public sphere

While Londoners knew their own particular wards, parishes and neighbourhoods, few were familiar with the entirety of the fast-growing metropolis.[34] Commentators lauded the city's expansion as evidence of England's growing wealth and power, and within the imperial metropolis residents might see and hear people speaking French, Dutch, Portuguese and Spanish, as well as Turkish and a variety of North African, West African, South Asian and even indigenous American languages.[35] The city's imperial and mercantile operations radiated out from a relatively small part of the City of London centred on Cornhill. Within and spreading out from that area, three institutions were of central importance in late seventeenth-century London for business, commerce and the nation's fast-growing empire: the printed news sheets and newspapers, coffee houses and the Royal Exchange. Figure 4 shows the concentration of key financial and imperial institutions and coffee houses located within an area of little more than 2,000 square yards. Print media, coffee shops and the Royal Exchange functioned as vital nexuses for the transmission of news and commercial information and for the conduct of business in Restoration London, and were of particular significance in the area surrounding the Royal Exchange. Many of those in London who owned enslaved people either worked closely with or were themselves people who worked in and around these institutions, and the area was a vital hub for the business of advertising and recapturing enslaved and bound freedom seekers.

The Royal Exchange

The Royal Exchange first opened in 1571 and continued in operation until it was destroyed in the Great Fire of London in 1666. A second building was rapidly erected on the same site, opening in 1669 and continuing to operate

[34] J. Strype, *A Survey of the Cities of London and Westminster: Containing the Original Antiquity, Increase, Modern Estate and Government of Those Cities. Written at first in the Year MDXCVIII, By John Stow, Citizen and Native of London* (London, 1720), i. 4.

[35] Harding, 'City, capital, and metropolis', p. 123; Griffiths, *Lost Londons*, pp. 2–4, 23–4; J. Selwood, *Diversity and Difference in Early Modern London* (Farnham, 2010).

Figure 4. Institutions around the Royal Exchange shown in detail from *London &c. Actually Surveyed, by Wm. Morgan* (London, 1682), Library of Congress (additions by the author). The East India Company was at EIC from 1638 onwards; the Royal African Company was at RAC1 between the 1660s and 1677, and at RAC2 from 1677 onwards; and the Bank of England was at BANK from 1694. Key coffee houses around the Royal Exchange were Jamaica (J1); Garraway's (G1); Jonathan's (J2); Lloyd's (L); Maryland (M1); Virginia (V1); Carolina (C1); Bowman's (B1); Cole's (C2); Elford's (E); Batson's (B2); Marine (M2); Royal (R); Garter (G2); Vernon's (V2). There were many other coffee houses.

Figure 5. Robert White, 'The Royall Exchange of London'
(London, 1671), Folger Shakespeare Library.

there until well into the nineteenth century: only St Paul's cathedral cost more
to rebuild, a clear indication of the importance of the exchange (Figure 5).[36]
The Royal Exchange was the single most significant venue for merchants and
members of the business and trading communities, and it was a vital base for
the colonization, trade and empire that was transforming England from a minor
European to a major global power.[37] At the turn of the eighteenth century one
observer described the exchange and what occurred there as follows:

> Shops and businesses filled the building's two floors, but much of what made it
> significant occurred in the courtyard and public places where one would think
> all the World was converted into News-Mongers and Intelligencers; for that's the
> first Salutation among all Mankind that frequent that Place: What news from
> *Scandaroon* and *Aleppo?* Says the *Turkey* Marchant. What Price bears Currants at

[36] Zahedieh, *The Capital and the Colonies*, p. 82.
[37] N. Glaisyer, *The Culture of Commerce in England, 1660–1720* (Woodbridge, 2006), pp. 27–34.

Figure 6. Detail from Wenceslaus Hollar, 'Byrsa Londinensis vulgo the Royal Exchange' (1644?), Folger Shakespeare Library. A female hawker selling newspapers is visible on the left at the front of the crowd. The illustrations of freedom seekers by Triona Lawrence are based on newspaper advertisement descriptions of freedom seekers used in this book and have been inserted by the author to give an impression of such people trailing their enslavers in this environment.

Zant? Apes at *Tunis?* ... What News of such a Ship? Say's the *Insurer.*[38]

Different areas of the Royal Exchange were associated with particular trade goods or trading regions, as illustrated by a January 1690 advertisement in the *London Gazette* for 'a Sugar House, ready fitted with three Pans, and all Utensils' and available for rent in Southwark. The advertisement enjoined interested parties to make enquiries 'at Exchange time on the Barbadoes Walk' of the Royal Exchange.[39] A 1677 directory of the names and addresses of London's bankers and merchants included some who went so far as to give the various 'walks' on the exchange as their place of business, as in the case of John Gold, Thomas Gurden and George Ravenscroft on the Turkey Walk, and Sir Matthew Halworthy, Thomas Hardwick and Sir Stephen White on the Spanish Walk.[40] The New England, Carolina, Virginia, Jamaica and Barbados walks were clustered together in the south-western corner of the exchange.

Coffee Houses

As adjuncts to the Royal Exchange, a large number of coffee houses provided key meeting places for the exchange of news. Pepys went regularly 'to the Exchange, and a Coffee House', and on one such occasion he went 'to the Exchange, and meeting [Captain John] Shales, he and I to the Coffee-house, and there talked of our victualling matters'.[41] Such meetings and interactions were commonplace, and between 1650 and the early 1700s coffee houses spread rapidly in London, providing sociable spaces for Londoners engaged in trade, commerce, government and politics. After little more than a decade London had eighty-two coffee houses, and by the turn of the eighteenth century there were several hundred in the capital.[42] Avoiding the intoxication and revelry of inns and taverns and serving the colonial staples of coffee and chocolate along with all of the latest news sheets and newspapers, coffee houses were highly significant sites of socialization and business. Brian Cowan has illustrated their significance by exploring the diaries and journals of Londoners to assess how often late seventeenth-century men of business frequented these institutions. Pepys recorded visiting them at least ninety-nine times during the 1660s as they were taking root in the capital. Between 1672 and 1680 Robert Hook made at least sixty-four coffee house visits, and by the turn of the eighteenth century

---

[38] Brown, *Amusements Serious and Comical*, p. 44.
[39] 'IN Holland's Leagur ... a Sugar House', *London Gazette*, 9 Jan 1689.
[40] S. Lee, *The Little London Directory of 1677: The Oldest Printed List of the Merchants and Bankers of London* (London, 1863).
[41] Pepys, *Diary*, 14 July 1665; 13 Nov. 1663.
[42] M. Ellis, *The Coffee House: a Cultural History* (London, 2004), p. 103.

Figure 7. Interior of a London coffee house, drawing by unknown artist (*c.*1690–1700). © The Trustees of the British Museum. The illustration conveys how these establishments were simultaneously places of business and of sociability; the newspapers and paperwork shown, and the more open discussions and conversations and the smaller group meetings they allowed, all illustrate how Pepys and his contemporaries used these establishments.

they were so ubiquitous that James Brydges made some 280 coffee house visits over five years between 1697 and 1702. These diarists probably made many more coffee house visits than they recorded in their sometimes perfunctory diary entries. Together they demonstrate that London's coffee houses were leading venues for accessing printed news and oral rumour, for discussing business deals and professional matters, for ruminating on the arts and sciences, and for more idle social chatter and gossip (Figure 7). News was as integral to coffee houses as the coffee and chocolate they served, and Pepys was typical in going 'to the Coffee-house to hear newes'.[43] Upon arrival, customers greeted their fellow patrons with the question 'What news?', and newspapers and newsbooks were placed on tables for customers to read and discuss. The informal gossip and exchange of information was as important as the printed news and, even

[43] Pepys, *Diary*, 14 Nov. 1664.

though he was well connected through his work for the government, Pepys often found coffee houses a faster and more accurate conduit for fresh news.[44]

By the end of the seventeenth century Garraway's, Jonathan's and Lloyd's had emerged as particularly important coffee houses, each of which was within a few yards of the exchange and not much further from the offices of the East India and Royal African companies and the Bank of England. Edward Lloyd established his coffee shop on Tower Street in 1686, and Lloyd's soon became a meeting place for ship owners and captains, the merchants whose goods they transported, and the consortia that provided insurance for these voyages. Lloyd's moved to Lombard Street in 1691, and within a year had begun publishing lists of shipping. Early in the eighteenth century the group of marine insurance underwriters came together in Lloyd's rented rooms at the Royal Exchange.[45] Garraway's, Jonathan's and Lloyd's probably hosted negotiations for the sale and purchase of enslaved people, both those labouring in the colonies and those brought to London.

The small area in which these coffee houses were concentrated is revealed in Morden and Lea's somewhat impressionistic view of London stretching northwards from the banks of the Thames just west of the northern entrance onto London Bridge (which appears in the south-eastern corner of Figure 8). Much of this area had been destroyed by the Great Fire in 1666, and the monumental column marking the place where the fire started lies just above the bridge. Church towers and spires provided the landmarks that enabled Londoners to situate themselves in the densely built and populated City of London, and they reveal the contours of the financial area in and around Cornhill. The Royal Exchange (marked on the map by the number 71) was one of the few civic buildings as tall as churches, and the central tower atop the main entrance on Cornhill dwarfed the nearby church of St Bartholomew Exchange (number 70). Fewer than 250 feet south of the exchange lay St Edmonds Church (number 76) on Lombard Street. The couple of hundred square yards between the exchange and St Edmonds contained London's greatest concentration of coffee houses: together with the exchange, these formed the nexus for much of the City's commercial and colonial business, and they played a pivotal role in newspaper advertisements for the recovery of enslaved freedom seekers.

The immediate environs of the Royal Exchange had the greatest concentration of coffee houses, especially in and around Exchange Alley and Birchin Lane, across Cornhill from the exchange's southern entrance. Exchange Alley was filled

[44] B. Cowan, *Social Life of Coffee: the Emergence of the British Coffeehouse* (New Haven, Conn., 2005), pp. 30, 108–9; Ellis, *The Coffee House*, pp. 55–6, 67. See also S. Pincus, '"Coffee politicians does create": coffeehouses and Restoration political culture', *Journal of Modern History*, lxvii (1995), 807–34.

[45] Ellis, *The Coffee House*, pp. 169–70.

London

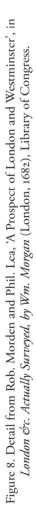

Figure 8. Detail from Rob. Morden and Phil. Lea, 'A Prospect of London and Westminster', in *London &c. Actually Surveyed, by Wm. Morgan* (London, 1682), Library of Congress.

Figure 9. Marcellus Laroon, 'London Gazette here' (woman selling newspapers), in *The Cryes of the City of London Drawne after the Life* (London, 1711), plate 56. Folger Shakespeare Library.

with 'divers eminent Coffee Houses, as Garraways, Jonathans, Barkers, Elmers, chiefly frequented by Brokers, Stockjobbers, Frenchmen, Jews, as well as other Merchants and Gentlemen'.[46] Like other financial and imperial institutions such as the Royal Exchange, the Bank of England and the offices of the East India and Royal African companies, coffee houses were male environments, although on occasion women ran or worked in them.

Newspapers

As Jürgen Habermas and others have argued, spaces such as the Royal Exchange and the numerous surrounding coffee shops combined with the printed newspapers that circulated within and beyond such spaces to create a new public sphere.[47] Printers, particularly those producing newsletters,

---

[46] Strype, *A Survey of the Cities of London and Westminster*, i. 163.

[47] J. Habermas, *The Structural Transformation of the Public Sphere: an Inquiry into a Category of Bourgeois Society*, trans. T. Burger (Cambridge, [1962] 1989).

newspapers and all manner of ephemeral notices and advertisements, fed a steady diet of news and information to readers in their homes and places of work, in taverns and within coffee houses and the Royal Exchange. Printed communication linked the East India Company, the Royal African Company and other operations such as the companies colonizing Virginia and the Carolinas with merchants and investors in the City. Printers were vital in translating the flow of information for consumption by those with interests in commerce as well as for more general audiences. There were a good number of stationers and printers within or relatively close to the exchange and hawkers, many of them female, patrolled the area selling pamphlets and newspapers (Figure 9). 'For a penny', enthused Henry Peacham in 1669, 'you may have all the news in *England*, and other Countries.'[48]

Readers could find all manner of information on the columns or walls of the exchange. At the end of the seventeenth century one observer noted that within the exchange 'Advertisements hang as thick round the Pillars of each Walk, as Bells about the Legs of a *Morrice-Dancer*'.[49] Brown described the varied subject matter of these printed notices:

> Why first here is a *Ship* to be sold, with all her Tackle and Lading. There are virtuous Maidens that are willing to be transported with *William Penn* into *Maryland*, for the Propagation of *Quakerism*. In another is a *Tutor* to be hir'd, to instruct any Gentleman's Children in their own Families … In another Column in a *Gilded Frame* was a Chamber-Maid that wanted a Service; and over her an old Batchelor that wanted a Housekeeper. On the Sides of these were two less Papers, one containing an Advertisement of a Red-headed Monkey, lost from a Seed Shop in the *Strand*, with two Guineas Reward to him or her that shall bring him home again with his Tail and Collar on.[50]

In the early eighteenth century the Gresham Committee, which supervised the exchange, charged customers 2 shillings and 6 pence for the display of a notice or an advertisement that had been created by the printers who plied their trade in and near to the exchange.[51] This was a significant amount, more than an unskilled male labourer in the mid seventeenth century might have earned for two days of work.[52]

---

[48] H. Peacham, *The Worth of a Penny; or, A Caution to Keep Money* (London, 1669), p. 21.

[49] N. Ward, *The London Spy Compleat*, ed. R. Straus (London, 1924), p. 68.

[50] Brown, *Amusements Serious and Comical*, pp. 37–8. See also M. Harris, 'Exchanging information: print and business at the Royal Exchange in the late seventeenth century', in *The Royal Exchange*, ed. A. Saunders (London, 1997), pp. 188–97.

[51] Harris, 'Exchanging information'; Glaisyer, *The Culture of Commerce in England*, pp. 34–5.

[52] J. Humphries and J. Weisdorf, 'The wages of women in England, 1260–1850', *Journal of Economic History*, lxxv (2015), 405–47, at p. 432.

Few of these ephemeral printed notices have survived but the advent of newsbooks and newspapers made it possible for printed notices and advertisements to reach far larger audiences beyond the immediate environs of the Royal Exchange. By no means all of these early publications were printed, however, and manuscript newsletters dominated the early to mid seventeenth century and continued well into the period of newspaper publication during the Restoration era. Scribally produced and reproduced newsletters communicated both domestic and international news but did not contain advertisements. However, the notices and advertisements published in the printed newspapers that succeeded newsletters echoed the wealth of information that might have appeared on the printed sheets affixed to walls and columns in the exchange and in coffee houses and taverns throughout London. In March 1681, for example, the master of a ship '*bound for* Ashley River *in* Carolina' advertised in a newspaper printed on Cornhill, a stone's throw from the exchange, for anyone '*minded to transport themselves, Servants, or Goods*' to contact him 'at the Jamaica *Coffee-House* in Miles *Ally, and on the Exchange all Exchange time*'.[53] Any person who found a pocket book with a 'Silver Pen, and several Writings in it', whose owner had lost it 'betwixt the *New Exchange* and *London Bridge*', could return it to the office of a printer in Lombard Street.[54] A single issue of the *City Mercury* in January 1675 listed other items lost, numerous houses and commercial properties for sale, a ketch to be auctioned at 'Mr. *Hain's* Coffee-house in *Birchin* Lane', and sought out 'a very good Ship … fit for the *Virginia* Trade', inviting anyone with such a vessel to bring details to the *City Mercury* printing office at the exchange.[55] Similarly, a single issue of the *London Gazette* includes notices announcing the departure of 'about 20 Sail of Merchant Ships' from the Thames, the recent arrival in Bristol of a ship that had sailed from Antigua, the availability of 'several Shops proper for all forms of Trades', bankruptcy proceedings against Seymor Wood and the availability for purchase of 'several Hundred choice Canary Birds'.[56] During the second half of the seventeenth century newspapers played an increasingly significant role in the transmission of information, especially in London, and those who did not subscribe could read them in coffee houses or purchase them from female hawkers at the exchange and elsewhere in central London.

[53] 'The *Ship St.* Christopher', *Smith's Protestant Intelligence: Domestick and Forein*, 14 March 1681. For much of the later 17th century 'exchange time' occurred between 11 a.m. and noon and between 5 p.m. and 6 p.m. See N. Glaisyer, 'Merchants at the Royal Exchange, 1660–1720', in *The Royal Exchange*, pp. 198–202.

[54] 'One Pocket Book', *London Gazette*, 5 Dec. 1672.

[55] *The City Mercury; or, Advertisements concerning Trade*, 27 Jan. 1675.

[56] *London Gazette*, 4 March 1695.

The earliest newspaper advertisements appeared in the 1640s within early printed newsbooks.[57] By the early 1650s, for example, an issue of *The Perfect Diurnall of Some Passages and Proceedings of and in relation to the Armies in England, Ireland, and Scotland* (London) ended with a half page of advertisements, all for books and pamphlets published and sold by six different London printers.[58] However, given that many newsbooks were relatively short-lived and with small circulations, advertising in their pages was not necessarily a useful strategy. Of 117 English newsbook titles published between 1649 and 1660, only twenty-nine contained advertisements.[59] Longer-lasting newspapers such as *Mercurius Politicus* contained more advertisements, and one issue in June 1659 included numerous notices for books and pamphlets; an advertisement for a nursery supplying fruit trees, plants and flowers; a notice seeking a lost horse; and a runaway advertisement for a servant named Richard Smith. While many servants and apprentices eloped, their employers tended not to advertise for them unless they had committed a crime. In this case Smith had left his employer, a goldsmith in Cheapside, taking with him 'Pearls and Jewels, and Rings with Diamonds, and much gold to a great value'.[60] An analysis of advertisements in English newsbooks suggests that well over half were for books; almost 20 per cent for goods and services; about 15 per cent for 'physicians' and cures; just under 5 per cent for lost, found or stolen goods; and just under 2.5 per cent for runaways.[61]

On Wednesday, 22 November 1665, Pepys recorded in his diary the publication of the first issue of the *Oxford Gazette*, noting that the newspaper was 'very pretty, full of newes, and no folly in it'.[62] When London's outbreak of plague had diminished sufficiently, the *Gazette* relocated to the capital, where, as the *London Gazette* (Figure 10), it would serve as a vital conduit of information for many within and beyond the city. Pepys regularly referred to

[57] R. S. King, 'The manuscript newsletter and the rise of the newspaper, 1655–1715', *Huntington Library Quarterly*, lxxix (2016), 411–37; P. Arblaster, 'Posts, newsletters, newspapers: England in a European system of communications', in *News Networks in Seventeenth Century Britain and Europe*, ed. J. Raymond (London, 2006), pp. 19–34; J. Raymond, *The Invention of the Newspaper: English Newsbooks, 1641–1649* (Oxford, 1996), pp. 20–79.

[58] *The Perfect Diurnall of Some Passages and Proceedings of and in relation to the Armies in England, Ireland, and Scotland*, 7 Feb. 1652.

[59] J. McElligott, 'Advertising and selling in Cromwellian newsbooks', in *Buying and Selling: the Business of Books in Early Modern Europe*, ed. S. Graheli (Leiden, 2019), pp. 467–86; J. McElligott, *Royalism, Print and Censorship in Revolutionary England* (Woodbridge, 2007).

[60] '*Tuesday June the seventh … Richard Smith*', *Mercurius Politicus, comprising the Sum of Foreign Intelligence, with the Affairs now on foot in the Three Nations of England, Scotland, and Ireland, for Information of the People*, 9 June 1659.

[61] McElligott, 'Advertising and selling in Cromwellian newsbooks', p. 475.

[62] Pepys, *Diary*, 22 Nov. 1665.

𝕹𝖚𝖒𝖇. 2278

The London Gazette.

Published by Authority.

From **Thursday** August 18. to **Monday** August 22. 1687.

THE following Addresses have been Presented to the King, which His Majesty received very Graciously.

The humble Address of the Mayor, Recorder, Aldermen, and Assistants of Your Majesties Loyal Corporation of Tavistocke in Your County of Devon.

Great SIR,

IT having pleased Your Sacred Majesty, by Your late Royal Declaration, most Graciously to signifie Your Resolution of Protecting, Supporting, and Maintaining Your Archbishops, Bishops, and Clergy, and all Your other Subjects of the Church of England, in the free Exercise of their Religion as by Law Establisbed.

We being in Duty and Gratitude obliged, do most humbly present Your Majesty our ineffable Thanks for these and all other Your Royal Favours and former Assurances, shewn and made to the Church of England: And we do hereby unanimously and sincerely profess and declare, that we shall, to the Period of our Lives, endeavour to demean our selves as becomes the True Sons of the Church of England,

And Your Majesties most Loyal, and Obedient Subject and Servants.

To the King's most Excellent Majesty,

The Humble Address of Your Majesties Loyal and Obedient Subjects, the Dissenters of the Borough of Cockermouth, and places adjacent in the County of Cumberland, and in the name of divers others in the Western parts of the said County.

May it please Your Majesty,

WHereas in your Majesties late Declaration for an intire Liberty of Conscience unto all Your loving Subjects, You have been Graciously pleased to Declare, as Your constant Principle and Judgment; That Conscience ought not to be constrained, nor People forc'd in matters of meer Religion; and that such force shall not be attempted during Your Majesties Reign; Adding Your Gracious purpose to concur with Your Two Houses of Parliament, in a Work so transcendently Good and Glorious: To which let English Mankind say Amen.

Wherefore having solemnly given Thanks to God, who hath set over these Nations, so Wise and Gracious a Prince, making Justice and Equity the standard of His Throne; than which nothing can contribute more, to the Strength, the Wealth, and Glory of the English Nation; We Your Majesties most Dutiful Subjects, as in Duty bound, and by Your most indulgent Grace and Favour obliged, do hereby offer up unto Your Majesty, our most hearty Thanks and Acknowledgments; praying for Your Majesties long and prosperous Reign over these Your Kingdoms, and ever ready to approve our selves,

Your Majesties most Peaceable,
Loyal, and Obedient Subjects.

To the King's most Excellent Majesty,

The humble Address of divers of Your Majesties most Dutiful and Loyal Subjects, Dissenters in and about London, being Merchants, Tradesmen, and others, on occasion of Your Majesties late Declaration,

Most Gracious Soveraign,

WHen we reflect on the various difficulties through which the special Providence of God accompanied You to the Throne of Your Royal Ancestors; and of Your Wise and Gracious Conduct since; We cannot but conclude, the Almighty hath raised You up (like Moses) to be the Deliverer of his People from the Yoak and Bondage of Penal Laws, a Slavery and Darkness worse than that which punished Egypt: In sense therefore of our Duty to Almighty God, and in Duty and Gratitude to Your Self, by whose Hand we receive so great a Blessing: We presume to offer both to him and You, our solemn Thanks and Praises for the same.

By this Expedient Your Majesty will make Your Government easie and delightful to Your Self and People, augment their Trade, encourage Strangers, encrease Your Subjects, and gain the Empire of all their Hearts, banishing from thence all Fears and Jealousies.

By this Your Majesty hath distinguished and set the Bounds of Your own Dominion from that of Heaven it self; You have given to God and Man their due, and yet preserved Your own Right; and hereby Your Majesty will obtain this Glory to be admired and imitated by Your neighbouring Princes; or envied for Your own, and Subjects Felicity.

May the Almighty God who hath given You the Wisdom and Courage to attempt so great a Work, assist Your Majesty and Your next Great Council to compleat the same. And may Your Majesty long Live and enjoy the Reward thereof here; and in the World to come, an everlasting Crown of Glory. So prayes,
Your Majesties most Loyal and Obedient Subjects.

To the King's most Excellent Majesty,

The Humble Address of Your Majesties most Dutiful and Loyal Subjects, the Dissenters in Leathward in the County of Cumberland,

IT having pleased Almighty God, (and for which we bless his Name for ever) to put it into the Heart of Your Majesty to issue forth Your late Gracious Declaration for Indulgence and Liberty of Conscience to all Your loving Subjects, for the free exercise of their Religion: And Your Majesty having thereon publickly declared to the World, upon the most just and true Reasons and Principles of Nature and Christianity. That it hath been Your Majesties constant Sence and Opinion, (and as contrary to Your Royal Inclination, as to the Interest of Government) That Conscience ought not to be constrained, nor People forced in matters of meer Religion, in regard the success in all former ages, has not answered the Design, so as to reduce these Kingdoms to an exact Conformity: But that the difficulty is invincible. And being assured of your firm Resolution of adding this Liberty to the perfect enjoyment of our Property (the two things Men most value) which Your Majesty has Graciously

Figure 10. Front page of the four-page *London Gazette*, 22 August 1687 (<https://www.thegazette.co.uk>).

this newspaper in his diary, sometimes relating how he shared its contents with others or arranged for notices to be published in it.[63] At his death Pepys owned an almost complete run for the years between 1665 and 1703, as well as long runs of other London newspapers such as *Mercurius Publicus*, the *Intelligencer* and the *Newes*.[64] His dependence on this and other newspapers appears to have been typical among political, governmental and commercial figures.

The *London Gazette* was England's first broadsheet newspaper, and during the second half of the seventeenth century its significantly higher print runs and circulation increased the effectiveness of the paid advertisements that appeared regularly on the third and fourth pages. Uniquely, the *London Gazette* was both a private, commercially produced publication and a state-sanctioned and officially authorized publication run with the authority of the secretary of state. The king and his ministers disapproved of a free press and the Licensing Act of 1662 meant that by the end of 1666 the *London Gazette* was the nation's only legal newspaper. The chaos of the Exclusion Crisis resulted in parliament failing to renew the Licensing Act, and between 1679 and 1682 almost forty newspapers exploded onto the scene, but apart from this brief period the *London Gazette* was London's and England's sole legal newspaper between August 1666 and February 1688. Following the accession of James II, the Licensing Act was renewed until the freedom to publish newspapers was restored in 1695, although what printers produced remained carefully monitored.[65]

The publishers of the *London Gazette* were licensed and paid by the government to produce officially sanctioned news, and according to its colophon they intended the newspaper 'for the use of some Merchants and Gentlemen'. The periodical press in London was heavily restricted in its reporting of domestic political news and events, advertising was a freer space for publishers and readers, and advertisements rapidly became an integral feature of the newspaper. The printed advertisements displayed in such venues as the Royal Exchange were ephemeral and are largely lost to us, but the advertisements in newsbooks and newspapers have survived. Their potentially huge circulations made the *London Gazette* and the newspapers that would follow attractive to potential advertisers. Estimates vary widely, from print runs of between 13,000 and 15,000 for each

[63] Pepys, *Diary*, 14 Dec. 1666; 4 May 1666. For the sale of newspapers in London, see Glaisyer, *The Culture of Commerce*, pp. 33–4.

[64] *Mercurius Publicus, Comprising the Sum of Forraign Intelligence*; *The Intelligencer, Published for Satisfaction and Information of the People*; *The Newes, Published for Information and Satisfaction of the People*. See K. Loveman, *Samuel Pepys and his Books: Reading, Newsgathering, and Sociability, 1660–1703* (Oxford, 2015), p. 83.

[65] J. Sutherland, *The Restoration Newspaper and its Development* (Cambridge, 1986), pp. vii–viii, 2–25.

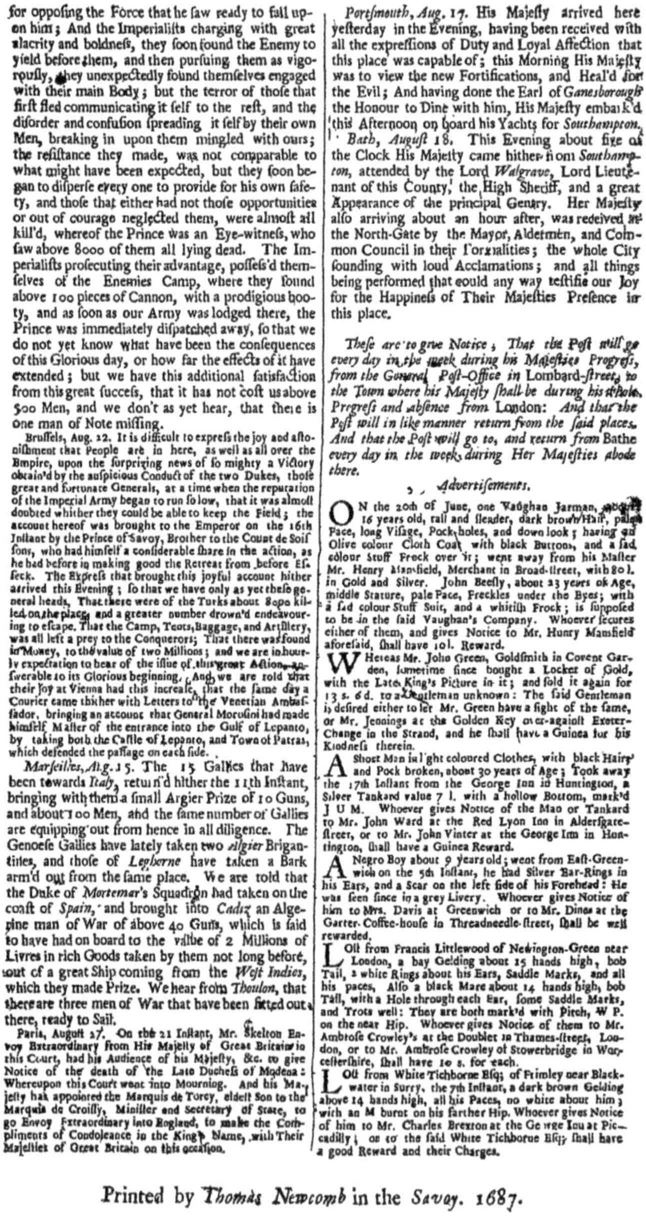

for oppoſing the Force that he ſaw ready to fall upon him; And the Imperialiſts charging with great
alacrity and boldneſs, they ſoon found the Enemy to
yield before them, and then purſuing them as vigo-
rouſly, they unexpectedly found themſelves engaged
with their main Body; but the terror of thoſe that
firſt fled communicating it ſelf to the reſt, and the
diſorder and confuſion ſpreading it ſelf by their own
Men, breaking in upon them mingled with ours;
the reſiſtance they made, was not comparable to
what might have been expected, but they ſoon began to diſperſe every one to provide for his own ſafe-
ty, and thoſe that either had not thoſe opportunities
or out of courage neglected them, were almoſt all
kill'd, whereof the Prince was an Eye-witneſs, who
ſaw above 8000 of them all lying dead. The Imperialiſts proſecuting their advantage, poſſeſs'd themſelves of the Enemies Camp, where they found
above 100 pieces of Cannon, with a prodigious boo-
ty, and as ſoon as our Army was lodged there, the
Prince was immediately diſpatched away, ſo that we
do not yet know what have been the conſequences
of this Glorious day, or how far the effects of it have
extended; but we have this additional ſatisfaction
from this great ſucceſs, that it has not coſt us above
500 Men, and we don't as yet hear, that there is
one man of Note miſſing.

Bruſſels, Aug. 22. It is difficult to expreſs the joy and aſto-
niſhment that People are in here, as well as all over the
Empire, upon the ſurprizing news of ſo mighty a Victory
obtain'd by the auſpicious Conduct of the two Dukes, thoſe
great and fortunate Generals, at a time when the reputation
of the Imperial Army began to run ſo low, that it was almoſt
doubted whither they could be able to keep the Field; the
account hereof was brought to the Emperor on the 16th
Inſtant by the Prince of Savoy, Brother to the Count de Soiſ-
ſons, who had himſelf a conſiderable ſhare in the action, as
he had before in making good the Retreat from before Eſ-
ſeck. The Expreſs that brought this joyful account hither
arrived this Evening; ſo that we have only as yet theſe general heads. That there were of the Turks about 8000 killed on the place, and a greater number drown'd endeavour-
ing to eſcape. That the Camp, Tents, baggage, and Artillery,
was all left a prey to the Conquerors; That there was found
in Money, to the value of two Millions; and we are in houſe-
ly expectation to hear of the iſſue of this great Action, An-
ſwerable to its Glorious beginning. And we are told that
their Joy at Vienna had this increaſe, that the ſame day a
Courier came thither with Letters to the Venetian Ambaſ-
ſador, bringing an account that General Moroſini had made
himſelf Maſter of the entrance into the Gulf of Lepanto,
by taking both the Caſtle of Lepanto, and Town of Patras,
which defended the paſſage on each ſide.

Marſeilles, Aug. 15. The 15 Galleys that have
been towards Italy, return'd hither the 11th Inſtant,
bringing with them a ſmall Argier Prize of 10 Guns,
and about 100 Men, and the ſame number of Galleys
are equipping out from hence in all diligence. The
Genoeſe Galleys have lately taken two Algier Brigan-
tines, and thoſe of Legherne have taken a Bark
arm'd out from the ſame place. We are told that
the Duke of Mortemar's Squadron had taken on the
coaſt of Spain, and brought into Cadiz an Alge-
rine man of War of above 40 Guns, which is ſaid
to have had on board to the value of 2 Millions of
Livres in rich Goods taken by them not long before,
out of a great Ship coming from the Weſt Indies,
which they made Prize. We hear from Thoulon, that
there are three men of War that have been fitted out
there, ready to Sail.

Paris, Auguſt 27. On the 21 Inſtant, Mr. Skelton Envoy Extraordinary from His Majeſty of Great Britain in
this Court, had his Audience of his Majeſty, &c. to give
Notice of the death of the Late Dutcheſs of Modena:
Whereupon this Court went into Mourning. And his Majeſty has appointed the Marquis de Torcy, eldeſt Son to the
Marquis de Croiſſy, Miniſter and Secretary of State, to
go Envoy Extraordinary into England, to make the Com-
pliments of Condoleance in the King's Name, with Their
Majeſties of Great Britain on this occaſion.

Portſmouth, Aug. 17. His Majeſty arrived here
yeſterday in the Evening, having been received with
all the expreſſions of Duty and Loyal Affection that
this place was capable of; this Morning His Majeſty
was to view the new Fortifications, and Heal'd for
the Evil; And having done the Earl of Ganesborough
the Honour to Dine with him, His Majeſty embark'd
this Afternoon on board his Yachts for Southampton.

Bath, Auguſt 18. This Evening about five of
the Clock His Majeſty came hither from Southampton, attended by the Lord Walgrave, Lord Lieutenant of this County, the High Sheriff, and a great
Appearance of the principal Gentry. Her Majeſty
alſo arriving about an hour after, was received at
the North-Gate by the Mayor, Aldermen, and Common Council in their Formalities; the whole City
ſounding with loud Acclamations; and all things
being performed that could any way teſtifie our Joy
for the Happineſs of Their Majeſties Preſence in
this place.

Theſe are to give Notice, That the Poſt will go
every day in the week during his Majeſties Progreſs,
from the General Poſt-Office in Lombard-ſtreet, to
the Town where his Majeſty ſhall be during his whole
Progreſs and abſence from London: And that the
Poſt will in like manner return from the ſaid places.
And that the Poſt will go to, and return from Bathe
every day in the week during Her Majeſties abode
there.

Advertiſements.

ON the 20th of June, one Vaughan Jarman, about
16 years old, tall and ſlender, dark brown Hair, pale
Face, long Viſage, Pock-holes, and down look; having an
Olive colour Cloth Coat with black Button, and a ſad
colour Stuff Frock over it; went away from his Maſter
Mr. Henry Mansfield, Merchant in Broad-ſtreet, with 80 l.
in Gold and Silver. John Beeſly, about 23 years of Age,
middle Stature, pale Face, Freckles under the Eyes; with
a ſad colour Stuff Suit, and a whitiſh Frock; is ſuppoſed
to be in the ſaid Vaughan's Company. Whoever ſecures
either of them, and gives Notice to Mr. Henry Mansfield
aforeſaid, ſhall have 10 l. Reward.

WHereas Mr. John Green, Goldſmith in Covent Garden, ſometime ſince bought a Locket of Gold,
with the Late King's Picture in it; and ſold it again for
13 s. 6 d. to a Gentleman unknown: The ſaid Gentleman
is deſired either to let Mr. Green have a ſight of the ſame,
or Mr. Jennings at the Golden Key over-againſt Exeter-
Change in the Strand, and he ſhall have a Guinea for his
Kindneſs therein.

A Short Man in ſad coloured Clothes, with black Hair
and Pock broken, about 30 years of Age; Took away
the 17th Inſtant from the George Inn in Huntington, a
Silver Tankard value 7 l. with a hollow Bottom, mark'd
J O M. Whoever gives Notice of the Man or Tankard
to Mr. John Ward at the Red Lyon Inn in Aldersgate-
ſtreet, or to Mr. John Vinter at the George Inn in Huntington, ſhall have a Guinea Reward.

A Negro Boy about 9 years old; went from Eaſt-Green-
wich on the 5th Inſtant, he had Silver Bar-Rings in
his Ears, and a Scar on the left ſide of his Forehead: He
was ſeen ſince in a grey Livery. Whoever gives Notice of
him to Mrs. Davis at Greenwich or to Mr. Dine at the
Garter-Coffee-houſe in Threadneedle-ſtreet, ſhall be well
rewarded.

LOſt from Francis Littlewood of Newington-Green near
London, a bay Gelding about 15 hands high, bob
Tail, a white Rings about his Ears, Saddle Marks, and all
his paces, Alſo a black Mare about 14 hands high, bob
Tail, with a Hole through each Ear, ſome Saddle Marks,
and Trots well: They are both mark'd with Pitch, W P.
on the near Hip. Whoever gives Notice of them to Mr.
Ambroſe Crowley's at the Doublet in Thames-ſtreet, London, or to Mr. Ambroſe Crowley of Stowerbridge in Wor-
ceſterſhire, ſhall have 20 s. for each.

LOſt from White Tichborne Eſq; of Frimley near Black-
water in Surry, the 7th Inſtant, a dark brown Gelding
above 14 hands high, all his Paces, no white about him;
with an M burnt on his farther Hip. Whoever gives Notice
of him to Mr. Charles Brexton at the George Inn at Pic-
cadilly; or to the ſaid White Tichborne Eſq; ſhall have
a good Reward and their Charges.

Printed by *Thomas Newcomb* in the *Savoy*. 1687.

Figure 11. Back page of the four-page *London Gazette*, 22 August 1687.
The advertisements include one for a nine-year-old 'Negro Boy' who
had eloped and another for two White servants who had eloped, as
well as for several lost horses (<https://www.thegazette.co.uk>).

issue of the *London Gazette* in October 1666 to between 4,000 and 7,000 per issue during the third quarter of 1678. The detailed printers' accounts for May 1695 to February 1697 and for November 1705 to November 1707 reveal that sales averaged nearly 10,000 copies per issue. This included almost 1,000 issues given away to government officials who were the source of some of the news and information within its pages and who received their copies gratis in return for this service. Other copies were supplied to subscribers, both individuals and institutions such as coffee houses and taverns, while hawkers sold them in and around the exchange and other public venues.[66]

Over the course of the second half of the seventeenth century the volume of newspaper advertising increased steadily, and by 1705 Daniel Defoe observed that 'the principal support of all the public papers now on foot depends on advertisements'.[67] Advertisements had rapidly expanded from notices for books to include medical cures and treatments, lost or stolen property including animals, lotteries, houses for sale or rent, auctions, bankruptcy proceedings, various goods for sale, and notices advertising for the apprehension of people who were lost or who had run away, including soldiers, apprentices, servants and bound or enslaved people of colour.[68] It was in the newspapers of Restoration London that the English Atlantic world's first runaway slave advertisements appeared, with well over 200 notices for lost or freedom-seeking people of colour, all published before the advent of the very first North American and Caribbean newspapers. Newspapers were destined to play a vital role in the pursuit of escaped enslaved people in colonial North America and the Caribbean, but the practice had been invented, developed and honed for more than half a century in London before its adoption in the first newspapers to appear in England's New World colonies (Figure 11).[69]

Advertisements for animals that had strayed or been stolen were rather more common than notices for runaway servants. Apart from advertisements for books and other publications, notices concerning missing animals such

---

[66] N. Glaisyer, '"The most universal intelligencers": the circulation of the *London Gazette* in the 1690s', *Media History*, xxiii (2017), 256–80, at pp. 257–8; N. Glaisyer, '"Published by authority": the *London Gazette*, 1665–1780', *População e sociedade*, xxxii (2019), 65–80, at pp. 68–9.

[67] D. Defoe, quoted in A. Downie, *Robert Harley and the Press: Propaganda and Public Opinion in the Age of Swift and Defoe* (Cambridge, 1979), pp. 111–12. See also C. J. Sommerville, *The News Revolution in England: Cultural Dynamics of Daily Information* (New York, 1996), pp. 69–70.

[68] R. B. Walker, 'Advertising in London newspapers, 1650–1750', *Business History*, xv (July 1973), 112–30.

[69] J. E. Taylor, 'Enquire of the printer: newspaper advertising and the moral economy of the North American slave trade, 1704–1807', *Early American Studies: an Interdisciplinary Journal*, xviii (2020), 287–323.

as horses and dogs were perhaps the most common paid announcements during the first half-century of English newspapers. Sometimes two or three appeared in a single issue, as when three advertisements for a total of seven horses appeared in the 28 August 1656 issue of the *Mercurius Politicus*. These advertisements rapidly assumed a fairly standard format, including a description of the missing animal and information about where and when they disappeared, to whom and where they could be returned, and the amount of any reward. In June 1656, for example, an advertisement appeared in the *Mercurius Politicus* for an 'Iron grey Gelding about fourteen handful high, six years old, with a long Tail, much inclined to white, and a white Face', believed to have 'strayed' from Lockington in Leicester two weeks earlier; anyone returning the horse there or to an address in Cripplegate, London, was promised a reward of twenty shillings. Even Charles II advertised in the newspapers when his 'black Dog, between a Greyhound and a Spaniell' was supposed stolen, for the animal 'would never forsake his Master'.[70] And, just a few weeks before her wedding to William III of Orange, Charles's niece Mary lost her much-loved 'little Spaniel' named Pert, prompting her own advertisement and detailed description and the promise of a substantial two-guinea reward for the animal's safe return.[71]

The first advertisements for servants who had eloped began appearing in London's newspapers in the mid-1650s. Many of London's households included one or more servants but, despite their having contracted to work for one year and to receive wages, these young people and those who employed them did not think of domestic service as simply and solely employment per se, for they were subsumed into the families and households in which they worked. When a man, or less commonly a woman, spoke of his or her household or family they were usually referring to live-in servants as well as family members. Law and custom dictated that servants owed obedience to their employers, and they were subject to the same authority and even physical punishment that a head of household might apply to his children and even his wife.[72] Despite this patriarchal relationship and the contract between employer and servant, it was not unusual for servants to leave before the end

---

[70] 'Advertisements', *Mercurius Politicus*, 28 Aug. 1656; 'One Iron grey Gelding', *Mercurius Politicus*, 19 June 1656; 'Advertisement. We Must call upon you again for a black Dog', *Mercurius Publicus*, 5 July 1660.

[71] 'Sunday the 21 instant … lost from *St. James's*, a little Spaniel Bitch', *London Gazette*, 25 Oct. 1677. See also J. Van der Kiste, *William and Mary: Heroes of the Glorious Revolution* (Stroud, 2003), pp. 45–8.

[72] Kussmaul, *Servants in Husbandry*, p. 9; S. D. Amussen, *An Ordered Society: Gender and Class in Early Modern England* (New York, 1988), pp. 37–40; I. K. Ben-Amos, 'Service and the coming of age of young men in seventeenth-century England', *Continuity and Change*, iii (1988), 41–64, at p. 42; M. Merry and P. Baker, '"For the house herself and one servant":

of their service, perhaps to escape punishment, to seek a better situation or a different kind of work, or for any of a wide range of reasons.[73]

In this labour-rich environment there is little evidence that employers were unduly concerned about contracted servants who eloped from their service. Pepys's diary records a high rate of turnover among servants in his London household, with some being discharged, others leaving of their own volition and yet more departing on mutual agreement. Over a ten-year period six remained in his service for between a year and eighteen months, seven for between six months and a year, five for between three and six months, and eight for less than three months, including a servant girl who ran away on her second day of work 'and we heard no more of her'. High turnover among servants was normal, and as newspaper advertisements developed in London during the second half of the seventeenth century only a very small proportion of employers made use of print media in pursuit of servants who had eloped.[74]

However, when servants stole property and took it with them employers were more inclined to publish runaway advertisements, and these notices were aimed at recovery of property and the apprehension and punishment of a thief as much as the return of a contracted servant. One of the earliest advertisements for a runaway servant appeared in the *Mercurius Politicus* on 11 September 1656, seeking out 'The Apprentice of *John Portman*, Goldsmith, at the Unicorn in *Lombard-Street*', who 'is run away, having taken a considerable summe of money with him in Spanish Pistolets and English Gold'. This advertisement described the 'bold confident' nineteen-year-old and offered a sizeable reward of £10 and expenses for his capture. Two notices placed together advertised for Daniel Midleton, 'a servant to Sir *Matth. Thomlinson*' in Westminster who had run 'away from him with certain goods of his', and for Daniel Neech who had 'run from his Master with several sums of money' and was 'supposed to be about the City'. Thus runaway servants were commonly advertised for as thieves who had stolen money, clothing, horses and other items of value. Employers did not hesitate to advertise for and pursue, for example, a servant who stole a gold picture frame set with rubies and diamonds. When an absconding maid named Nan stole from her mistress many items of fine clothing made of satin,

---

family and household in late seventeenth-century London', *London Journal: a Review of Metropolitan Society Past and Present*, xxxiv (2009), 205–32.

[73] Ben-Amos, 'Service and the coming of age', pp. 54–5.

[74] Over a 10-year period 12 servants remained with Pepys for two or more years, while these 26 were in service for much shorter terms. See Pepys, *Diary*, 20 Aug. 1663. See *The Diary of Samuel Pepys*: x, *Companion*, ed. R. Latham (Berkeley, Calif., 1983), p. 196; Earle, *The Making of the English Middle Class*, p. 221.

silk and lace, a newspaper advertisement used twenty words to describe Nan but eighty words to detail the items she had stolen. Theft on this scale was a serious crime, potentially punishable by execution: the inconvenient absence of a fairly easily replaced servant was of far less concern.[75]

Given that servants who had escaped with stolen property might hope to disappear into London's large population of servants and working people, employers used advertisements to provide details that might help identify the runaways in the large urban crowd. As runaway advertisements became more common, they emerged as some of the most developed descriptions of personal appearance that appeared in newspapers, often including depictions of bodily characteristics and apparel. News articles and other newspaper content, both foreign and domestic, seldom featured such bodily descriptions, but advertisers sought to describe individuals in ways that would resonate among readers and render identification more probable. These notices might indicate age, height, body type, complexion, hairstyle and clothing, as well as including descriptions of how individuals held and conducted themselves. But the lexicon of servitude and of skin tone and colour was not as yet fully racialized, and a binary Black and White identification system had not yet crystallized. The terms used to describe the bodily appearance of White runaways reflected contemporary understandings of aptitude, ability and character while also reflecting beliefs about the effects of body humours and weather on colouring and demeanour. A runaway servant might be 'of a bold confident behaviour' or be less self-possessed and display 'a down look, black hollow eyed … [with] a little stooping as [to] shoulders'.[76] Employers who had invested in good clothing for their servants might be all the more inclined to describe it in detail, as in the case of twenty-one-year-old Robert Bateman who eloped wearing 'a black hat on, with a small silver Band, his Breeches, Doublet and Cassock of a middle gray'.[77] 'A Black haired Maid, of a middle stature thick set, with big breasts' eloped from the Pall Mall house of her mistress, taking with her an abundance of expensive clothing that did not belong to her, and wearing 'a greyish Cloth Wastcoat turned, and a Pink-coloured Paragon upper Petticoat, with a green Tammy under one'.[78]

---

[75] 'The Apprentice of John Portman', *Mercurius Politicus*, 11 Sept. 1656; 'Advertisements. Daniel Middleton … [and] Daniel Neech', *Mercurius Politicus*, 4 Nov. 1658; 'A Young French-man … hath robbed his Master', *The Public Intelligencer, Communicating the Chief Occurrences and Proceedings Within the Dominions of England, Scotland, and Ireland*, 21 Feb. 1659; 'A Black haired Maid … did … steal away from her Ladies house in the Pal-mall', *Mercurius Publicus*, 31 May 1660.

[76] 'The Apprentice of John Portman', *Mercurius Politicus*, 11 Sept. 1656; 'Daniel Middleton about 30 years of age', *Mercurius Politicus*, 4 Nov. 1658.

[77] 'Robert Bateman, having run away', *Mercurius Politicus*, 17 June 1658.

[78] 'A Black haired Maid', *Mercurius Publicus*, 31 May 1660.

These advertisements featured a wide range of terms to describe the appearance of runaway English children and adults, and terms such as 'fresh', 'pale', 'swarthy', 'ruddy', 'brown' and 'dark' were used by advertisers to describe the skin tone of White men and women who had eloped. Twenty-two-year-old Walter Finch was 'flaxen haired, whitely faced' and Evan Jones was 'a lusty Man, and whitely coloured'.[79] Others were identified along similar lines as having notably light complexions: Charles Billingsly had 'a sallow complexion', Edward Chiffins was 'a fair Complexioned Youth', and William Harman had a 'pretty fresh complexion, a round visage, full of pockholes, grey eyes and a down look'.[80]

There were a range of terms to describe the colouring of those who did not have such pale countenances. Eighteen-year-old John Bingham had 'a fresh ruddy Complexion, [and] lank flaxen Hair', and John Jackson was similarly described as having 'a ruddy Complexion and lank whitish hair'.[81] Samuel Greenwood had a 'Redish-face', while William Hincham was described as having 'a fresh colour, but his complexion a little tann'd with the Weather'.[82] Edmund Fowler had a 'swarthy Complexion, short black Hair, [and] stammers in his Speech', while Jonathan Paine had 'a swarthy yellow Face'.[83] Others had noticeably darker complexions as in the case of Thomas Lewes and fourteen year-old Charles Russell, both of whom had a 'Brown Complexion'.[84] Some had particularly dark countenances, as in the case of John Plat who was 'of a darkish Complexion, with short thin black Hair', or Thomas Blackborn who had both 'a down look' and 'a black complexion'.[85]

Thus, well before racial slavery became a feature within English society, gradations of whiteness functioned as markers of status and modesty, particularly for women. At the beginning of the seventeenth century Thomas Campion had sung the praises of the 'country maid' Amaryllis, affectionately describing her as a 'Nutbrowne lasse'. This reference

---

[79] 'Whereas *Walter Finch* a little fellow aged about 22 years', *Mercurius Politicus*, 2 Oct. 1656; 'Thomas Walby … Evan Jones', *London Gazette*, 23 May 1687.

[80] '*Charles Billingsly*', *Public Intelligencer*, 19 Dec. 1659; 'One Edward Chiffins', *London Gazette*, 21 Jan. 1684; 'William Harman', *London Gazette*, 24 Feb. 1687.

[81] 'John Bingham', *London Gazette*, 23 April 1685; 'ONE John Jackson', *London Gazette*, 19 Sept. 1689.

[82] 'Run away … Samuel Greenwood', *London Gazette*, 30 June 1692; 'William Hinchman', *London Gazette*, 19 Aug. 1686.

[83] 'ON Tuesday … one Edmund Fowler', *London Gazette*, 21 July 1684; 'RUN away … Jonathan Paine', *London Gazette*, 21 Aug. 1690.

[84] 'Thomas Lewes, *Servant*', *London Gazette*, 31 Jan. 1684; 'Charles Russell', *London Gazette*, 2 Sept. 1689.

[85] 'THE 14th … John Plat', *London Gazette*, 23 May 1687; 'Thomas Blackborn, aged about 19', *London Gazette*, 11 Oct. 1677.

to Amaryllis's skin colouring was Campion's only description of her physical attributes, and it presented her in stark contrast to the women who displayed their class and modesty through natural or cosmetically produced white skin of the type seen in portraits of Elizabeth I and other elite women of the Tudor and Stuart eras.[86] Throughout the seventeenth century, newspaper advertisements seeking out White servants, soldiers and apprentices continued to describe their wide range of skin colourings and appearance, and many were described as having darker skin. In contrast, people of colour who eloped and were advertised for in London newspapers during the second half of the seventeenth century were generally described in simple and rudimentary terms as 'Black', 'Blackamoor' or 'Indian', suggesting that these words denoted race rather than skin colouring. The only exceptions were those with lighter skin tones who were referred to as 'mulatto' or as 'tawny'.

Yet, as England's trading outposts in South Asia and West Africa and colonies in the Caribbean and North America developed, and as the transatlantic slave trade and plantation slavery took root, runaway advertisements for people of colour represent one clear instance of the ways in which Londoners and English people began constructing themselves more generally as different from people of colour. Using late Elizabethan and early Stuart theatre, Gary Taylor has argued that the 'ideology of whiteness … originated in London, as a self-consciously symbolic fiction'.[87] Runaway advertisements for both Black and White people contributed to this process. It was in the newspapers of seventeenth-century London that the printed trope of the 'runaway slave' was developed, and later advertisements in the Caribbean and North America built upon the formulas Londoners had used to describe both escaped Whites and people of colour. Caribbean and North American runaway slave advertisements of the eighteenth and nineteenth centuries would deploy a range of terms to describe the physical appearance of enslaved freedom seekers. In slave societies filled with many thousands of people of similar appearance, subtle differences were vital for the correct identification of runaways who might otherwise melt away into the larger population of free and enslaved people of colour.[88] But these runaway slave advertisements had first appeared in

[86] T. Campion, 'I care not for these Ladies' (1601), in *The Works of Thomas Campion: Complete Songs, Masques, and Treatises with a Selection of Latin Verse*, ed. W. R. Davies (New York, 1970), p. 22.

[87] G. Taylor, *Buying Whiteness: Race, Culture, and Identity from Columbus to Hip Hop* (New York, 2005), pp. 141–2.

[88] See eg S. P. Newman, 'Hidden in plain sight: escaped slaves in late eighteenth- and early nineteenth-century Jamaica', *William and Mary Quarterly/OPEN OI* (July 2018)

the London press where notices seeking out people of colour did not need such detailed descriptions, and it was in advertisements for White servants that employers had developed the most detailed descriptions of skin tone and appearance.

The differences are readily apparent in advertisements that appeared in the *London Gazette* on 8 September 1684, including one for a freedom-seeking person of colour and another for a White servant who had eloped. The former was described in an advertisement that did not refer to skin colour, where the freedom seeker is described as 'A Negro of a middle stature about 21 years of age, [who] hath a low voice, speaks broken English' and who was wearing 'a black Hatt and Gold colour Ribbon, and a Frize Sute sad Cloth Colour'. The description of the runaway servant was rather more detailed about his appearance and skin colouring: 'THomas Parker Apprentice to Mr. Thomas Moody … being about 15 years of age, and of small stature, with Pockholes in his Face, short hair, a lively Countenance, a black Hatt, and a loose sad coloured Serge Coat with Loops upon it'.[89] There were thousands, perhaps even tens of thousands, of boys like Thomas Parker in London, and if Thomas Moody was to have any chance of regaining his apprentice the description he published needed sufficient detail to enable people to recognize the runaway boy. However, although there was a significant population of enslaved and free people of colour in the capital, their numbers were small enough to render detailed physical descriptions less necessary. Moody thought that by identifying this runaway as a twenty-one-year-old 'Negro' of middle stature, who spoke English in a deep voice, he had provided sufficient information to enable others to identify the unnamed freedom seeker. Despite English advertisements often being less detailed than those later published in the Caribbean and North America, the process of advertising and recording observable details about freedom seekers nonetheless made use of a lexicon of terms about skin tone, body type and mannerisms that served to commodify those who dared elope.[90]

The metropole

By the dawn of the eighteenth century, London had become one of the largest capital cities in Europe and the metropolitan heart of a rapidly

---

<http://oir.htmdevelopment.com/open_oi/hidden-in-plain-sight/hidden-in-plain-sight-escaped-slaves-in-late eighteenth-and-early-nineteenth-century-jamaica> [accessed 25 May 2020].

[89] 'A Negro' and 'Thomas Parker Apprentice', *London Gazette*, 8 Sept. 1684.

[90] For an excellent analysis of the significance of how Black bodies were described in North American runaway advertisements see S. Block, *Colonial Complexions: Race and Bodies in Eighteenth-Century America* (Philadelphia, Pa., 2018), pp. 35–59.

growing and ever more lucrative empire. Each year the hundreds of ships that travelled between London and England's colonies and trading posts testified to the city's imperial power: a directory of London merchants in 1677 listed almost 2,000 involved in overseas trade.[91] By 1700 England had colonies from Jamaica to Barbados to Bermuda in the Caribbean and the Atlantic, and from New Hampshire to South Carolina in North America; a string of fortified trading posts along almost 3,000 miles of the West African coast between the Gambia River and Angola; and an even larger number of trading posts in South Asia including major outposts in Surat, Bombay, Bengal and Madras. Colonization of North America and the Caribbean, the trade with West Africa and the fast-growing transatlantic slave trade, and the lucrative trade with South Asia were intimately linked and interdependent. Indeed, merchants, investors and others were simultaneously engaged in all of these areas, as in the case of Thomas Smythe, who led the East India Company between 1603 and 1621, during which time he secured a second royal charter for the Virginia Company and served as this organization's treasurer. In 1615, as the leader of the Somers Isles Company, he took control of the colony of Bermuda, and in the years that followed the island became involved in the trafficking of enslaved Africans.[92]

Slavery was an increasingly significant foundation of England's rising empire. Between 1651 and 1675 English ships carried an estimated 25,731 enslaved people to the Americas, but between 1676 and 1700 that number increased more than tenfold to 272,200.[93] As fast as England's slave trade grew, so too did the trade in the goods produced by enslaved labourers in the colonies. Annual tobacco imports rose from 1.8 million pounds in the 1630s to 22 million pounds in 1700, while sugar imports grew from an estimated 3,750 tons in 1651 to roughly 23,500 tons by 1700.[94] Both the transatlantic slave trade and the trade in the commodities grown and processed by enslaved labour in the colonies were vital foundations of English imperial power and wealth.

Yet slavery was not an abstract and distant institution for enslaved people brought to London in the later seventeenth century. Londoners who claimed

---

[91] S. Lee, *The Little London Directory of 1677* (London, 1863). See N. Zahedieh, 'Making mercantilism work: London merchants and the Atlantic trade in the seventeenth century', *Transactions of the Royal Historical Society*, ix (1999), 143–58.

[92] J. Eacott, *Selling Empire: India in the Making of Britain, 1600–1830* (Chapel Hill, N.C., 2016), p. 23.

[93] Estimates from Slave Voyages: Trans-Atlantic Slave Trade – Database <https://www. slavevoyages.org/voyage/database> [accessed 12 March 2021].

[94] C. G. A. Clay, *Economic Expansion and Social Change: England, 1500–1700* (Cambridge, 1984), p. 168; R. S. Dunn, *Sugar and Slaves: the Rise of the Planter Class in the English West Indies, 1624–1713* (Chapel Hill, N.C., 1972), p. 203.

ownership of these people were themselves part of the vast imperial project, and their dedication to the expansion and preservation of the slave trade and slavery included the development of a system for the recapture of any enslaved or bound person of colour who dared reject their subordination by attempting escape. It was in London that enslavers developed and perfected the runaway slave advertisement, making use of the new medium of newspapers to assert their control of those who sought freedom.

2. The Black community

The presence of a growing community of people of colour in seventeenth-century London is revealed by their appearance in surviving parish records.[1] More than 700 men, women and children were identified as people of colour in parish records between 1600 and 1710. Usually including a name, a date and a racial label, these records include 417 (59 per cent) baptisms, 40 (6 per cent) marriages and 248 (35 per cent) burials. There were surely many more Black people whose race was not recorded or who did not feature in these records.

Baptism, marriage or burial usually occurred in the parish in which the person resided and, given that many of these people lived in the homes of those for whom they laboured, we see people of colour spread out across London and its suburbs. A significant number were in the new and affluent areas around Westminster, for example, where they worked in well-to-do households. Others who served on ships or who worked in the maritime communities of the East End and south of the Thames were clustered in those areas. At least fifteen of the forty marriages were so-called Fleet marriages, irregular ceremonies that took advantage of a legal loophole to avoid the usual processes and charges by having a clergyman marry a couple on land that was outside of church control, usually a prison. This may suggest that people of colour were less rooted in their home parishes or, more probably, that like many White Londoners they did not have the means to undertake a regular marriage. By the late seventeenth and early eighteenth centuries perhaps half or more of the city's weddings were Fleet marriages.[2]

---

[1] All references to London baptism, marriage and burial records in this chapter are drawn from the digitized London parish records available through http://ancestry.co.uk. I am grateful to Peter Elmer for sharing data accumulated as he researched the 'Early Modern Practitioners' project (https://practitioners.exeter.ac.uk/about), and to Laurence Ward of the London Metropolitan Archives (LMA) who shared data from their 'Switching the Lens' dataset, https://search.lma.gov.uk/scripts/mwimain.dll?logon&application=UNION_VIEW&language=144&file=[lma]through-the-lens.html&utm_source=col&utm_medium=web&utm_campaign=switching-the-lens.

[2] For more on Fleet marriages see R. Probert and L. D'Arcy Brown, 'The impact of the Clandestine Marriages Act: three case-studies in conformity', *Continuity and Change*, xxiii (2008), 309–30; R. Brown, 'The rise and fall of the Fleet marriages', in *Marriage and Society: Studies in the Social History of Marriage*, ed. R. B. Outhwaite (London, 1981), pp. 117–36; J. Boulton, 'Clandestine marriages in London: an examination of a neglected urban variable', *Urban History*, xx (1993), 191–210.

Figure 12. Map of London area showing approximate locations of baptisms, marriages and burials of Black Londoners, 1600–1710. Map by Anthony King.

Baptisms
Marriages
Burials

1600-1710

Although many of these records of baptism, marriage or burial contain only a few words, they nonetheless hint at more complete life stories. Samuel Cesar (*sic*) was baptized at St John's in Wapping on 14 June 1702. White people baptized in the church that month were described in such terms as 'son of John Clark labourer', but seventeen-year-old Samuel Cesar appeared in the register as 'a black born in Ginney [*sic*]'.[3] Jane, 'an East India black [and] a servant of Mr. Crump', was christened in St Alfege in Greenwich on 13 August 1694. The words 'She knows not her name' were scrawled in the baptismal register, explaining why she was the only person baptized that month with no last name.[4] In October 1681 an African of unknown age was buried in the churchyard of St Bride's in Fleet Street. He is unnamed in the parish register and, like so many enslaved and bound people of colour, he was recorded by the name of a White person as 'Sir William Poole's Moore'.[5] It seems probable that this was the Sir William Pool who had briefly captured Tobago from the Dutch in 1672.[6]

When infants were baptized the records sometimes recognized that both parents were people of colour. Josiah Jheronomy, the 'black-moore sone of Thomas Jheronomy, black-moore, living in the ward', was baptized at St Botolph, Aldgate, on 1 September 1613. Earlier that year Thomas Jheronomy had married Hellen Millian in the same church, and in the register the couple were described as 'two black-moores'.[7] Similarly on 17 September 1695 Peter Daniel, 'a Mariner', married Elizabeth Almeda: in the parish register the couple were described as 'both of Stepney, both blacks'.[8] Two years later, on 3 March 1697, William Munday and Mary Sanders, 'Moores Both', were

[3] Baptism of Samuel Cesar, 14 Jan. 1701/2, Baptisms, Parish Register 1665–1707, St John of Wapping, p. 245. LMA, London, England, P93/JN2/004. All such references are to the digitized records at <www.ancestry.co.uk>.

[4] Baptism of Jane, 13 Aug. 1694, Christenings, Parish Register 1680–1721, St Alfege, Greenwich, p. 85. LMA, London, England, P78/ALF/002.

[5] Burial of Sir William Poole's Moore, 24 Oct. 1681, Buriails, Parish Register, 1673–1695, St Bride, Fleet Street. LMA, London, England, P69/BRI/A/005/MS06540/002.

[6] Agents of Barbados to Council of Trade and Plantations, enclosing memorial relating to islands of Tobago and St Lucia, William Bridges, Scotland Yard, 30 Dec. 1699, 'America and West Indies: December 1699, 18–31', in *Calendar of State Papers Colonial, America and West Indies: xvii, 1699 and Addenda, 1621–1698*, ed. C. Headlam (London, 1908), pp. 575–86, *British History Online* <http://www.british-history.ac.uk/cal-state-papers/colonial/america-west-indies/vol17/pp575-586> [accessed 3 April 2020].

[7] Baptism of Josiah Jeronomy, 1 Sept. 1613, Christenings, Parish Register, 1558–1625, St Botolph Aldgate, p. 144. LMA, London, England, P69/BOT2/A/001/MS09220. Marriage of Thomas Jheronomy and Helen Millian, 9 Feb. 1613, Marriages, Parish Register, 1558–1625, St Botolph Aldgate, p. 70. LMA, London, England, P69/BOT2/A/001/MS09220.

[8] Marriage of Peter Daniel and Elizabeth Almeda, 17 Sept. 1695, Marriages, Parish Register, 1694–1713, Holy Trinity, Minories. LMA, London, England, P69/TRI2/A/010/MS09245.

married at Holy Trinity, Minories.[9] On other occasions interracial couples brought infants to church for baptism. On 18 November 1706 three different members of one family were baptized at St John's in Wapping. Elizabeth Grigg and Phoebe Grigg, aged seven months and ten years respectively, were baptized alongside their mother Ann Grigg, a thirty-year-old native of Barbados. Ann was married to Thomas Grigg of Parrott Alley, almost certainly a White man.[10] London was home to both Black and interracial couples who formed families and households whose simple daily lives would have been impossible in the developing plantation colonies.

But many of London's population of people of colour were single, and most were young and separated from their birth families. Yet the surviving records enable us to learn more about enslavers such as Sir William than about Samuel Cesar, Jane or the man identified only as 'Sir William Poole's Moore'. We know that these people of colour were present in London, and that the adults who were baptized or married had chosen to engage with the local Christian community. Many of London's people of colour were in their teens or even adults when they were baptized, and perhaps this suggests that baptism was their own choice rather than something required of enslaved children by their masters and mistresses. Undoubtedly, there were more such people present in London who were not identified by race in the surviving records, or for whom such records no longer survive. Many more are absent because they were not baptized, married or buried while they were in London and so do not feature in these particular records. However, the people of colour who were recorded in parish registers attest to what Daina Ramey Berry compellingly describes as the 'soul values' of enslaved people, the determination to resist and reject bondage on the basis of a defiant awareness of their 'internal, personal, and spiritual valuation of themselves'.[11]

Even if we know little about members of London's community of people of colour, we can trace the contours of that community. We know a good deal about gender and a little about the age groups of the people appearing in church records. The gender of 664 of the 705 is clear, and of these 24 per cent were female and 76 per cent male. Precise ages were rarely recorded, but in 353 cases it is apparent whether the person recorded was an adult or a child. Of these just over half (181) were boys, girls or 'young', while 172 were aged 19 or older. However, given that these records tended to include only the ages of

[9] Marriage of William Munday and Mary Sanders, 3 March 1697, Marriages, Parish Register, 1683–1754, Holy Trinity, Minories, p. 160. LMA, London, England, P69/TRI2/A/008/MS09243.

[10] Baptism of Elizabeth, Phoebe and Ann Grigg, 18 Nov. 1706, Christenings, Parish Register, 1665–1707, St John of Wapping, p. 280. LMA, London, England, P93/JN2/004.

[11] D. R. Berry, 'Soul values and American slavery', *Slavery & Abolition*, xlii (2021), 201–18, at p. 203.

children, it is probable that most of a further 328 whose age was not recorded were adults. Among those aged 18 or younger, 134 (77 per cent) were male and 41 (23 per cent) female. A total of 172 records clearly indicated that the person being baptized, married or buried was an adult, and of these 45 (26 per cent) were female and 127 (74 per cent) male. It seems clear that males constituted approximately three quarters of London's community of people of colour.

These records are generally imprecise about the status of the person who was being baptized, married or buried. Some were probably enslaved, others were free, and many more were in a liminal state between these categories, bound to serve a particular person and living much as an employed English servant might live, yet perhaps believing themselves vulnerable to being sent or taken back to a colony where enslaved status might easily be reimposed upon them. Only one was explicitly identified as a 'slave', a word used surprisingly rarely to describe people of colour in seventeenth-century London. In November 1662 Emanuell Fernande, buried in the graveyard of St Benet Fink in the City of London's Broad Street ward, was identified in the parish register as 'Mr Adams friends slave a blackamore'.[12] Situated on Threadneedle Street perhaps fifty yards north-east of the Royal Exchange, this church was in the heart of the City of London's mercantile district.

In other instances the parish registers hint at enslaved status, or at least a subservient role that was qualitatively different from that of White servants. Margaret and her daughter Katherine were both baptized on 15 December 1710 in St John's in Hackney. Only their first names were recorded, and Margaret was described as 'Madm. Mitchel's Negro'.[13] The lack of a surname and the possessive label both suggest that Madame Mitchell may well have regarded Margaret and Katherine as her property, not least because free servants who had children were usually fired by their employers. Similarly, on 7 June 1696 Daniel Locker was baptized at St Paul's in Shadwell in the heart of the East End shipping districts. Locker was described in the register as being twenty years old and 'a Black that serves Mr Robert Davies a Shipwright against ye Mast Yard' in Wapping, which lay adjacent to Shadwell.[14] Two months earlier Phenex Negro was baptized in the same church, and he was described in the register as 'a Black that Served to Jane Moss Tobacconist', again in Wapping.[15]

---

[12] Burial of Emanuell Fernande, 20 Nov. 1662, Burials, Parish Register, St Benet Fink, p. 40. LMA, London, England, P69/BEN1/A/010/MS04098.

[13] Baptism of Margaret and Katherine, 15 Dec. 1710, Baptisms, Parish Register of St John, Hackney, p. 110. LMA, London, England, P79/JN1/024.

[14] Baptism of Daniel Locker, 7 June 1696, Baptisms, Parish Register, 1695–1702, St Paul, Shadwell. LMA, London, England, P93/PAU3/114.

[15] Baptism of Phenex Negro, Baptisms, 7 April 1696, Parish Register, St Paul Shadwell, 1670–1711, p. 275. LMA, London, England, P93/PAU3/001.

For some people of colour, baptism may have served as the prelude or the postscript to escape. Church membership represented integration into a vital institution of English society and recognition of the equality of Black and White parishioners in the eyes of God. Church membership must have dissolved some of what made people of colour appear different and alien, and enabled the creation of friendship and community across racial lines, all of which may have facilitated escape. The baptismal records of the church of St Philip and Jacob in Bristol show that on 16 April 1693 'Daniel Poole a black' was baptized. Four months later an advertisement appeared in the *London Gazette* for 'A Negro Boy aged about 20, speaks English very well, his name is Daniel Poole … run away from his Master at Bristol'. Apparently Poole was taken up, for two months later another advertisement in the *London Gazette* sought out 'A Negro Boy named Daniel Poole'; the different clothing described in these two advertisements suggests two separate escape attempts rather than one prolonged absence.[16] We cannot know whether or not baptism had encouraged this young man to try repeatedly to escape but it may have given him some sense of membership of a community beyond his master's household. His determination to be free is clear, and the advertisements in the *London Gazette* suggest that Poole's pursuers believed he was headed for or was already in the capital.

Regardless of their status, Africans and South Asians were a conspicuous part of the workforce in the maritime communities that served ships going to and returning from West Africa, South Asia and the Caribbean and North American colonies. Boys and men of colour served on these ships, sometimes as the enslaved property of ship captains and officers and at other times as free men, and they too appear in these parish records. A scant ten words describes the death and burial of one such unnamed man at St John's in Wapping. The man's cause of death, his racial identity, and where he had worked were recorded simply as 'fever d[ied] black man from on bord of a ship', and his age, status and identity are lost forever.[17]

Peter Black, who was recorded as 'Mr Lowman's Blackmore', was buried in the churchyard of St George the Martyr in Southwark in November 1692.[18] In Greenwich, the fast-growing hub of Royal Naval and commercial shipping (Figure 13), Zephania was identified as 'an Indian belonging to

[16] Baptism of Daniel Poole, 16 April 1693, Christenings, Parish Register, St Philip and Jacob, 1671–1699, Bristol, 7, P/St P&J/R/1/4; 'A Negro Boy aged about 20', *The London Gazette*, 31 Aug. 1693; 'A Negro Boy named Daniel Poole', *London Gazette*, 30 Oct. 1693.

[17] Unnamed Burial record, Burials, 25 Nov. 1697, Parish Register, St John Wapping, 1665–1707, p. 111 recto. LMA, London, England, P93/JN2/023.

[18] Burial of Peter Black, Buryalls, Nov. 1692, p. 84 verso. LMA, London, England, P92/GEO/142.

Figure 13. Jan Griffier, *A View of Greenwich from the River with Many Boats*, 1700–10, Yale Center for British Art.

Mrs Elizabeth Johnson' when she was baptized in February 1687.[19] Elizabeth Johnson's father-in-law had inherited a large shipbuilding yard in Blackwall, close to Greenwich, and her uncle had served in Bengal in the East India Company before becoming involved with the West African trade. He was eventually appointed governor of the British forts in West Africa, dying in 1719 in Cape Coast Castle on the Gold Coast.[20] Also in Greenwich 'Captain Robinsons black-boy' William Christian was baptized on 5 February 1662, one of a number of boys of colour in these parish records who were identified with ship captains.[21] Twenty years later Theophilus Foy, 'a blackamore belonging to Capt John Castle', was baptized in the same parish.[22] Other boys and men of colour were identified with ships as well as captains, as in the case of William Newport who was baptized at St Dunstan and All

[19] Baptism of Zephania, Christening, 25 Feb. 1687, Parish Register of St Alfege, Greenwich, p. 42. LMA, London, England, P78/ALF/002.

[20] For details of Henry Johnson (1659–1719) see <http://www.histparl.ac.uk/volume/1660-1690/member/johnson-sir-henry-1659-1719>, and for William Johnson (*c.*1660–1718) see <https://www.historyofparliamentonline.org/volume/1660-1690/member/johnson-william-1660-1718> [accessed 26 March 2020].

[21] Baptism of William Christian, Christenings, Feb. 1706, Parish Register of St Alfege, Greenwich, p. 197. LMA, London, England, P78/ALF/002.

[22] Baptism of Theophilus Foy, 3 Sept. 1685, Christenings, 1684, Parish Register of St Alfege, Greenwich, p. 27. LMA, London, England, P78/ALF/002.

Saints Church in Stepney in 1694, and was recorded in the parish register as 'a Negro belonging to Capt Lucas the Ship Elizabeth'.[23]

On occasion it is possible to speculate beyond the few words of these parish records. For example, we cannot know – but it seems probable – that the unnamed 'Black servant to Capt[n] Beasley' who was buried at St Dunstan and All Saints in Stepney on 12 August 1704 was the property of Edward Beasley, captain of the London-based slave ship *Betty*.[24] The ship had transported 190 West Africans to Jamaica two years earlier.[25] One of the two owners of that ship was Benjamin Quelch, from whom an unnamed sixteen-year-old 'Negro Maid' had escaped in December 1702, not long after the *Betty* had returned to London.[26] Almost a month later she remained at liberty and a second advertisement named her as Bess: both of these notices promised a guinea reward to anybody who would bring her or information about her to Lloyd's coffee house.[27] Thus the evidence suggests that it is possible that both Bess and the unfortunate boy buried in the East End two years later had suffered on the slave-trading voyage of the *Betty* and then been brought back to London as the personal property of the ship's captain and owner.

Elizabeth was described as 'Eliz: Capt: Swans black' in the record of her burial in the churchyard of St Nicholas Deptford in December 1683. She may well have sailed on the London-based slave-trading ship *Carlisle* which, under the command of Captain Charles Swan, had brought over 400 enslaved people from Cabinda on the Angola coast to Jamaica. Having arrived in Jamaica in September 1681, the *Carlisle* would have been back in London later that year or in early 1682.[28] Maria Moore, her race furnishing her with an imposed last name for the register, was baptized at St Dunstan and All Saints in Stepney on 24 January 1694. She was identified in the parish register as 'Maria Moore a black Servant to Capt: James Brusser of Ratcliffe 19 years old'.[29] This was probably James Brusser, who captained several slave-trading voyages. Thus Maria Moore may well have been on Brusser's ship the *Blossom*, no more than

[23] Baptism of William Newport, 16 Sept. 1694, Christenings, Parish Register of St Dunstan and All Saints, Stepney. LMA, London, England, P93/DUN/259.

[24] Burial of unnamed person, 12 Aug. 1704, Parish Register of Burials, St Dunstan and All Saints, Stepney, 1701–1715. LMA, London, England, P93/DUN/128.

[25] Voyage of the *Betty*, Voyage 24142 in Slave Voyages: Trans-Atlantic Slave Trade – Database <https://www.slavevoyages.org/voyage/database> [accessed 26 March 2020].

[26] 'A Negro Maid', *The Flying Post; or, The Post-Master*, 12 Dec. 1702.

[27] 'A Negro Maid … named Bess', *The Post Man: And The Historical Account*, 2 Jan. 1703.

[28] Unnamed Burial record, 8 Dec. 1683, Buried, Parish Register of St Nicholas, Deptford, 1664–1735, p. 246. LMA, London, England, P78/NIC/003; Voyage of the *Carlisle*, Voyage 9897 in Slave Voyages: Trans-Atlantic Slave Trade database.

[29] Maria Moore, Christening, 24 Jan. 1694, Parish Register of St Dunstan and All Saints, Stepney, 1656–1710. LMA, London, England, P93/DUN/259.

sixteen years old when the ship reached Jamaica in October 1689, before she arrived with him in London in the early summer of 1690.[30]

As Maria shows, not all the people revealed in London parish records as having been enslaved by or bound to ship captains were young males. An unnamed 'Negro Girl of Capt Listock of Limehouse' was laid to rest in the church yard of St Dunstan and All Saints in Stepney in late March 1690.[31] Three other people were buried on the same day, all of whom were graced with a name. Girls and women of colour may have served as domestic servants to ship captains, especially if these men had wives and families. However, these unfortunate people may very well have been sexual victims: young women enslaved or held in bound service to men were even more vulnerable to rape than White servants were. We may glimpse some of the suffering endured by one woman of colour who chose to end her own life. Perhaps the pastor of the church of St George the Martyr in Southwark recognized this when he laid to rest in consecrated ground the body of 'Sarah Goulding a blackamore [who had] hang[ed] herself'. Normally anyone who committed the mortal sin of suicide was denied a Christian burial.[32]

Most of the younger Black people who served Londoners were male, however, and many of these attended elite members of society. On 6 December 1691 'Daniel Mingoe an Indian boy servant to Lady Ann Godwin' was baptized in the church of St Katherine Cree in Aldgate ward of the City of London.[33] Sinoben, identified as 'the Earl of Dorsetts Blackamoor', was buried on 30 January 1664 at St Bride's Fleet Street on the western edge of the City of London, while in 1697 fifteen-year-old Thomas Williams was baptized in St Alfege in Greenwich as 'A Negro belonging to Sir Richard Reynes'.[34] On 12 November 1684 mother and daughter Margaret and Frances were baptized at St Pancras, Euston Road. They were described in the register as 'Two Blacks of my Ld Baltimore's', and a few months later on 12 March 1685 'Thomas a black child of Lord Baltimore'

[30] Voyage of the *Blossom*, Voyage 9659 in Slave Voyages: Trans-Atlantic Slave Trade database.

[31] Unnamed Burial record, 26 March 1690, Parish Register of St Dunstan and All Saints, Stepney, 1684–1694. LMA, London, England, P93/DUN/280.

[32] Sarah Goulding, Burial record, 5 Jan. 1669, Buriall, Parish Register of St George the Martyr, Southwark, Parish Register, 1664–1735, p. 85 recto. LMA, London, England, P78/NIC/003.

[33] Daniel Mingoe, baptism record, 6 Dec. 1691, Baptizings, Parish Register of St Katherine Cree, 1664–1735. LMA, London, England, P78/NIC/003.

[34] Sinoben, Burial record, 30 Jan. 1664, Burialls [*sic*], Parish Register of St Bride Fleet Street, 1653–1699, p. 139 verso. LMA, London, England, P69/BRI/A/005/MS06540/001. Thomas Williams, baptism record, 5 June 1697, Christenings, Parish Register of St Alfege, Greenwich, 1538–1812, p. 107. LMA, London, England, P78/ALF/002.

was buried in the church yard of St Giles in the Fields.[35] Charles Calvert, the third Lord Baltimore, had returned from Maryland to London in 1684, presumably bringing these enslaved servants with him. The Lords Baltimore had endeavoured to bring as many enslaved Africans to Maryland as possible to support the colony's rapidly growing tobacco plantations. Lord Baltimore's proprietorial control of the colony founded by his grandfather would end with the Glorious Revolution a few years later, but he and his family's control of enslaved people like Thomas would last far longer.[36]

Even though the racial descriptors recorded by London clerics in these parish records were often quite imprecise, we can still detect some patterns. Sixty-eight people were identifiably South Asian, and these people were usually described as Indian or East Indian. One of these was also described as mulatto, while thirteen South Asians were labelled as Black and two described as 'negro'. In general, however, the term 'negro' appears to have been reserved for Africans and their descendants, and 175 people were recorded in London's parish registers with this term appended to their names or records. Even more Africans were described in some way as 'moor', including 157 as 'blackamoor', thirty-eight as moor, and three as 'tawnymoor'. Twenty-five were identified as African born, often with references to specific locations such as Guinea or Madagascar, while others were labelled more generically as Ethiopian or Barbary. The largest single racial descriptor was 'black', which was used as a single-word racial descriptor in 225 records, as well as in some records as a secondary label, as in the case of 'Negro black' or 'Indian black', evidence that the term was applied to both Africans and South Asians.[37]

During these early days of England's empire only a handful of people were identified as having originated in the American and Caribbean colonies; probably more came from these areas, but this was not mentioned in church records. Isaac Sandy was baptized on 15 March 1702 in the church of St Mary in Stratford-le-Bow in the East End, and described in the register as 'a Black about

---

[35] Margaret and Frances, baptism record, 12 Nov. 1684, Christenings, Parish Register of St Pancras Old Church, 1538–1812. LMA, London, England, P90/Pan1/001. Thomas, Burial record, 12 March 1684/5, Burialls [sic], Parish Register of St Giles in the Fields, Holborn, 1668–1719. LMA, London, England, P69/BRI/A/005/MS06540/001.

[36] J. G. Morris, *The Lords Baltimore* (Baltimore, Md., 1874), p. 42. In 1664 Governor Calvert had written to the second Lord Baltimore to reassure him that the latter's efforts to ensure the Royal African Company would bring large cargoes of enslaved Africans to Maryland would meet with success. George Calvert to Lord Baltimore, 27 April 1664, in *Documents Illustrative of the History of the Slave Trade to America*, ed. E. Donnan (Washington, D.C., 1935), iv. 9.

[37] In all of these church records and in the runaway slave newspaper advertisements it was comparatively rare for South Asians to be identified by the terms 'negro', 'blackamoor' or 'moor'.

18 yeares of age. Born at Barbados'. Also baptized in the church on this day was fourteen-year-old Thomas Adams, also born in Barbados, and following these records appear the words 'these 2 boys Belongs to Mr Barwick Marchant'.[38] Anthony Black, who was baptized at St Nicholas in Deptford on 28 January 1704, appears in the parish register as 'an Indian born at Maddras', one of a number of people identified as coming from a specific part of South Asia.[39]

These church records identify Black people across Greater London from Greenwich to Putney and from St Pancras to Lambeth, and more than anything else they suggest the ubiquity of Africans and South Asians in early modern London. However, almost half (45 per cent) of the baptisms, marriages and burials were recorded in the registers of parishes within the City of London itself, an area of little more than one square mile. This was where many of the merchants and investors in colonial ventures lived and worked, as did those who worked for them in their homes and businesses. The shipping and mercantile areas of the East End accounted for a further 23 per cent, while 13 per cent came from the communities hugging the southern banks of the Thames from London Bridge eastward to Greenwich. The remainder were from the areas to the immediate west, north and south of the City of London, with 16 per cent in and around Westminster and 3 per cent in London's other suburbs.

Certain parishes and wards were particularly prominent, especially in the areas to the south and east of the City adjacent to the Thames. Sixty-eight of the records came from Stepney, thirty-four from Whitechapel, and twenty-five from Wapping, while south of the river twenty-five came from Southwark, and nineteen each from Deptford and Greenwich. While baptisms, marriages and burials of people of colour took place all over the London area, there was a noticeable concentration of such ceremonies to the west of the city near Westminster. A remarkable fifty-three took place at St Martin in the Fields and a further thirty-seven at St Giles in the Fields, two thirds of them baptisms and the remainder all burials. Although some affluent areas were developing around this part of London, the 'Rookery' was a particularly poor area: perhaps the label 'St Giles blackbirds' applied to residents of this area may have signalled the presence of a noticeable population of colour.[40] Whatever the reason, the churches of St Martin in the Fields and St Giles in the Fields were clearly popular among members of London's Black population.

---

[38] Isaac Sandy and Thomas Adams, baptism records, 15 March 1702, Parish Register of St Mary, Stratford-le-Bow, 1647–1724, p. 285. LMA, London, England, P88/MRY1/003.

[39] Anthony Black, baptism record, 28 Jan. 1704, Parish Register of St Nicholas, Deptford, 1702–1718, p. 13. LMA, London, England, P78/NIC/004.

[40] G. H. Gerzina, *Black London: Life before Emancipation* (Hanover, N.H., 1995), p. 19.

The marriages of Black adults and the christening of Black children all suggest that some people of colour were free and independent, but many more who appear in London's parish records were enslaved or bound in service and many lived in a liminal state between these two extremes. In most cases the precise status of people of colour recorded in seventeenth- and early eighteenth-century church records for the London area is far from clear, but taken together the records clearly indicate the existence of a small yet significant community of Africans and Asians in the capital. The City of London and the maritime communities of the East End and south of the Thames were still relatively small, occupying no more than a few square miles in total, and so, although London's Black population was heavily outnumbered by White people, it would not have been unusual to see men, women and children of colour living and working in the capital.

The apparent otherness of these men, women and children may encourage historians to see them as outsiders and strangers with limited agency, within yet apart from London society.[41] Many of Restoration London's Black people were what Ira Berlin described as 'Atlantic Creoles', people who 'might bear the features of Africa, Europe or the Americas in whole or in part' but whose new cosmopolitan identities transcended their origins.[42] While parish records, and most especially the newspaper advertisements at the heart of this book, provide evidence of the subordination of bound people of colour, they simultaneously suggest agency within and degrees of membership in London society. On the one hand, in the heart of London enslavers and their allies were working to consolidate the institution of racial slavery, an effort designed to confirm the subordinate status of many people of colour. On the other hand, the very existence of these parish records and newspaper advertisements serve as evidence that Black people, many of them children, sought a degree of agency, whether through baptism, marriage or resistance to their bondage by escaping. Even in death their burial in London's churchyards marked these people as Londoners – men, women and children who were accorded the same Christian rituals as any White person. Thus 'John Cooke, a Blackamoor' was baptized at St Peter, Cornhill, on 7 November 1683; fourteen years later 'John Cooke a man a black from off Salt Peter bank'

---

[41] This point has been made by O. Nubia, '"Blackamoores" have their own names in early modern England', in *Black British History: New Perspectives*, ed. H. Adi (London, 2019), pp. 15–36, at p. 17.

[42] I. Berlin, *Many Thousands Gone: the First Two Centuries of Slavery in North America* (Cambridge, Mass., 1998), p. 17.

was buried at St Mary Whitechapel.[43] Saltpetre Bank was a small area of southern Whitechapel, close to Wapping, and it lay less than one mile east of St Peter, Cornhill. It would be extremely unlikely that two men named John Cooke would be identified as Black in adjacent London parishes some fourteen years apart, and thus these records provide evidence of the relatively long period of life and work of this one late seventeenth-century Black Londoner.

Escape was the means by which many Black Londoners grasped at the possibility of independence. Freedom seekers hoped to improve their situations by asserting control over the conditions of their life and employment – and over their own bodies. They did so in London, and, while some sought to escape the city, many others appear to have anticipated a life of freedom living and working as free Black Londoners in the heart of a nation that was rapidly expanding involvement in and profit from the transatlantic slave trade and plantation slavery.

---

[43] John Cooke, baptism record, 7 Nov. 1683, Parish Register of St Peter, Cornhill, 1538–1774, p. 74. LMA, London, England, P69/PET1/A/001/MS08820. John Cooke, Burial record, 13 Oct. 1697, Parish Register of St Mary, Whitechapel, 1695–1812. LMA, London, England, P93/MRY1/005.

3. Freedom seekers in Restoration London

... a little Negro *Boy of about 13 years of age ... has been seen much to frequent* Fleet Street *and the* Strand *...* (1664)

A Negro Boy, his name Africa, *by his growth seeming to be about 12 years old ... speaks some English, Dutch, and Blacks ...* (1678)

Run away ... a Negro about 16 years of age, pretty tall, he speaks English, but slow in Speech ... he is called by the name of Othello ... (1685)

Run away the 30th of January, a Negro Man of Tawny Complexion, with Mosse Hair, middle stature, with a Down Cast Look, he walks with his Chin in his Bosom, having a piece of one of his Ears cut of, with a Brass Collar about his Neck, he talks very bad English, and is called Ned, and will readily answer to that Name. (1689)

An Indian black Girl, aged about 15, with a Brass Collar about her Neck, in a Drugget Gown and a Painted-Callico Petticoat ... (1690)

A Black Boy, an Indian, about 13 years old, run away... having a Collar about his Neck with this Inscription, the Lady Bromfield's Black in Lincolns Inn Fields ... (1694)

A Negro, named Quoshey, aged about 16 years ... run away from Bell-Wharf ... branded on his left Breast with E.A. but not plain, and shaved round his Head ... (1700)[1]

There were many Africans and South Asians in Restoration London. During the second half of the seventeenth century English colonists, traders, sailors and adventurers brought more and more people of colour back to the British

---

[1] ' ... a little *Negro* Boy', *The Newes, Published for Satisfaction and Information of the People*, 8 Dec. 1664; 'A Negro Boy', *The London Gazette*, 12 Sept. 1678; 'Run away ... a Negro', *London Gazette*, 5 Jan. 1685; 'Run away the 30th of January', *London Gazette*, 7 March 1689; 'An Indian black Girl', *London Gazette*, 22 Sept. 1690; 'A Black Boy, an Indian', *London Gazette*, 10 Sept. 1694; 'A Negro, named Quoshey', *London Gazette*, 30 Dec. 1700.

Isles, and most especially to the metropole.[2] Restoration London was within, and indeed essential to, the contact zone between English investors, merchants, planters and bound Africans and South Asians, and as such it was a venue in which at least some English understandings and practices of racial slavery were constructed. How many of the men, women and children of colour brought to the seventeenth-century city were enslaved? Who were they and what can we learn of their lives and existence? We cannot fully answer these questions, and in many cases the only surviving records of these people are newspaper advertisements for those who escaped or were lost, short notices that reveal precious little about the individuals in question.

Some Africans and South Asians in London were enslaved, others were held in an often ill-defined state of bondage, while a few were or eventually became nominally free employees. Their status is blurred by the language people in England used to describe them, for during much of the seventeenth century the words 'slave' and 'slavery' were more commonly used by English people of themselves rather than applied to bound Africans and South Asians. During the Exclusion Crisis the earl of Shaftesbury declared in the House of Lords that 'Popery and Slavery, like two sisters, go hand-in-hand', and a sermon celebrating King William's displacement of James II enthused that his reign would prevent both the 'inslaving of

[2] There is a growing historiography related to people of colour in early modern London and England, although there has been less work on slavery and freedom seekers in the foundational later 17th century. See eg M. Kaufman, *Black Tudors: the Untold Story* (London, 2017); K. Chater, *Untold Histories: Black People in England and Wales during the Period of the British Slave Trade, c.1660–1807* (Manchester, 2009); G. Gerzina, *Black London: Life before Emancipation* (New Brunswick, N.J., 1995); C. Molineux, *Faces of Perfect Ebony: Encountering Atlantic Slavery in Imperial Britain* (Cambridge, Mass., 2012); K. F. Hall, *Things of Darkness: Economies of Race and Gender in Early Modern England* (Ithaca, N.Y., 1995); I. Habib, *Black Lives in the English Archives, 1500–1677: Imprints of the Invisible* (Aldershot, 2008); S. D. Amussen, *Caribbean Exchanges: Slavery and the Transformation of English Society, 1640–1700* (Chapel Hill, N.C., 2007); F. O. Shyllon, *Black Slaves in Britain* (Oxford, 1974); N. Myers, *Reconstructing the Black Past: Blacks in Britain, 1780–1830* (London, 1996); P. Fryer, *Staying Power: the History of Black People in Britain* (London, 1984); J. Walvin, *The Black Presence: a Documentary History of the Negro in England* (London, 1971); *Slavery and the British Country House*, ed. M. Dresser and A. Hann (Swindon, 2013); P. D. Fraser, 'Slaves or free people? The status of Africans in England, 1550–1750', in *From Strangers to Citizens: the Integration of Immigrant Communities in Britain, Ireland and Colonial America, 1550–1750*, ed. R. Vigne and C. Littleton (Brighton, 2001), pp. 254–60; V. C. D. Mtubani, 'African slaves and English law', *Pula: Botswana Journal of African Studies*, iii (1981), pp. 71–5. We know far less about South Asians in 17th-century London, but there is a little more work in this field for the 18th century: see E. Rothschild, *The Inner Life of Empires: an Eighteenth-Century History* (Princeton, N.J., 2011), pp. 87–91, 291–9, and E. S. Filor, 'Complicit colonials: Border Scots and the Indian empire, c.1780–1857' (unpublished University College London PhD thesis, 2014), pp. 205–14.

our Bodies ... [and] the Inslaving of our Souls'.[3] When this new king had arrived in Exeter, his procession included '200 Blacks brought from the Plantations of the *Neitherlands* in *America*' to attend the horses of the cavalrymen, wearing 'Imbroyder'd Caps lin'd with white Fur, and plumes of white Feathers'.[4] Englishmen's celebration of their liberation from a more symbolic bondage was heralded by Africans whose enslavement was real.

English onlookers may very well have regarded these Black attendants as servants rather than as enslaved. The most widely used English translations of the Bible had all but eliminated the word 'slavery', employing instead the word 'servant' to describe the various forms of service and bondage represented in Scripture. Tyndale's version of Deuteronomy XXIII: 16, for example, represented an enslaved person who had escaped as 'the servant which is escaped from the master', and the practice of using the word 'servant' in place of 'slave' pervaded the King James and the Geneva Bibles. Most strikingly of all, the Israelites in Egypt were described in these Bibles as servants rather than as slaves, and the language of service and bond labour almost completely replaced the language of enslavement. The Egyptians 'caused the Children of Israel to Serve', who were rescued when God bought his chosen people 'out of the land of Egypt, out of the house of bondmen'.[5] The Bible was the most ubiquitous printed work in seventeenth-century England, and in its pages (as well as in thousands of religious tracts and sermons) the 'usages of "servant" to denote "slave" – following the Hebrew *'eved*, Greek *doulos*, and Latin *servus* – continued to be used throughout the seventeenth century'.[6]

In England service and servitude were a continuum encompassing both the nominally free labour of many young English men and women and the bound labour of Africans, some South Asians and some indigenous people. In contrast, the word 'slave' tended to appear in English polemics with reference to an English person's or a Protestant's loss of religious or political freedom. This included English sailors, merchants and others captured and held by

[3] John Marshall, *John Locke: Resistance, Religion and Responsibility* (Cambridge, 1994), p. 111; *England's Call to Thankfulness for her Great Deliverance from Popery and Arbitrary Power by the Glorious Conduct of the Prince of Orange (now King of England) in the year 1688 in a sermon preach'd in the parish-church of Almer in Dorsetshire on February the 14th, 1688 by John Olliffe* (London, 1689), pp. 3–4.

[4] *A True and Exact Relation of the Prince of Orange his Publick Entrance into EXETER* (London, 1688). I am grateful to Judith Spicksley for drawing my attention to this event.

[5] Deuteronomy XXIII: 16, *Five Books of Moses [Pentateuch]* [Tyndale Bible] (Antwerp, 1530); Exodus II: 13, *The Bible: Translated according to the Ebrew and Greeke ...* [Geneva Bible] (London, 1611), p. 22; Jeremiah XXXIV: 13, *The Holy Bible ...* [King James Version] (London, 1611).

[6] N. Tadmor, *The Social Universe of the English Bible: Scripture, Society, and Culture in Early Modern England* (Cambridge, 2010), p. 100; see also pp. 82–118.

North African states, a cause célèbre in Restoration England. In his diary Pepys recorded meeting Captain Mootham and Mr Dawes, 'who have been both slaves … [in Tangiers and] did make me fully acquainted with their condition there'. Throughout the seventeenth century Englishmen such as John Rawlins, William Oakeley and Thomas Phelps wrote accounts of their enslavement, while their stories spread still further through ballads such as 'The Algiers Slaves Releasement' or the catchily titled 'The Lamentable Cries of at Least 1500 Christians: Most of Them Being Englishmen … [in] Turkish Slavery'.[7]

Of course, the language of slavery and servitude was starkly different in Barbados, Virginia and the other plantation colonies where it quickly became important to differentiate between White servants on the one hand and enslaved Africans and indigenous people on the other. In these colonies the difference between a White servant and a Black enslaved person was profound. But in seventeenth-century England the differences were less visible and linguistic imprecision far more common, with the result that during the second half of the seventeenth century the word 'servant' covered both White workers and bound people of colour. Consequently, although there are fleeting impressions of Africans and South Asian people of colour in early modern English records, it is often very difficult to determine their precise status. Some appear in parish records, others in runaway advertisements in London newspapers seeking the recapture and return of people of colour who had escaped. In London the Atlantic world's very first runaway slave newspaper advertisements conceptualized and defined the very concept of the runaway slave, though these notices seldom included the word 'slave'.[8] In seventeenth-century English newspapers the word 'slave' was seldom applied to people of colour.

---

[7] *The Diary of Samuel Pepys: Daily Entries from the 17th Century London Diary*, 8 Feb. 1661 <https://www.pepysdiary.com/diary> [accessed 24 Jan. 2021]; J. Rawlins, *The Famous and Wonderful Recovery of a Ship of Bristol, called the Exchange, from the Turkish Pirates of Argier* (London, 1622); W. Okeley, *Eben-ezer or a Small Monument of Great Mercy Appearing in the Miraculous Deliverance of John Anthony, William Okeley, William Adams, John Jephs and John Carpenter from the Miserable Slavery of Algiers …* (London, 1675); T. Phelps, *A True Account of the Captivity of Thomas Phelps, at Machiness in Barbary* (London, 1685); *The Algiers Slaves Releasement; or, The Unchangeable Bost-Swain* (London, 1671); *The Lamentable Cries of at Least 1500 Christians: Most of Them Being Englishmen (Now Prisoners in Argiers under the Turks) …* (London, 1624), repr. in *Naval Songs and Ballads*, ed. C. H. Firth (London, 1908), xxxiii. 88–9, 31–3. See also R. C. Davis, *Christian Slaves, Muslim Masters* (Basingstoke, 2004), pp. 3–68.

[8] Traditionally historians have used the term 'runaway slave' for those who attempted to escape enslavement. This term is somewhat problematic given that it labels the person as a 'slave' and therefore denies them individuality or even a small degree of agency by defining them as an object and property. Moreover, the term may be read as implying an almost unquestioning acceptance of the categorization of escape as an illegal act, a theft of property. The term 'freedom seeker' acknowledges the individuality and agency of the person who

Whether they were regarded as servants or as enslaved, these freedom seekers of Restoration London are as elusive to us as they often were to those who pursued them. In North America and the Caribbean it is occasionally possible to trace in great detail the lives of eighteenth- and nineteenth-century freedom seekers who were the subject of newspaper advertisements, sometimes in remarkable detail, as in the case of Ona Judge who escaped from George and Martha Washington.[9] But, even beyond such well-documented individuals, freedom seekers in the English colonies and the early United States escaped from a system of slavery that has left numerous sources including plantation records, medical and military records, the diaries and personal papers of slave-owners, merchants and travellers; the log books and papers of crew members of slave ships; and so forth. Although it is only rarely possible to hear the voices of the enslaved in the voluminous records of slavery compiled by slave-holders, such records can nonetheless yield a great deal of information about racial slavery in the round, and historians have made use of them to deepen their understanding of freedom seekers, the kinds of slavery they escaped from, the particular reasons for their flight and something of their hoped-for destinations and lives. While the individuals often elude us, their situations and strategies may start to come into focus.[10]

There are precious few of these contextual records in seventeenth-century England, and in every instance freedom seekers in Restoration London can be glimpsed only in a single newspaper advertisement. These freedom seekers appear insubstantial, little more than archival ghosts who can barely be glimpsed in the few dozen words drafted by those eager to reclaim their human property. Sometimes we do not even know their names, and we know next to nothing of their lives before or after this moment of attempted escape. Were those who ran away, prompting these advertisements, seeking permanent freedom or *petit marronage*, a temporary absence from slave-holders and their working environments?[11] Often there was a delay of at least several days between the disappearance of a freedom seeker and the

---

resisted enslavement by escaping, although it too is problematic in that its more positive tone may obscure the very real risks taken by such people and their continued status as fugitives from their masters and the law. I prefer 'freedom seeker' and will use this more often but I shall use 'runaway slave' too, in the hope that using both will illuminate the tension between the agency and the objectification of those who escaped embodied by newspaper advertisements.

9 E. A. Dunbar, *Never Caught: the Washingtons' Relentless Pursuit of their Runaway Slave Ona Judge* (New York, 2017).

10 One recent attempt is S. P. Newman, 'Hidden in plain sight: escaped slaves in late-18th and early-19th century Jamaica', *William and Mary Quarterly*, June 2018 <https://oireader. wm.edu/open_wmq> [accessed 5 Oct. 2020].

11 One of the best studies of *petit marronage* is M. P. Nevius, *City of Refuge: Slavery and Petit Marronage in the Great Dismal Swamp, 1763–1856* (Athens, Ga., 2020).

publication of an advertisement, perhaps reflecting a more than temporary absence. Did these freedom seekers try to find sanctuary in London's small community of people of colour or among White Londoners? These questions cannot be answered, and the challenge is to read between and beyond the lines of these advertisements and the related sources to which they lead, and endeavour to imagine the enslaved and to discern the actions, assumptions and attitudes of the English men and women who were at the metropolitan heart of a nascent empire built on slavery and exploited labour.

To undertake such work is to accept the challenge of investigating and reconstructing the histories of these freedom seekers without implicitly reaffirming the violent theft of identity and humanity inherent in racial slavery. However, these surviving advertisements and other related records, taken together, afford some scope for speculation about the broader parameters of this community, about gender ratios, average ages, linguistic abilities, clothing and so on among the freedom seekers who featured in newspaper advertisements. From this schematic data we may be able to imagine an ecology of personal histories, experiences, motivations and attitudes among London's enslaved people.[12]

It is the gender disparity that is most striking in the 212 advertisements for freedom seekers published in London between 1655 and 1704 (see Table 1). Only thirteen (6 per cent) of the advertisements were for female freedom seekers, while 199 (94 per cent) were for males. The ages or age categories of 171 of the freedom seekers were included by the people writing and posting these 212 advertisements.[13] When they are compared with

---

[12] Saidiya Hartman has written that every historian of the enslaved 'is forced to grapple with the power and authority of the archive and the limits it sets on what can be known, whose perspective matters, and who is endowed with the gravity and authority of historical actor' (S. Hartman, *Wayward Lives, Beautiful Experiments: Intimate Histories of Social Upheaval* (New York, 2019), p. xiii). Hartman has been a major force in conceptualizing and articulating the problem of the 'violence' of the archive, leading with her tremendously powerful work on the Middle Passage in S. Hartman, *Lose your Mother: a Journey along the Atlantic Slave Route* (New York, 2007). Since then historians like Marisa J. Fuentes have taken us further in trying to answer the questions she poses in the introduction to her powerful book on enslaved women in Barbados: 'How do we narrate the fleeting glimpses of enslaved subjects in the archives …? … How do we construct a coherent historical accounting out of that which defies coherence and representability? How do we critically confront or reproduce these accounts to open up possibilities for historicizing, mourning, remembering, and listening to the condition of enslaved women?' (M. J. Fuentes, *Dispossessed Lives: Enslaved Women, Violence, and the Archive* (Philadelphia, Pa., 2016), p. 1). For a variety of perspectives on this archival and historical challenge, see the essays featured in a special issue of the journal *History of the Present* entitled 'From Archives of Slavery to Liberated Futures?', edited by B. Connelly and M. Fuentes, vi (2016), 105–215.

[13] The database of advertisements compiled by the author that form the basis of this study includes 212 freedom-seeking people of colour who escaped and were advertised for in London

Characteristic of freedom seekers	London (1655–1704)	Jamaica (1775–1823)	Virginia (1730–1787)	South Carolina (1730–1787)
Males	94%	76%	88%	77%
Females	6%	24%	12%	23%
Age 8–19	60%	37%	17%	26%
Age 20–29	31%	33%	45%	44%
Age 30–39	8%	19%	26%	20%
Age 40–49	1%	9%	10%	9%
Age 50 +	0%	2%	2%	1%

Table 1. Freedom seekers in London and in the colonies. Information about freedom seekers in Virginia and South Carolina has been drawn from B. G. Smith and R. Wojtowicz, *Blacks who Stole Themselves: Advertisements for Runaways in the Pennsylvania Gazette, 1728–1790* (Philadelphia, Pa., 1989), table 1, p. 13. Data for Jamaican runaways is from the author's own research.

freedom seekers in the plantation colonies during the eighteenth and early nineteenth centuries (when the earliest colonial newspaper advertisements make such a comparison possible), the higher gender imbalance and the striking youth of London's runaways becomes apparent. The youngest of London's freedom seekers was eight years old and the oldest a mere forty. A significantly greater proportion of London's freedom seekers were aged nineteen or younger than was true in Jamaica, while London's younger freedom seekers outnumbered those in South Carolina by a ratio of well over 2:1, and those in Virginia by a ratio of more than 3:1. When imprecise indicators of age such as 'boy', 'girl' or 'young' are included, the age groups of 175 of London's freedom seekers are known, and 107 (62 per cent) appear to have been aged nineteen or younger. As there were no newspapers and runaway advertisements in the colonies during the seventeenth century, it is impossible to compare seventeenth-century freedom seekers in London with those in the Caribbean and North America. However, we know that during these earliest years of the plantation system slave-traders and planters sought out adult males. The resulting gender imbalance and high mortality rates meant that stable families and children did not emerge quickly, and

between 1655 (when the first such advertisement appeared) and June 1704 (the date on which a runaway advertisement first appeared in a newspaper in Britain's New World colonies). These advertisements were gathered by means of research in digitized newsletters and newspapers from this era. Keyword searching proved unreliable as 17th-century printing does not always lend itself to optical character recognition, so review of each issue was required in most cases.

so an even higher proportion of seventeenth-century freedom seekers in Jamaica, Virginia and South Carolina was most probably adult.

Female freedom seekers were somewhat older than their more numerous male counterparts. The ages of twelve of the thirteen female freedom seekers for whom advertisements survive were recorded in these newspaper notices, and the thirteenth was an adult recorded as 'a Negro Woman, named Minke'.[14] Two were fifteen years old, two were sixteen, one was eighteen, four were twenty, and one each were twenty-five, thirty-five and forty (the latter is the oldest person in the entire data set). Three of the thirteen were South Asian: Sarah, the forty-year-old, was described as an 'Indian woman'; Corney as 'East-India tawney'; and an unnamed fifteen-year-old as an 'Indian black Girl'.[15] The remaining ten were all African. Six of these were described in advertisements as 'negro', two of whom were aged twenty, two aged sixteen, one aged thirty-five and one described as a 'woman'. Two were labelled as 'Black', one of whom was aged twenty and the other fifteen, while two described as 'Blackamoor' were aged eighteen and twenty. South Asians thus constituted 23 per cent of female freedom seekers, which aligns with the 24 per cent of male freedom seekers who can be identified as coming from the same area. It is possible, perhaps even probable, that the ages of female freedom seekers indicate that some had been trafficked to London by enslavers who exploited them sexually: freely given consent would have been impossible in these circumstances and, whether or not the sexual acts imposed on them were violent, they would have constituted rape.

Among the males who eloped the age profile was rather different. Of 159 males whose ages were recorded, 62 per cent appear to have been aged nineteen or younger. At least some, perhaps a majority, had been young boys transported from Africa who were retained by ship captains and officers rather than being sold to planters and colonists, and twenty three had escaped from ships. Other boys and young men served planters and colonists as domestic servants, and continued this work when they accompanied their masters to London, a practice that would continue for more than a century.

During the second half of the seventeenth century racial slavery and the enslaved themselves were strongly associated with London, and advertisements for freedom seekers associated most of them with particular parishes and wards in and around the capital. A total of twenty-five appear to have escaped from outside London, and the advertisements associated them specify locations

---

[14] 'RAN away from her Mistress, Penelope Meade, a Negro Woman, named Minke', *London Gazette*, 3 Jan. 1703.

[15] 'Strayed or spirited … Sarah', *London Gazette*, 19 Jan. 1680; 'Run away … an East-India tawney Maid', *London Gazette*, 6 Aug. 1691; 'An Indian black Girl', *London Gazette*, 22 Sept. 1690.

Figure 14. Map of London showing approximate locations from which freedom seekers eloped, 1655–1704. Not all newspaper advertisements reveal this information. Map by Anthony King.

from Ipswich to Bristol and from Plymouth to Wrexham. Locations such as Windsor, Sudbury and Kingston were fairly close to London: only seven were more than 100 miles from the capital, and ten were within fifty miles. It is possible that enslaved people were being taken to other places in the British Isles, and perhaps some escaped. But newspapers were rare outside London during most of this period, and the small number of advertisements for freedom seekers who eloped outside of the city tended to assume that the runaways either had escaped while in London or were heading there. Beyond the twenty-five who appear to have eloped from outside London and the twenty-three from ships (almost all anchored on the Thames), the remainder most probably ran away in and around London, and a total of 126 can be clearly associated with escape in the capital. Thirty-eight different wards, parishes and villages were mentioned as the places from which freedom seekers had eloped, from the village of Chelsea to Greenwich (Figure 14).

The City of London stretched east of the Tower of London, encompassing little more than one square mile, yet it accounted for twenty-six (28.6 per cent) of the 126 freedom seekers who eloped from named areas in the greater London area. Although urban growth was uniting the City of London with Westminster, the two areas remained differentiated and, along with neighbouring areas such as Chelsea, Westminster and the area west and north of the City, accounted for a further nineteen (20.9 per cent) freedom seekers. The third focal point of early modern London was south of the Thames and centred on Southwark and, together with areas as far west as Putney and especially the fast-growing mercantile and shipbuilding centres of Rotherhithe, Deptford and Greenwich to the east, account for another thirteen (14.3 per cent) runaways. The most significant area was the fast-growing East End on the northern banks of the Thames, from St Catherine's immediately east of the Tower of London, north to Hackney and then east along the river to Poplar and the Blackwall shipbuilding yard. Encompassing Stepney, Limehouse, Shacklewell, Bromley-by-Bow, Shadwell, Ratcliff, Whitechapel and Wapping, this area accounted for twenty-nine (31.9 per cent) of the freedom seekers associated with particular parts of greater London; by the turn of the eighteenth century the proportion of London's freedom seekers escaping from the East End was growing fast.

The racial delineators used by the White men and women who placed newspaper advertisements were vague and imprecise in comparison with those that would become common in the eighteenth century as the British empire solidified and racial slavery and racial inequality became institutionalized. Racial denominators of various kinds appear in all 212 advertisements, and some 24 per cent of those who can clearly be identified as either African or South Asian appear to have come from India. Advertisements featured a variety of terms to describe these people, often in combination as in 'East India Mallatto', 'East India tawney' or 'Indian black'. Twenty-one of the forty-seven South Asians were described as 'Black', twenty simply as 'Indian' or 'East Indian', and six were described in advertisements as 'tawney' or 'mulatto', perhaps an indication of skin tones that were often not as dark as those of first- or even second-generation Africans. It is possible that there may have been indigenous Americans among these forty-seven, but other evidence within the advertisements makes clear that most if not all of the freedom seekers labelled as 'Indian' were South Asians. Only one of the 212 advertisements may have been for an indigenous American, 'a Spanish Indian man called Diego or James, of Low Stature, Tawny Complexion, flattish Nose' who had eloped from William Smith in Battersea.[16]

The use of 'Black' for both South Asians and Africans is a clear indicator of the linguistic imprecision around race during these early years of slavery and empire. Fifteen of the 212 freedom seekers who appear to have been bound servants of colour were labelled as 'black', two as 'mulatto' and one as 'tawney', but, with no other information within the advertisements or that can be discovered about the people from whom they escaped, there is no way of telling whether they were of African or South Asian origin. Indeed, the word 'black' was itself no clear guide, for seventeenth-century English people continued to use 'black' to describe some White English men and women with reference to their complexion or dress. When two servants named Richard Cleyton and Robert Ekin escaped in 1658, a newspaper advertisement described them as 'proper black men, about 26 years of age'.[17] At this time the term 'black man' or 'black woman' might refer to people wearing black, especially those who were clothed in this way in their capacity as paid professional mourners. The advertisement for Cleyton and Ekin went on to note that both men were dressed 'in Mourning', confirming that what might at first appear a racial label actually referred to their profession. Sergeant Warren advertised for 'Owen Crane a black man with lank Hair', one of six soldiers who had deserted from the army, including their names and a brief description. His name and the description of Crane's hair suggest that in this advertisement the word 'black' referred to complexion or appearance and not to race.[18] In many cases the word

---

[16] 'Run away from his Master … Diego or James', *London Gazette*, 10 Aug. 1685.

[17] 'Richard Cleyton and Robert Ekin', *Mercurius Politicus, comprising the Sum of Forein Intelligence, with the Affairs now on foot in the Three Nations of England, Scotland, and Ireland, for Information of the People*, 25 March 1658.

[18] 'William Chamberlain… Owen Crane', *London Gazette*, 9 May 1689. For more on the use of the word 'black' to describe the complexion of White British people see M. S. Dawson, 'First impressions: newspaper advertisements and early modern English body imaging, 1651–1750,' *Journal of British Studies*, l (2011), 277–306, at 292–5, 302–6.

'Black' was capitalized when referring to South Asians and Africans, while the uncapitalized 'black' more often referred to White English people.

By the mid eighteenth century, when slavery and accompanying constructions of race had solidified, British newspaper advertisements occasionally identified South Asians as 'Negro', a racial othering of all subordinated people of colour across the far-flung British empire. Thus Peter Paul, who escaped in London in April 1746, was described in a newspaper advertisement as 'an East-Indian Negro, or Lascar'.[19] However, during the earlier period between 1655 and 1704 Englishmen's ideas of colour and race were still developing and the term 'Negro' appears to have been applied by advertisers almost exclusively to Africans. One hundred and forty-six (75 per cent) of the 194 runaways whose race can be identified were African, while forty-seven (24 per cent) were South Asian. Among the African freedom seekers 62 per cent were labelled 'Negro', a further 4 per cent as 'Black Negro' or 'Negro Black', 9 per cent as 'Black', 16 per cent as 'Blackamore' or 'Moor', 3 per cent as Madagascan, 2 per cent as being from Guinea or the Gold Coast, 3 per cent as a 'tawney'-coloured 'Negro' or 'Blackamore', and under 1 per cent as 'Mulatto'. There were no doubt mixed-race children born on slave ships, in the plantations and perhaps even in Britain who might have been described as 'Mulatto' or 'Tawney', but during this early period of English involvement in the transatlantic slave trade and plantation slavery a majority – probably a large majority – of the enslaved were African born. Only one possibly South Asian freedom seeker was identified as 'A Tall Slender Negro' in the opening words of an advertisement that went on to note that he 'came from the East-Indies in the [ship] Loyal Merchant'.[20] Perhaps this thirty-year-old man was an African seafarer who had served aboard this ship that had just returned from the Indian Ocean, or perhaps he was one of the first South Asians to be identified as a 'Negro' in an English runaway advertisement. But this advertisement appeared in 1701, and the seventeenth-century advertisements in this database identified only Africans with the term 'Negro'.

There is no evidence of what became of the freedom seekers. Some were probably recaptured and remained enslaved, whether as personal servants, attendants and workers in England or back in the colonies. Others, no doubt, accompanied their masters on return trips to the colonies, and if they served the ship captains who owned them they might easily have been sold at a handsome profit in plantation colonies eager for new workers. Perhaps some were sent from England to the colonies when they were no longer needed or wanted: attractive young page boys might have been less

[19] 'Whereas one Peter Paul', *The Daily Advertiser*, 21 April 1746.
[20] 'A Tall Slender Negro', *The Post Man: and The Historical Account*, 30 Sept. 1701.

desirable as they grew older. Quashy was one such unfortunate man. He was the property of Anthony Bigg, a doctor and Jamaican plantation owner who in the early eighteenth century had returned to Bristol. Bigg may have been the son of Abraham Bigg, who in the early 1660s had been listed with the duke of York, the earl of Carlisle, George Lord Berkeley, Sir James Modyford and Sir John Colleton as early shareholders in the Royal African Company monopoly of the transatlantic slave trade.[21] When Anthony Bigg died in 1722 he left his Jamaican plantation, 'which was bought and purchased by my father', to his wife and his niece, as well as large cash sums to his sister and other relatives. But his will also identified 'my Negroe Boy named Quashy', who was not destined to remain in England; instead Bigg ordered his executors to proceed 'with all possible speed after my death to transport and send away' Quashy 'to my Executors residing in the Island of Jamaica to be disposed of with my Residency'.[22]

Although it was unusual for testators to make a provision of this kind, it was not uncommon for enslavers to send enslaved people from London to the colonies for sale or redeployment. Thus Samuel Pepys and his housekeeper grew tired of what he described as the 'lying, pilfering ... [and] other mischievous' behaviour of his enslaved servant Sambo, who was no longer a child. Believing him to have grown too 'dangerous to be longer continued in a sober family', Pepys contrived to have some Admiralty watermen kidnap Sambo and place him aboard HMS *Foresight*, a naval frigate built by Jonas Shish in Deptford that was at the time being fitted out for a voyage to the West Indies. On 11 September 1688 Samuel Pepys instructed Captain Edward Stanley of HMS *Foresight* to transport Sambo to the plantations and there sell him to a planter; after subtracting any costs incurred, the captain was to invest the proceeds in whatever goods he thought best and return them or any profits they produced to Pepys. Nearly a decade earlier Stanley had helped capture and then taken control of the *Prize of Algier*, and while under his command an insurrection by enslaved people broke out on this captured ship during which several of them were killed. Captain Stanley knew well the force and violence needed to subordinate enslaved people.[23]

---

[21] Grant to the Royal African Company, 10 Jan. 1663, 'America and West Indies: January 1663', in *Calendar of State Papers Colonial, America and West Indies: v, 1661–1668*, ed. W. N. Sainsbury (London, 1880), p. 408 <http://www.british-history.ac.uk/cal-state-papers/colonial/america-west-indies/vol5/pp119-122> [accessed 21 Jan. 2021].

[22] Will of A. Bigg, of Bristol, Gloucestershire, 2 Nov. 1722, National Archives, PROB 11/588/6.

[23] For details of the slave insurrection on the *Prize of Algier* see Stanley, Lieutenant, HMS *Adventure*, on board the *Prize of Algier*, Court Martial Papers, Records of the Admiralty, National Archives, ADM 1/5253/13, ff. 13–15. For further information on Pepys and Sambo

While slavery in London was far removed from the extreme violence and horrors of the Caribbean and the southern colonies, being sold into colonial slavery nevertheless remained a very real threat to the enslaved in the capital. Perhaps Sambo had been one of the many enslaved boys transported to London who then grew into men who were less visually appealing to the English as personal attendants and who did not hide their resistance to the terms of their bondage. However benign bound service and slavery in Restoration England may appear, it was still slavery and the threat of a far worse and more violent form of unfreedom was always present.

Just occasionally we glimpse the possible paths of freedom seekers, as in the case of Tom Black, 'A Black Boy about 15 or 16 years of age' who eloped from Covent Garden in June 1686. Three months later another advertisement was placed by Sir Thomas Janson of Tunbridge Wells, announcing that he had possession of 'A Black Boy, about 15 years old, supposed to have Run away from his Master'.[24] Tunbridge Wells was about thirty miles south-east of the City of London, nestled in the countryside of West Kent. Was the young boy taken up by Janson the same one who had escaped three months earlier, and if so what had taken him down into Kent? Had he travelled alone or with others? What these advertisements suggest are the possibilities for freedom seekers: while escape was difficult and forging a new life challenging, there appear to have been possibilities for some who challenged their status. The case studies in Part II detail individual freedom seekers and those who claimed them, sometimes exploring the possible outcomes of their bids for freedom.

If we can glimpse freedom seekers and their lives and experiences in the aggregate, we can see their enslavers in far greater detail, an interlinked community of ship captains, merchants, investors and colonial speculators, gentry and aristocrats who were engaged together in the development of racial slavery in the English Atlantic World. While this imbalance of knowledge implicitly replicates the power dynamics of enslavement itself, it can nonetheless reveal a good deal about the enslaved and slavery in Restoration London, providing a firmer foundation for speculation about these all but forgotten victims of the early stages of English, and then British, transatlantic slavery.

The development of racial slavery was as much an English as a colonial story, and it was a London story in particular. However different slavery may have appeared in the metropole, during the early years of the transatlantic slave trade and colonial plantations the institution was as real and as present

---

see C. Tomalin, *Samuel Pepys: the Unequalled Self* (New York, 2002), pp. 177, 405–6; A. Bryant, *Samuel Pepys: iii, The Saviour of the Navy* (Cambridge, 1938), p. 270. These events took place well after Pepys had ceased keeping a diary.

[24] 'A Black Boy about 15 or 16', *London Gazette*, 28 June 1686; 'A Black Boy, about 15 years old', *London Gazette*, 20 Sept. 1686.

in the capital as it was in the colonies. And, as racial slavery was a feature of Restoration London, so too was resistance by escape. During the seventeenth century escape from slavery was constructed, defined and dealt with by slave-holders in two important ways: through the laws and slave codes created in the colonies that determined how this crime against property should be recognized and punished, and in the runaway advertisements published in London newspapers that detailed these individual acts of rebellion and promised rewards for the recapture and return of those who rebelled by escaping.

The story of how freedom seekers were constructed by Londoners in newspaper advertisements as 'runaway slaves' reflects the larger narrative of the significance of London and Londoners in the creation of plantation slavery. An interconnected web of aristocrats, gentry, merchants, bankers, coffee shop owners, craftsmen, shipwrights, ship captains and their families in the capital emerge from these newspaper notices, revealing the connections between those who owned or directly benefited from the traffic in and exploitation of enslaved people both in the colonies and in London. The merchant trading offices and coffee shops around the Royal Exchange in the heart of the City of London, the dockland and shipping communities hugging the northern and southern banks of the River Thames, and the wealthy sections of the fast-growing areas to the west of the City of London were all home to the people who owned or were complicit in racial slavery. Just as planters and colonial assemblies were in the process of creating and defining racial slavery through laws and legal codes, enslavers and their accomplices in London were participating in their own domestic process of defining slavery as they understood it, circumscribing the lives of the people in London whom they claimed as property and moving against what they interpreted as theft, namely the act of escaping and stealing one's own body.

The runaway slave advertisement would become the most ubiquitous evidence of resistance by the enslaved in the English, and then British, societies of the Caribbean and North America, and later in the United States. We can never fully know the enslaved who inhabited Restoration London but we can see and learn from the world that held them in thrall, the people who owned and manacled them, the cold and alien city in which they found themselves, and the newspaper advertisements that spoke of but not really about them. Using our imagination, we can visualize something of their lives, their experiences, their hopes, their fears and their desperation. It is only when we look very hard and allow ourselves to wonder, to imagine and to feel that we can begin to see these people not merely as the subjects of enslavement and new metropolitan practices and understandings of slavery but, rather, as individuals who reacted against the people and the system that held them in bondage so very far from home.

Part II

The freedom seekers

4. *Jack*: boys

*A Guinea Negro Boy, about 8 years old, named Jack, straight limb, no
mark in his face, in a black cloth suit, and a black Serge Frock over them,
and on his head a black Cloth Permission Cap, he strayed away from Mr.
Peter Paggens in Cross-lane, on St. Mary Hill near Billingsgate, on the
3d instant, about 6 in the afternoon. Whoever shall bring the said Negro
Boy to the above said Mr. Paggens, or discovers where he is, so that he
may be had again, shall have 20 s. Reward.*

The London Gazette, 9 June 1690

Racial slavery became commonplace in England's Caribbean and
Chesapeake colonies during the second half of the seventeenth century
and planters strove to acquire enslaved adults, mostly African but some
indigenous Americans. Children were less desirable than the 'Choyce
Young Negros Who will be fit for plant serwice', the healthy young adult
males Henry Drax sought for his Barbados plantation.[1] Over the course of
the century more than 173,000 enslaved people disembarked in the colonies
of Virginia, Maryland, the Carolinas, Antigua, Barbados and Jamaica, and
of these almost 166,000 (96 per cent) went to Caribbean plantations, where
they suffered horrifyingly high mortality rates.[2] In the Caribbean colonies
enslaved adult workers died far more frequently than children were born,
and planters replaced them with enslaved adults newly arrived from Africa
who could immediately work and be productive until they too succumbed.
This was not yet a mature plantation society containing social and familial
units, and planters who sought nothing other than labour from the people
they owned viewed children as having little value.

The situation was very different in Restoration London, however, where
young boys dominated the city's enslaved community (Figure 15). The ages
or age groups of freedom seekers were included in 201 of the 212 newspaper
advertisements between 1655 and 1704, and 56 per cent of these were aged

---

[1] H. Drax, 'Instructions which I would have observed by Mr Richard Harwood in
the Mannagment of My plantation', in P. Thompson, 'Henry Drax's instructions on the
management of a seventeenth-century Barbadian sugar plantation', *William and Mary
Quarterly*, 3rd series, lxvi (2009), 565–604, at p. 585.

[2] Slave Voyages: Trans-Atlantic Slave Trade – Database <https://www.slavevoyages.org/
voyage/database#statistics> [accessed 4 May 2020].

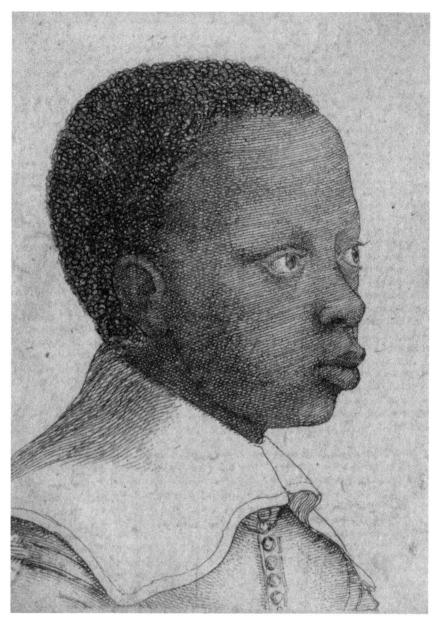

Figure 15. Wenceslaus Hollar, 'Portrait of an African Boy',
17th century, Folger Shakespeare Library.

nineteen or younger (or were described as 'boy' or 'young' male). Among the male freedom seekers whose age was included in advertisements, 49 per cent were aged seventeen or younger and 15 per cent were no older than 12.

The labour of enslaved children in Restoration England was dramatically different from that undertaken by the enslaved in the Caribbean and Chesapeake colonies, where planters needed adults to undertake arduous agricultural labour to raise and process tobacco, sugar and other staple crops. Enslaved boys assisted ship captains, merchants and others as cabin boys, messengers and the like, and some became the page boys and personal attendants of men and women rich enough to purchase them. Those who were dressed in smart liveries advertised the wealth and success of the people who were profiting from England's rapidly expanding colonial ventures and commodity trades: during the early 1660s, for example, Samuel Pepys was attended by an English boy named Wayneman Birch, dressed in an attractive livery and wearing a sword. This clothing demonstrated that the wearer was not expected to undertake the hard and dirty work done by many household servants, especially girls and young women. Adolescent males employed in this way attended the head of household from dawn to dusk, perhaps preparing his clothes and helping him dress and undress, cutting and combing his hair, and even shaving and washing him. A servant of this kind was expected to keep himself sufficiently clean, well dressed and presentable to reflect well on the master he attended about town.[3]

Some of London's liveried servant boys were enslaved or bound Africans or South Asians, and a few of these tried to escape their service. Jack was 'A Guinea Negro Boy, about 8 years old', who had 'strayed away from Mr. Peter Paggens' in Billingsgate. The word 'strayed' suggests that Jack may have lost his way rather than escaped, although, given the value of a young enslaved boy, he might also have been kidnapped. A young boy born perhaps in West Africa, who had endured separation from his family and the horrors of the Middle Passage, Jack found himself in London far from everyone and everything that was familiar to him and may have eloped with no clear idea of a destination or what he might do. Despair may have occasioned this child's actions.

Jack was described in the advertisement as being from Guinea and well dressed 'in a black cloth suit, and a black Serge Frock over them', along

[3] H. Summerson, 'Servants of Samuel Pepys' (2006), *Oxford Dictionary of National Biography* <https://doi.org/10.1093/ref:odnb/93850> [accessed 8 March 2019]; J. J. Hecht, *The Domestic Servant Class in Eighteenth-Century England* (London, 1956), p. 120; I. K. Ben-Amos, *Adolescence and Youth in Early Modern England* (New Haven, Conn., 1994), pp. 151–2; P. Earle, *The Making of the English Middle Class: Business, Society and Family Life in London, 1660–1730* (Berkeley, Calif., 1989), p. 223.

with 'a black Cloth Permission Cap' that he could wear in locations where males traditionally uncovered their heads. Jack's dress reflected the wealth and status of his master Peter Paggen, a Huguenot merchant in London who had begun as a ship captain transporting tobacco from the Chesapeake Bay region to London. Paggen became one of the capital's leading tobacco merchants and was appointed their colonial agent in London in 1692 by the General Assembly of Maryland, when he expanded his trading interests to include trafficking in enslaved people. Between 1699 and 1706 he was the co-owner of at least twenty-six ships that undertook transatlantic slave trading voyages, almost all destined for England's fastest-growing and most profitable colony of Jamaica. Paggen was deeply invested in the slave trade and plantation slavery, and intimately connected with the network of London traders who were building and profiting from this endeavour: in 1703, for example, he joined with Sir Bartholomew Gracedieu and others in petitioning the Council of Trade and Plantations to allow and encourage the resettlement and defence of Port Royal following the devastating Jamaican earthquake of 1692.[4] Upon his death Paggen left his wife the substantial income from £20,000 worth of stock in the United East India Company (the Dutch East India Company) and the Bank of England, and, having already provided one daughter with a dowry of £16,000, he left £10,000 of stock in trust for a second daughter. His daughter Catherine's second husband was Sir Humphry Morice, a leading London slave-trader and governor of the Bank of England; Morice named one of his slave ships in honour of his wife Catherine. The wealthy community of investors in slavery and plantations were, as Paggen and his family illustrated, not even one step removed from the actual ownership of enslaved people.[5]

---

[4] Sir B. Gracedieu et al. to the Council of Trade and Plantations, 26 April 1703, in *Calendar of State Papers Colonial: North America and the West Indies, 1574–1739*: xxi, *26 April 1703*, pp. 380–2 <https://www.british-history.ac.uk/cal-state-papers/colonial/america-west-indies/vol21/pp377-394> [accessed 28 Sept 2021]. For biographical details of Paggen see W. A. Pettigrew, *Freedom's Debt: the Royal African Company and the Politics of the Atlantic Slave Trade, 1672–1752* (Chapel Hill, N.C., 2013), pp. 64–5, 72.

[5] Slave Voyages: Trans-Atlantic Slave Trade database; 'An Act Appointing Peter Pagan Merch[t] to be Agent for this their Majest[s] Province of Maryland, 8 June 1692', Assembly Proceedings, 10 May–9 June 1692, in *Proceedings and Acts of the General Assembly of Maryland: Proceedings and Acts of the General Assembly of Maryland, April, 1684–June, 1692*, xiii, ed. W. H. Browne (Baltimore, Md., 1894), p. 467; Will of P. Paggen of Wandsworth, Surrey, 15 July 1720, National Archives, PROB 11/575/141. For a brief discussion of Paggen and his career see Pettigrew, *Freedom's Debt*, p. 64. Paggen's daughter Catherine had first married William Hale, but after his death she married Humphry Morice. See 'Notes of Wills and Acts of Administration', *Proceedings of the Huguenot Society of London*, i (1885), p. 304. For Humphry Morice and his naming of slave ships see J. A. Rawley, *London, Metropolis of the Slave Trade* (Columbia, Mo., 2003), p. 44; E. Cruickshanks and S. Handley, 'Humphry Morice (c.1671–1731)', in *The History of*

The trade in enslaved people and the crops they raised had made Paggen an extremely wealthy man, and an attractive, well-liveried enslaved boy who attended him enabled Paggen to flaunt his wealth and its human source. Jack was almost certainly one of a number of servants living and working in Paggen's house, and, although his work and clothing may have made him appear more privileged than those tasked with the drudgery of cooking and cleaning, he was almost certainly less free than the servants who could change employer at the end of annual contracts or even leave the household at will and quite likely not be pursued for breach of contract. How did Paggen's use of Jack and his clothing to display success and wealth feel to an eight-year-old whose life and person were being deployed to embody the success of another person, his life and individuality stripped away in the few words of an advertisement and an anonymizing uniform? An unnamed 'Guinea Negro Boy', he was less than a person, an adjunct to Paggen rather than an individual. Almost certainly torn from his mother, his family and his culture at a very tender age, where could he have found comfort, friendship and love? Perhaps in Paggen's household and from other servants, but to the Paggens he was valuable property as much as he was a family member.

Samuel Pepys owned an enslaved 'neager-boy' who had been given to him in 1675 by Lieutenant Howe of the *Phoenix*. It appears that Pepys owned this unnamed boy for five years before selling him in June 1680.[6] It is unclear if this boy ever attempted escape, but the brief notes of his existence and the years he spent in the Pepys household remind us that there were almost certainly many more enslaved boys who did not escape or who were not the subject of advertisements than there were young freedom seekers who appear in the pages of Restoration London's newspapers. The courage of the children and young adults who did elope, and the terror of those who were kidnapped – quite possibly to be sold – are not easily communicated in the few dry words of advertisements. An 'East India slim-Boy, aged about 14' eloped in late January 1689.[7] He could be returned for the reward of one guinea to Margaret Cooper on Threadneedle Street, just north of the Royal Exchange. A different Jack, 'whose Indian name is Mottaw', was between eleven and twelve years old when he eloped in early November 1690.[8] The

---

Parliament: the House of Commons, 1690–1715, ed. D. Hayton, E. Cruickshanks and S. Handley (Woodbridge, 2002) <http://www.historyofparliamentonline.org/volume/1690-1715/member/morice-humphry-1671-1731> [accessed 22 June 2020].

[6] Pepys's receipt of this boy, and his subsequent sale of a boy, are recorded in his papers and occurred after the conclusion of his diary keeping. See C. Tomalin, *Samuel Pepys: the Unequalled Self* (New York, 2002), pp. 177, 405–6.

[7] 'RUN away … an East India slim Boy', *London Gazette*, 7 Feb. 1689.

[8] 'Run away … Jack', *London Gazette*, 4 Dec. 1690.

'blue stroke between his Eye-brows' may have been a Hindu *bindi*, a brightly coloured marking representing the third, invisible eye.[9] If so, perhaps Jack kept marking himself in this way to connect himself to his home, his family and his culture. The blue stroke and Mottaw's pierced ears, which would have been unusual in London at this time, were described in the advertisement, along with his clothing, in the hope of identifying the freedom seeker, yet he had already been absent for almost a month when the advertisement appeared.

Peter, who was about thirteen years old, escaped from Gilbert Bruning's home near Drury Lane in mid-September 1687.[10] This boy had arrived from Surinam some three years earlier and had learned to speak 'pretty good English'. Having spent almost one quarter of his life in the city, Peter had no doubt learned his way around London and he had perhaps made friends and forged relationships that made escaping more practical. Gilbert and his brothers Francis and John had been planters in Surinam under both Dutch and English rule, and Gilbert and John had owned 'as considerable a plantation in Surinam as any Englishman'. Peter had probably accompanied Bruning from that colony back to London, serving him as a well-dressed personal attendant.[11] Described by Bruning as 'well favour'd', Peter apparently looked the part of an attractive, young enslaved servant; when he eloped he was dressed accordingly 'in a sad hair colour Cloth Sute lin'd with the same colour, his Coat faced with Red Cloth, and white Pewter Buttons'. Smart without being as ostentatiously attired as the expensively liveried enslaved servants of some men and women, Peter was nevertheless far better dressed better than most of the capital's young White servants. When Bruning died six years later he left plantations in Surinam and Antigua to various family members. It is unclear whether Peter, or for that matter any of the other enslaved or bound servants in London, was still with the family and considered a part of the 'goods and chattels in England, Holland and the Island of Antigua' that Bruning left to his wife. Bruning's legacy of the 'goods and chattels' of his Surinam plantation probably included enslaved people, and so the absence

---

[9] M. G. Anthony, 'On the spot: seeking acceptance and expressing resistance through the *bindi*', *Journal of International and Intercultural Communication*, iii (2010), 346–68, at p. 347.

[10] 'RUN away ... Peter', *London Gazette*, 22 Sept. 1687.

[11] Petition of G. Bruning to the King, 22 Oct. 1674, 'America and West Indies: October 1674', in *Calendar of State Papers Colonial, America and West Indies*: vii, *1669–1674*, ed. W. Noel Sainsbury (London, 1889), pp. 610–15 <http://www.british-history.ac.uk/cal-state-papers/colonial/america-west-indies/vol7/pp610-615> [accessed 5 May 2020]. See also A. Games, 'Cohabitation, Suriname-style: English inhabitants in Dutch Suriname after 1667', *William and Mary Quarterly*, 3rd series, lxxii (2015), 195–242, at pp. 236–7.

of any specific mention of people as property does not necessarily mean that Peter or somebody like him was not part of Bruning's estate.[12]

Many of the enslaved boys in the capital had arrived on ships on which they had served as the cabin boy and attendant of the captain, who often then sold the boy on. An unnamed 'Mollatta Boy about Eleven years of Age' was described as having a 'yellow Complexion, [and] wooly Hair like a Negro'.[13] He had eloped from 'Capt. John Symonds of his Majesty's Navy' who had captained HMS *Tiger*, an older frigate recently rebuilt in the Deptford shipyard of John Shish.[14] According to Symonds, the boy, who had escaped about ten days earlier, 'has been seen several times about Town', perhaps enjoying his escape from the hard life aboard ship.

One resourceful young freedom seeker gives us an impression of the possible routes to freedom available to these children and young adults. In November 1673 an eleven-year-old 'black Boy' who 'goes by the name of *William Moorfield*' eloped from Thomas Lewis on Crutched Friars, which lay immediately north of the Navy Office and just to the west of the Tower of London.[15] Four months later an advertisement specified that William might be returned to Lewis or to 'John Knight, at the King's great Wardrobe, in the *Savoy*'. The identity of Knight is unclear: he may have been an official with responsibility for naval supplies or have worked for the treasurer of the Customs House, since at that time men with that name and those positions appear to have resided at or near by the Savoy.[16]

Remarkably, we know a little more about what the freedom seeker himself achieved, for just over a year later Lewis readvertised for Moorfield, by now a 'Black Boy about twelve years old', who had escaped once again. But in this second advertisement Lewis noted that during Moorfield's earlier attempt at freedom, after he had escaped 'near five Moneths past', he had 'put himself into service with Mr. *Gorey*, living near *Mulgrave house* at *Charing Cross*'.[17] In short, Moorfield had sought, like many White servants, to enter service as a paid free worker. What is perhaps most remarkable is that Gorey's home was no more than two miles from Thomas Lewis's home whence Moorfield had escaped, and no more than 1,000 yards west

[12] Will of G. Bruning, Gentleman of Saint Giles in the Fields, Middlesex, 22 July 1693, National Archives, PROB 11/415/304.

[13] 'A Mollatta Boy', *The Post Boy*, 7 June 1701.

[14] R. Winfield, *British Warships in the Age of Sail, 1603–1714: Design, Construction, Careers and Fates* (Barnsley, 2009), pp. 118–19.

[15] 'A black Boy … by the name of *William Moorfield*', *London Gazette*, 2 March 1674.

[16] See eg records for 14 Sept. 1672 in *Calendar of State Papers, Domestic Series, May 18th to September 30th, 1672*: xiii, ed. F. H. Blackburne Daniel (London, 1899), p. 613, and J. T. Smith, *The Streets of London, with Anecdotes of their More Celebrated Residents* (London, 1849), p. 147.

[17] 'A Black Boy … goes by the name of *William Moorfield*', *London Gazette*, 9 April 1674.

along the Strand from John Knight's home at the Savoy. The size and density of London, together with the growing number of people of colour working in the households and businesses of a range of Londoners, appear to have made it possible for freedom seekers to hope to evade recapture while remaining in the City, hiding in plain sight as free paid workers of employers they had chosen. Moorfield escaped for the second time at the end of March 1674, only ten days or so after Gorey had returned him to Lewis. Gorey was clearly determined to prevent Moorfield from escaping again and so had arranged for the fitting of 'a Lock and Chain about his Neck', highly visible evidence both of Moorfield's enslaved status and of Lewis's determination that, after absenting himself for almost half a year, Moorfield would not escape again. The fitting of a collar and chain – a punishing restraint commonly used by enslavers in the colonies – makes clear that Lewis claimed Moorefield as enslaved property, for the imposition of such a restraint upon a free labourer was extremely unlikely. Employed servants who eloped usually were pursued only if they had stolen goods, and if caught they might be punished, but not by the fitting of restraints considered inappropriate for free Englishmen.

Enslaved boys might also seize the opportunities for freedom presented by the death or departure of the men who owned and had brought them to London. Toby, 'a lusty Negro Boy', was about fourteen years old when he escaped from Anthony Reynolds on 20 April 1691.[18] The advertisement placed by Reynolds stated that Toby 'lived formerly with Mr. Beacham against St. Lawrence Church by Guildhall'. It is possible that Toby was or had been the enslaved property of Edmund Beauchampe who had lived in that area: in his will Beauchampe described himself as both 'Mercer of London and … County Clerke of Somerset in the Province of Maryland', and he was in Maryland when he died in September 1691.[19] Although Toby was 'lusty' and so presumably in good health, he 'goes bending in the Back, and stammers much at his first speaking'. Stammering, especially when it was an occasional rather than a constant condition, might well reflect the psychological impact of the fear experienced by an enslaved person, in this case a child perhaps brought from Maryland to London (and perhaps from Africa to London before then) and left in the capital with a virtual stranger when Beauchampe returned to the Chesapeake. It is unclear what Toby's status was, for although the advertisement states that he had 'RUN away from' Reynolds it is not clear if Reynolds now owned Toby or was exercising temporary control over him.

[18] 'RUN away … Toby', *London Gazette*, 27 April 1691.
[19] Will of Edmund Beachamp, 10 April 1691, Somerset County Judicial Records 1691–1692, Archives of Maryland Online, cdv. 115–17 <http://aomol.msa.maryland. gov/000001/000405/html/am405--115.html> [accessed 5 May 2020].

The runaway advertisements for boys and young adult males who fled indicate that some, like William Moorfield, were able to remain free for extended periods and perhaps permanently. Typical of these are ten-year-old John Moor, who had been gone for over two weeks when an advertisement for him appeared; twelve-year-old Andrew, who had been absent for well over one month; fourteen-year-old Calib, who had been gone for almost the same length of time; and eleven-year-old William Moorfield, who had been absent for an impressive four months.[20] That so many could remain free for so long was an indication of the presence of a significant number of boys of colour in Restoration London, which enabled freedom seekers to blend into a larger population. While a few were the richly liveried attendants to extremely wealthy men and women, others were intended to show the wealth and success of affluent yet less prestigious people, and yet more were dressed in the working clothes of those who worked for ship captains, merchants and other traders and business people. Young boys from South Asia and Africa were not simply present in London: they were a part of the city, integrated into the rhythms of life and work of the bustling metropole of a fast-growing empire. Some eloped and, while many were recaptured, others may have been able to fashion some kind of life for themselves as Londoners and as the youngest members of the capital's community of people of colour.

---

[20] 'RUN away ... John Moor', *London Gazette*, 14 May 1691; 'Run away ... Andrew', *London Gazette*, 17 April 1690; 'Run away ... Calib', *London Gazette*, 12 Nov. 1685; 'A black Boy ... William Moorfield', *London Gazette*, 2 March 1674.

5. *Francisco/Bugge*: South Asians

An Indian, with a Red Jacket and Breeches much tarred, also his Cap.
A tall Man, long visage, some Pockholes in his face, and ill looked, aged
about 28, his Name Francisco, alias Bugge. Run away about 3 weeks
ago, from Capt. John Bowers. Whoever gives Notice of him to Capt.
Bowers aforesaid, at Elephant Stairs in Rotherhithe, or to Mr. Evance
Goldsmith at the Black Boy in Lombard-street, shall have a Guinea
Reward, and Charges.

The London Gazette, 5 March 1688

South Asians accounted for just under one quarter (24 per cent) of the enslaved men, women and children who eloped in London between 1665 and 1704. These forty-seven freedom seekers included three females aged forty, twenty and fifteen. The ages of thirty-four of the males were included in newspaper advertisements, ranging from twelve to thirty. Of these, 56 per cent were aged sixteen or younger and 76 per cent were no more than teenagers (aged nineteen years or younger). Almost half (45 per cent) were described in advertisements as Black, including two as Indian 'Black boy', four as 'East India Black' and nine as India or Indian 'Black'. One advertisement began by defining the freedom seeker as 'AN East India Mallatto', while five used the term 'tawney' to describe the skin colour of people delineated as Indian or East Indian. Twenty advertisements did not refer to skin colour but instead used the term 'Indian', while one described the freedom seeker as 'East Indian'.

The Portuguese, Dutch, French and English all traded enslaved people in East Africa, the islands of the Indian Ocean and India itself. Raids and warfare in areas such as the Bengali coast produced tens of thousands of enslaved people, while famine and natural disasters left others with little choice but to sell themselves or family members into slavery: for example, three severe famines in Madras between the 1640s and 1680s killed tens of thousands of people and forced many more into bondage. From the 1620s onwards the English East India Company made use of enslaved people in their fortified trading posts and port towns. While living and working in South Asia, Englishmen took enslaved people as personal servants: when the merchant Henry Pearle died in Bantam he ordered 'my Black Boy Peeter' to 'waite upon Agent Dawes' for a set period after which Peeter would be freed.[1] It is probable that many of the South Asians living and working in Restoration London had been brought back by Englishmen like Pearle.

The first advertisement for a South Asian freedom seeker appeared in the *Public Intelligencer* in March 1659, against the backdrop of the tense powerplay between the House of Commons, the army and Lord Protector Richard Cromwell.[2] 'A Tawny Indian with long black Hair' eloped from Sarah Daniel in Greenwich.[3] Mrs Daniel was married to an officer in the Royal Navy, and several years later she appeared regularly in the diary of Samuel Pepys as the daughter-in-law of his landlady in Greenwich when he briefly left London to escape the plague.[4] The freedom seeker was described in the advertisement as being 'of a reasonable tall stature, about eighteen years of age, in a red Cap, red Waste-coat, and a striped pair of Breeches of East-India Stuff'. The advertisement was situated mid-page between a notice for several religious books, one about a lost horse and another a stolen horse, and one with information about an attack on a man. Everyday life continued in the shadow of significant political and constitutional change: within a matter of weeks the army would trigger Cromwell's resignation, the dissolution of parliament and the beginning of the end for the republic. Perhaps such a chaotic period made escape more appealing and a new beginning appear more achievable for a well-dressed and perhaps well-qualified young man who had experience of living among and interacting with English people.

In his lively early eighteenth-century account of London and its people Thomas Brown imagined 'the Genius of an *Indian*' as his companion when he walked around the city, using this visitor to help him to describe London's sights and sounds. As Brown and his South Asian companion walked:

[1] Will of Henry Pearle, Merchant, 16 May 1671, National Archives, PROB 11/336/88. For more on the English and slavery in South Asia see R. B. Allen, *European Slave Trading in the Indian Ocean, 1500–1850* (Athens, Ohio, 2014), pp. 1–62, 108–40; R. B. Allen, 'Satisfying the "want for labouring people": European slave trading in the Indian Ocean, 1500–1850', *Journal of World History*, xxi (2010), 45–73; M. Bennett, 'The East India Company, transnational interactions, and the formation of forced labour regimes, 1635–1730' (unpublished University of Kent MA thesis, 2016), pp. 4–39; V. B. Platt, 'The East India Company and the Madagascar slave trade', *William and Mary Quarterly*, 3rd series, xxvi (1969), 548–77.

[2] R. Hutton, *The Restoration: a Political and Religious History of England and Wales, 1658–1667* (Oxford, 1986), pp. 23–41.

[3] 'A tawny Indian', *The Public Intelligencer. Communicating the Chief Occurrences And Proceedings Within the Dominions of England, Scotland and Ireland. Together with an Account of Affairs from Severall Parts of Europe*, 21 March 1659.

[4] *The Diary of Samuel Pepys: Daily Entries from the 17th Century London Diary*, 18 Dec. 1665; 20 July 1666; 6 Aug. 1666 <https://www.pepysdiary.com/diary> [accessed 9 April 2020]. John Daniel would later serve as a lieutenant on the *Royal Charles*: see 'John Daniel', <https://www.pepysdiary.com/encyclopedia/10018/#summary> [accessed 9 April 2020].

our *Indian* cast his Eye upon one of his own Complexion, at a certain Coffee-house … and being willing to be acquainted with his Country-man, gravely enquir'd what Province or Kingdom of *India* he belong'd to; but the sooty Dog could do nothing but Grin, and shew his Teeth, and cry, *Coffee, Sir, Tea, will you please to walk in, Sir, a fresh Pot upon my word.*[5]

Required to solicit trade and serve customers, a man like this might have been a paid employee but he might also have been enslaved. While Brown's imaginary South Asian visitor was surprised to find a countryman in London, what is more significant is that the encounter appeared routine to Brown himself. In London South Asians were far from unusual.

One of the South Asian brought to London who attempted escape was Francisco, also known as Bugge, who eloped in early February 1688.[6] About twenty-eight years old, Francisco was a 'tall Man, [with a] long visage' whose face was scarred by smallpox and, according to Captain John Bowers, he was 'ill looked', presumably meaning that Bowers judged his appearance to be unattractive. Francisco wore the clothing of a sailor, 'a Red Jacket and Breeches, much tarred, also his Cap'. This was not surprising given that Bowers had sailed to Bantam, Surat, Calcutta, Madras and Bengal for the East India Company, making at least four voyages between 1675 and 1687 in the *Persia Merchant*.[7] Bowers's residence in London was by Elephant Stairs in Rotherhithe, one of close to a dozen landing points in this small but busy maritime district. Several days later Bowers once again advertised for Francisco, who by this point had been at liberty for almost a month.[8]

In both of the advertisements Bowers stated that if recaptured Francisco could be brought to him in Rotherhithe or to 'Mr. Evance Goldsmith at the Black Boy in Lombard-street' in the heart of the City. Working in premises marked by an all too appropriate sign displaying a Black boy, Stephen Evance or Evans was both a goldsmith and a banker (Figure 16).[9] He was

---

[5] T. Brown, *Amusements Serious and Comical, Calculated for the Meridian of London* (London, [1700] 1702), p. 27.

[6] 'An Indian … his Name Francisco, alias Bugge', *London Gazette*, 5 March 1688.

[7] See eg *Persia Merchant*: Journal, 4 Jan. 1681–10 Feb. 1682, India Office Records and Private Papers, Marine Department Records (1600–*c*.1879), British Library, IOR/L/MAR/A/LXXVII; *Persia Merchant*: 'Instructions to Captain John Bowers of the Persia Merchant', 26 Sept. 1684, India Office Records and Private Papers, Letter Book VII (1682–1685), British Library, IOR/E/3/90 ff. 236v–237; *Persia Merchant*: Receipt Book (*c*.1688), India Office Records and Private Papers, Ships' Journals 1605–1705, British Library, IOR/L/MAR/A/LXXXV.

[8] 'An Indian … his name Francisco', *London Gazette*, 8 March 1688.

[9] Both Evans and Peter Percefull [Percival] were listed as operating 'at the Black Boy in Lumbard street' in S. Lee, *The Little London Directory of 1677: The Oldest Printed List of Merchants and Bankers of London* (London, 1878).

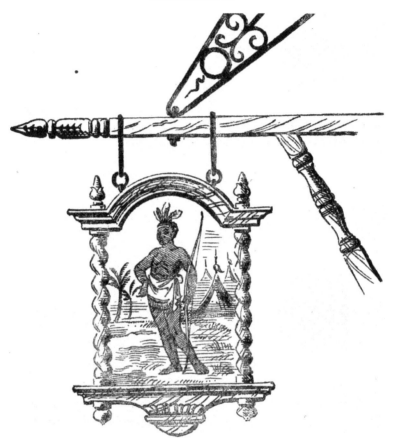

Figure 16. Representation of sign displaying the 'Black Boy' outside
the Lombard Street premises of Stephen Evance. From F. G. Hilton
Price, *The Signs of Old Lombard Street* (London, 1902), p. 82.

deeply involved in the trade of both the Royal African Company and the
East India Company, working to bring gold into England and to profit
from the nation's trade in both gold and silver. Evance's substantial loans to
the Crown helped earn him a knighthood and he embodied the interests of
the nascent financial sector in England's fast-developing trade with South
Asia and West Africa and the exploitation of those regions' people for profit.
Evance was a logical ally of a master such as Bowers.[10]

---

[10] See eg S. Mentz, *The English Gentleman at Work: Madras and the City of London, 1660–
1740* (Copenhagen, 2005), pp. 87, 149; J. Marshall, 'Whig thought and the revolutions of

Two years later Bowers once again advertised for a runaway, this time 'AN Indian black Girl, aged about 15, with a Brass Collar about her neck'.[11] Whereas Francisco's clothing indicated that he had served Bowers as a working sailor, this unnamed girl surely had an altogether different role in his household. Bowers's will revealed that he was married with children and grandchildren. The young South Asian girl who escaped from his household was prettily dressed in 'a Drugget Gown and a Painted-Callico Petticoat'. Presumably she was a domestic servant working for Bowers's wife, although it remains possible that she was escaping from a sexual bondage symbolized by the brass collar around her throat. The collar might suggest that she had already attempted escape and that Bowers was determined to do all he could to affirm his ownership of her and to make another escape attempt difficult.[12]

At least one of the South Asians who sought freedom in Restoration London escaped from a non-English household. In November 1681 an unnamed 'Tall slender *Indian* Tawney, about 18 years of age' eloped from the household of the conde de Castlemelhor in Somerset House, the royal palace on the bank of the Thames that was home to Catherine of Braganza, queen of England and wife of Charles II. Once an influential courtier in their native Portugal, Castlemelhor was one of Catherine's senior advisers.[13] At this time Lisbon was one of Europe's most racially mixed cities, and by the turn of the eighteenth century perhaps one fifth of its residents were people of colour, including some South Asians.[14] Many were enslaved, and when in 1662 Sir Edward Montagu, the earl of Sandwich, had escorted Catherine from Lisbon to England for her marriage to Charles II, he had purchased and brought with him 'a little Turk and a negroe, which are

1688–91', in *The Final Crisis of the Stuart Monarchy: the Revolutions of 1688–91 in their British, Atlantic and European Contexts*, ed. T. Harris and S. Taylor (Woodbridge, 2013), pp. 57–86, at p. 75; S. Quinn, 'Gold, silver and the Glorious Revolution: international bullion arbitrage and the origins of the English gold standard', *Economic History Review*, xlix (1996), 473–90, an examination of the years 1688–1700 based largely on Evance's bullion book record. See also H. Lancaster, 'Sir Stephen Evance' (2004), *Oxford Dictionary of National Biography* <https://doi.org/10.1093/ref:odnb/49172> [accessed 13 April 2020].

[11] 'AN Indian black Girl', *London Gazette*, 22 Sept. 1690.

[12] Will of John Bowers, Mariner of Rotherhithe, Surrey, 24 May 1707, National Archives, PROB 11/494/386.

[13] 'Run away ... a Tall slender Indian Tawney', *London Gazette*, 28 Nov. 1681. See also J. Mackay, *Catherine of Braganza* (London, 1937), p. 163; L. C. Davidson, *Catherine of Braganca, Infanta of Portugal & Queen-Consort of England* (London, 1908), p. 318.

[14] J. L. Vogt, 'The Lisbon Slave House and African trade, 1486–1521', *Proceedings of the American Philosophical Society*, cxvii (1973), 1–16; J. H. Sweet, 'The hidden histories of African Lisbon', in *The Black Urban Atlantic in the Age of the Slave Trade*, ed. J. Cañizares-Esguerra, M. D. Childs and J. Sidbury (Philadelphia, Pa., 2013), pp. 233–47.

intended for pages' in his household.[15] We know virtually nothing about this particular freedom seeker. The queen's Catholicism was extremely unpopular in Protestant England and it is possible that a runaway from her household might have met a favourable reaction from Londoners and safe harbour. No image of Catherine and her enslaved servants survives. However, Pierre Mignard's portrait of the duchess of Portsmouth, lady in waiting to Queen Catherine and a mistress of Charles II, displays an elite member of the royal court with an enslaved servant in attendance (Figure 17).

While the word 'slave' was not used in a single advertisement for South Asians who eloped in late seventeenth-century London, it is clear that some of those who ran away were held in perpetual bondage. Robert Goldesbrough had spent time in the East Indies, but by the late 1680s he was living as a pensioner in Chelsea, one of a number of former East India Company employees thus situated.[16] Goldesbrough had probably brought Andrew back with him, presumably as a personal servant, for despite his youth the boy spoke 'good English'. Goldesbrough's pension might indicate that he was in some way incapacitated and thus dependent on a bound servant. Andrew, however, resisted his bondage and Goldesborough had to take action to make escape more difficult. When Andrew eloped on 5 March 1690 he was hampered by 'a Steel Collar on (Engraven, Mr Robt. Goldesbrough of Chelsea …) a Steel Cuff about his Wrist, and an Iron Chain from the Collar to the Cuff on the outside of his Clothes'. Such restraints were clear emblems of enslaved status. Goldesbrough's advertisement was one of the few seventeenth-century notices with information about where the freedom seeker had gone, reporting that 'he was seen on the Western Road 4 or 5 weeks since, pretending to be going to one Mr. Griffins in Wiltshire'. Perhaps Andrew sought employment outside of London, earning a wage as a free person rather than labouring as enslaved property, or perhaps it was a ruse to gain free passage based on the practice of using young servants of colour to run errands and deliver messages. Either way, Andrew would have had to find a way of ridding himself of his shackles to stand any chance of remaining free and creating a new life for himself in England or further afield.[17]

[15] Pepys, *Diary*, 30 May 1662; *The Journal of Edward Montagu, First Earl of Sandwich, Admiral and General at Sea, 1659–1666*, ed. R. C. Anderson (London, 1929), p. 125.

[16] Goldesbrough was listed as a pensioner in various records and appears to have been resident in Chelsea before the Royal Hospital residence for army veterans opened in 1692. See eg *King's Warrant Book*, xii. 228–9, in 'Entry Book: July 1687, 16–20', in *Calendar of Treasury Books, Volume 8, 1685–1689*, ed. William A Shaw (London, 1923), pp. 1466–74. *British History Online* <http://www.british-history.ac.uk/cal-treasury-books/vol8/pp1466–1474> [accessed 28 Sept. 2021]. For references to Goldesbrough's time in India see A. Goldsborough, *Memorials of the Goldesborough Family, Collected, Collated and Compiled by Albert Goldsborough* (Cheltenham and London, 1930), p. 304.

[17] 'Run away … an Indian black Boy', *London Gazette*, 17 April 1690.

Figure 17. Pierre Mignard, *Louise de Kéroualle, duchess of Portsmouth*,
oil on canvas (1682), National Portrait Gallery. The jewellery, clothing
and adoring gaze of this presumably enslaved girl were intended to
show the wealth, privilege and benevolence of her mistress.[18]

---

[18] See D. Bindman and H. Watson, 'Court and city: fantasies of domination', in *The Image of the Black in Western Art*: iii, *From the 'Age of Discovery' to the Age of Abolition*: part iii, *The Eighteenth Century*, ed. D. Bindman and H. L. Gates (Cambridge, Mass., 2011), pp. 125–70, at pp. 266–7.

Figure 18. *East India Company Ships at Deptford* (c.1683). © National Maritime Museum, Greenwich, London. The large ship in the centre is likely to have been Grantham's ship *Charles II*. Grantham was knighted by the king on board the ship in February 1683 at the time of its launching.

It is possible that some of the people referred to simply as 'Indian' may have been Native Americans, but there is plenty of evidence within most of the advertisements to suggest that most if not all of these were South Asian. An advertisement in the *London Gazette* on 12 April 1688 sought out 'John Newmoone, alias Shackshoone, an Indian … low of stature, and swarthy complexion'. Shackshoone had eloped from the house of Sir Thomas Grantham in Sudbury on the outskirts of London, 'taking with him several things of value, designing to go beyond the seas'. Grantham had spent time in Virginia in the early 1670s and later in the decade had acted as an intermediary between Governor Berkeley and the colonial rebels under Nathaniel Bacon. As a merchant in London, Grantham shipped goods to and tobacco back from the colony, all of which might have suggested that Shackshoone was a Native American. Charles II had showed his appreciation of Grantham's efforts by knighting him and helping him secure a commission to captain the *Charles II*, an East India Company ship (Figure 18). Grantham then served in South Asia before returning to England in 1685, having negotiated a peaceful resolution to a mutiny in Bombay by Captain Richard Keigwin and his supporters, which resulted in the award of further honours by William and Mary.[19]

---

[19] 'One John Newmoone, alias Shackshoone', *London Gazette*, 12 April 1688. For more on Grantham's experiences in Virginia and India see T. Grantham, *An Historical Account of Some Memorable Actions, particularly in Virginia; also against the Admiral of Algier, and in*

While the label 'Indian', which Grantham employed in the 1688 advertisement, might have indicated that Shackshoone was either a Native American brought back from Virginia or a South Asian brought back from Bombay or elsewhere in South Asia, a separate advertisement proves that he was indeed South Asian. Eighteen months earlier Grantham had placed an advertisement in the *London Gazette* seeking the capture and return of 'an Indian called Shackshoon, and his Brother called Mahomet, brought from the East-India by Sir Thomas Grantham'.[20] The brothers had sailed from India to London on the *Charles II*, arriving a few months earlier. What happened to Mahomet? Was Grantham unable to retake possession of him? Had he escaped again or had he died? There were many ships leaving London for South Asia, and it is very possible that a young man seeking passage as a working sailor would have been able to secure a position, so it may have been possible for Mahomet to make his way back home.

Shackshoon's situation was unusual. The second advertisement described him as 'having a Child growing out of his side'. A newsletter dated 5 February 1687 reported that

> On Thursday at the Common Pleas was a trial between the monster (a man that hath a child growing out of his side) and Sir Thomas Grantham upon a writ *de homine replegiando*. Sir Thomas had contracted with him to come over from the Indies for six months and then to return, but has kept him like a slave longer and got a great deal of money by showing him; so he prays to be relieved according to law. The judges (it being a novel case, though the man has been christened since he came here) will consult all their brethren about it and have since ordered him to be bailed.[21]

The case reports describe Shackshoon as having 'the perfect shape of a child growing out of his breast as an excrescency, all but the head'. This is almost certainly a case of a parasitic twin in which one conjoined twin 'ceases development during gestation and becomes vestigial to the fully formed dominant twin'.[22] Grantham had brought Shackshoon from India 'and exposed [him] to the sight of the people for profit'. However,

---

the East Indies ... (London, 1716). See also P. Le Fevre, 'Sir Thomas Grantham' (rev. 2008), *ODNB* <https://doi.org/10.1093/ref:odnb/11297> [accessed 8 April 2020].

[20] 'Whereas an Indian called Shackshoon, and his Brother Mahomet', *London Gazette*, 8 Nov. 1686.

[21] Newsletter to John Fenwick at the *Swan*, Newcastle, 5 Feb. 1687, in *Calendar of State Papers, Domestic Series, of the Reign of James II, 1685–1689, Preserved in the State Paper Department of Her Majesty's Public Record Office 1893*: ii, *Jan 1686–May 1687*, ed. E. K. Timings (London, 1964), p. 359.

[22] C. DeRuiter, 'Parasitic twins' (16 Aug. 2011), *The Embryo Project Encyclopedia* <https:// embryo.asu.edu/pages/parasitic-twins> [accessed 8 April 2020].

Shackshoon had apparently 'turned *Christian* and was baptized', after which he 'was detained from his master' by sympathetic church members. Grantham 'claimed a property' in Shackshoon and employed a writ *de homine replegiando* to secure him; a local sheriff enforced the writ and returned Shackshoon to Grantham but without affirming the latter's rights of ownership. Chief Justice of the Common Pleas Edward Herbert ruled in favour of Grantham, ordering the sheriff to redraft his decision to confirm Grantham's rights over his enslaved property.[23]

Herbert tended to rule in favour of the interests of the king, and was to follow James II into exile. Given James's leadership of the Royal African Company and the English slave trade, it is hardly surprising that Herbert ruled thus.[24] Shackshoon's second escape a little over a year later is all the more understandable, and perhaps he had support and shelter from people who had supported him in his baptism and his legal struggle. Herbert was a political appointment by James II who was, in the words of one scholar, 'sadly deficient in professional knowledge'; his failure to report his cases in detail means that 'we are not even amused by his blunders, which are said to have been many and grievous'.[25] Herbert's decision must have been anything but amusing to Shackshoon, who was forced to return to a man who claimed ownership of and exploited him, and then to have that man's ownership of him legally confirmed. It is hardly surprising that a few months later Shackshoon once again attempted to gain his freedom. His physical condition cannot have made this easy, so it is hard to imagine his attempting escape without external aid.

Five years later, on 9 June 1703, an unnamed 'Negro Servt. Man of Sr. Tho. Grantham' was buried at St Mary's in Sunbury.[26] A year later Grantham himself died and his will stipulated that at least 200 guineas be spent on a marble memorial, which still exists, extolling Grantham as 'a most generous … benefactor'. One among numerous bequests to family and to the poor in two different parishes was his gift to 'any man or woman that shall be in my service at the day of my death the sum of five pounds apiece', but there

---

[23] Sir T. Grantham's Case, case 81 in *Modern Reports; or, Select Cases Adjudged in the Courts of King's Bench, Chancery, Common Pleas, And Exchequer*: iii, 5th edn, ed. T. Leach (London, 1793), p. 120. See also J. Campbell, *The Lives of the Chief Justices of England …* (Philadelphia, Pa., 1851), ii. 80–94.

[24] W. A. Pettigrew, *Freedom's Debt: the Royal African Company and the Politics of the Atlantic Slave Trade, 1672–1752* (Chapel Hill, N.C., 2013), pp. 28–31.

[25] Campbell, *The Lives of the Chief Justices of England*, pp. 80–94, at p. 82. See also J. R. Collins, 'Edward Herbert' (2005), *ODNB* <https://doi.org/10.1093/ref:odnb/13023> [accessed 8 April 2020].

[26] Burial of 'A Negro Servt. Man', 9 June 1703, Burials, Parish Register, St Mary, Sunbury. London Metropolitan Archives, London, England, DRO/007/A/01/001. Digitized copy of original consulted at https://www.ancestry.co.uk [accessed 15 May 2020].

THE OLD FOUNTAIN in the MINORIES

(taken down 1793) was formerly an Inn: the dining room was curiously orna-
mented, and over the fire place was a date, within a year of 1480. The timber works
were so firmly constructed, that Horses were employed to pull them asunder. The
court behind (now Fountain Court) was anciently called London Prentice Yard.

Published Aug. 10, 1791, by N. Smith, Rembrandt's Head, G. May's Buildings S. Martin's Lane, & I.T. Smith, in Frith S. Soho.

Figure 19. John Thomas Smith, 'The Old Fountain in the Minories'
(London, 1798). © The Trustees of the British Museum.

was no mention of Shackshoon.[27] Given that White Englishmen sometimes used the terms 'Black' and even 'Negro' to describe South Asians as well as Africans, it may have been Shackshoon who had predeceased Grantham one year earlier and whose baptism entitled him to a Christian burial.

The determination of some freedom seekers to achieve a greater degree of self-determination is all too clear. On 10 November 1690 the *London Gazette*

---

[27] Will of Sir Thomas Grantham of Sunbury, Middlesex, 6 Sept. 1704, National Archives, PROB 11/574/168. Memorial to Sir Thomas Grantham, Church Monuments listing, St Edburg's Church, Bicester, Oxfordshire <http://www.stedburgshistory.org.uk/monument_i.php> [accessed 8 April 2020].

included an advertisement for 'AN Indian Boy aged about 19' who had 'run away from William Johnson Esq; at Brumly near Bow'. Johnson reported that the unnamed runaway was 'bushy hair'd' and well dressed in 'a blew Livery lined with Orange-Colour and White, and Tin Buttons'. Bromley by Bow lay just north of Poplar in the fast-expanding East End of greater London, and the young freedom seeker could be returned to Johnson there or to a Captain Noble at the Fountain Tavern in the Minories in Portsoken ward in the north-eastern corner of the City of London (Figure 19).

Apparently this young freedom seeker was either captured or chose to return, for he eloped again four months later. This time Johnson advertised that the young man's name was Toby, 'pretty tall and slender, and his Hair newly cut off', that he was wearing his orange and blue livery and that a week earlier he had been 'seen in Essex the day he went away'. Again Toby was taken back; one month later he escaped for a third time. On this occasion Johnson described him as 'thin fac'd, his Head shaved, and the Hair a little grown'. Instead of his recognizable blue and orange lined livery, Toby eloped wearing 'an old Fustion Frock', the more anonymous working clothing of many White and Black Londoners. There were no further advertisements. Toby's bid for freedom may have succeeded and Johnson may have tired of the cost and trouble of pursuing him, or he may have been recaptured and punished to such an extent that he did not again escape and occasion yet another newspaper advertisement. Whatever his eventual fate, a succession of advertisements like these reveal Toby's courage and his determination to be free of Johnson.[28]

On rare occasions, advertisers indicated that freedom seekers had been seen since their escape. On 6 July 1702 'an Indian Black Boy' named Morall escaped 'from his Masters House in *Drury-Lane*' in the parish of St Giles in the Fields, which lay between the City of London and Westminster. About fifteen years old, long-haired and speaking 'very good English', Morall had left wearing 'a brown Fustian Frock, a blue Wastcoat and Scarlet Shagg Breeches'. The advertisement noted that since his escape a week earlier Morall had been seen in Hampstead, Highgate and Tottenham Court, all of them north of the residence from which he had escaped. If he had been in these places Morall was heading away from the river and the possibility of serving on a ship bound for India or indeed anywhere away from London, and so was presumably seeking a different life and employment

---

[28] 'AN Indian Boy', *London Gazette*, 10 Nov. 1690; 'RUN away the 19th instant … an East-India Black Boy named Toby', *London Gazette*, 26 March 1691; 'RUN away the 18th Instant … a pretty tall and slender East-India Black', *London Gazette*, 30 April 1691.

in or around London and its suburbs, away from Drury Lane.[29] Other freedom seekers, however, were almost certainly seeking to leave London and England aboard a ship and thus were engaged in 'maritime marronage', hoping to achieve the relative freedom and rough equality among working seafarers.[30] One such was an unnamed 'Slender middle sized India Black' who eloped from the service of Mrs. Thwaits in Stepney wearing a 'dark grey Livery with Brass Buttons'. Stepney was at the heart of the riverside docks and maritime communities of London's East End and, according to Mrs Thwaits, the freedom seeker was 'supposed to be gone on board some Ship in the *Downs*', the anchorage for ocean-going ships at the mouth of the Thames estuary.[31] It was not unusual for captains with insufficient crews to take on men from the Kent and Essex coastal communities on either side of the Downs: given that these men were ready to embark on lengthy voyages the captains probably did not ask questions or demand evidence of a volunteer's freedom to join the ship's company.

Mostly associated with ship captains, merchants and wealthy aristocrats, enslaved and bound South Asians in late seventeenth- and turn of the eighteenth-century London were generally young and male, serving as sailors, personal servants, liveried attendants and in a few cases maids and perhaps sexual victims. Together with parish registers recording the baptism, marriage and burial of South Asians, these newspaper advertisements testify to the presence of a small but noticeable community of people from India in greater London. Their status was even less clear than that of Africans, given that from the mid seventeenth century onwards the transatlantic slave trade and the rapid development of plantation slavery began to make African slavery a foundation of England's fast-growing economy and empire. While slavery and forms of unfreedom existed in India, they played a less well-known and visible role in England's increasing trade and empire building. The shackles worn by Andrew and by an unnamed South Asian girl and boy offer the starkest evidence that at least some of the South Asians who were the subject of London newspaper advertisements were attempting to escape from enslavement.[32]

---

[29] 'Went away from his Masters House … Morall', *The Flying Post; or, The Post-Master*, 14 July 1702. The same advertisement was printed in the *Post Man and The Historical Account*, 16 July 1702.

[30] N. A. T. Hall, 'Maritime Maroons: "grand marronage" from the Danish West Indies', *William and Mary Quarterly*, 3rd series, xlii (1985), 476–98.

[31] 'A Slender middle sized India Black', *The Post Man: and The Historical Account*, 13 June 1702.

[32] 'Run away … an Indian black Boy', *London Gazette*, 17 April 1690; 'An Indian black Girl', *London Gazette*, 22 Sept. 1690; 'A Black Boy, an Indian', *London Gazette*, 10 Sept. 1694.

6. 'A black Girl' and 'an Indian black girl': female freedom seekers

An Indian black Girl, aged about 15, with a Brass Collar about her Neck, in a Drugget Gown and a Painted-Callico Petticoat, Run away from Captain John Bowers in Rotherhith, on Monday night last. Whoever brings her to Captain Bowers aforesaid, shall have a Guinea Reward, and Charges.

The London Gazette, 22 September 1690

A black Girl, aged about 15 years, went away from her Master near 3 Weeks since; She had on a black Cloth Gown and Petticoat, with a brass Collar about her Neck, with this Inscription, John Campion at the Ship-Tavern at Ratcliff-Cross, his Negro. Whoever gives Notice of her to the said John Campion, shall have a Guinea Reward.

London Gazette, 5 November 1691

The very real female freedom seekers in Restoration London are all but invisible to us today, little more than ghosts in the archives. The words of those who sought them ring loud and clear across the centuries, and we can often learn a great deal about the people who claimed ownership or control of the enslaved and bound women of colour in London. But the thirteen girls and women can barely be glimpsed in the 872 words of newspaper advertisements that chronicled their escape: sometimes even their names are missing, and their silence within the archive is as complete as it is compelling.

Although they feature in only 6 per cent of advertisements for freedom seekers between 1655 and 1704, females probably comprised a significantly higher proportion of London's population of free and enslaved people of colour. Women and girls constituted 24 per cent of the 705 men, women and children of colour who were baptized, married or buried in London between 1600 and 1710 and whose gender was recorded in the surviving parish records. Fewer enslaved and bound females were brought back to Britain, and for whatever reasons a lower proportion of them attempted to escape.

Where enslaved boys often served White men as cabin boys and personal servants, enslaved girls and young women might work as the maids and personal attendants of White women and families. During these early days of the English slave trade and plantation agriculture there were relatively few White women in South Asia, West Africa or the developing plantations of Barbados, Antigua, Jamaica and the Carolinas. In Jamaica in 1673 a population of 2,006 White women was outnumbered by more than two to one by the 4,050 White men on the island, while on Antigua in 1678 the island's 544 White women were outnumbered by 1,236 White men.[1] During the early decades of plantation slavery and trade with South Asia it was predominantly men who brought enslaved people, generally boys or men, with them when they returned from the colonies to London or from trading or slave ship voyages. On occasion, enslaved people might be given as presents to White women in England. For example, Samuel Pepys recorded in May 1662 that the earl of Sandwich 'had a little Turk and a negroe, which are intended for pages to the two young ladies', his daughters;[2] but even here the people of colour selected to serve young elite women were boys and not girls.

The work of many of London's female servants was arduous, including incessant cleaning, food preparation, child care and personal attendance on the family of the householder. From the daily cleaning of kitchens, staircases and public entrances to the weekly washing of clothing and household linen, to the provision of water and fuel for fires and the emptying of chamber pots, the work of female servants was constant. Some female servants, especially in larger households, focused on the personal needs of the householder or his wife, keeping their clothing in order, helping them to undress or dress and ensuring that they themselves were sufficiently clean and well dressed that they could escort the householder's wife and children around town. Others worked in the householder's place of business, especially in inns, taverns and shops. A few of these female servants were adolescents and women of colour.[3]

We do not know the name of one female freedom seeker owned by a woman, nor do we know the name of her mistress. Described simply as 'A Negro Woman, short but thick, about 20 years of age', she was reported to have 'run away from her Mistress' on 4 July 1684. The advertisement stated that her ears were pierced and that she was wearing 'a Stuff Jacket buttoned down before, a Stuff Petticoat, black Shoos, and sad coloured Stockings … [and] a Cap with a blue Ribband on her Head'. She was dressed like many of London's female domestic servants, her 'stuff' jacket and petticoat made

---

[1] R. S. Dunn, *Sugar and Slaves: the Rise of the Planter Class in the English West Indies, 1624–1713* (Chapel Hill, N.C., 1972), pp. 155, 127.

[2] *The Diary of Samuel Pepys: Daily Entries from the 17th Century London Diary*, 30 May 1662 <https://www.pepysdiary.com/diary> [accessed 12 May 2020].

[3] P. Earle, *The Making of the English Middle Class: Business, Society and Family Life in London, 1660–1730* (Berkeley, Calif., 1989), pp. 221–3.

of lighter-weight woollen fabric. However, a difference between this freedom seeker and the many White domestic servants in the capital was made chillingly clear in a second advertisement published on 14 July. To the list of her clothes was added a further detail, that this woman was 'marked with a P and a B on her back'.[4] The layers of clothing she wore kept her warm but also served to obscure this brand, which had probably been applied at a slave-trading post on the West African coast, aboard a slave-trading ship or on a plantation. The violent scar would forever mark her as enslaved.

We shall never know the identity of this young woman or the reasons for her escape. Already free for ten days when the second advertisement was published, she achieved at least temporary freedom and may have found refuge in the growing Black communities south and east of the City of London or with a partner (Black or White) who concealed her. While legal unions between men and women of different races would soon be outlawed in colonies founded upon racial hierarchy, such marriages could and did occur in England. If she could pass as a free woman, there were employment opportunities as a maid, cook or domestic servant in London. Pepys's diary makes clear the ubiquity of such serving people and, while some of them were enslaved, others were quite possibly free. He included numerous references to Mingo, Sir William Batten's 'Black' servant, as well as the 'blackemore' servant of William Glanville; the death by plague of the merchant George Cocke's 'black' manservant; Jack, the Black servant of Sir William Penn; and Doll, 'a blackmoore' from the household of merchant William Batelier who briefly worked for Pepys and his wife.[5] We can get a sense of how Doll might have been dressed from Wenceslaus Hollar's 1645 portrait of a young African woman wearing the dress of a domestic servant (Figure 20).[6]

---

[4] 'A Negro Woman', *London Gazette*, 6 July 1684; 'A Negro Woman', *London Gazette*, 14 July 1684.

[5] For Mingo see Pepys, *Diary*, 27 March 1661, <https://www.pepysdiary.com/diary/1661/03/27/> [accessed 28 Sept. 2021]; 10 April 1661, <https://www.pepysdiary.com/diary/1661/04/10/> [accessed 28 Sept. 2021]; 21 March 1667, https://www.pepysdiary.com/diary/1667/03/21/ [accessed 28 Sept. 2021]; 4 Nov. 1665 https://www.pepysdiary.com/diary/1665/11/04/ [accessed 28 Sept. 2021]; and 14 Feb. 1661 <https://www.pepysdiary.com/diary/1661/02/14/> [accessed 28 Sept. 2021]; for Glanville's servant see Pepys, *Diary*, 27 Sept. 1665 <https://www.pepysdiary.com/diary/1665/09/27/> [accessed 28 Sept. 2021]; for Cocke's servant see Pepys, *Diary*, 31 Oct. 1665 <https://www.pepysdiary.com/diary/1665/10/31/> [accessed 28 Sept. 2021]; 27 March 1661 <https://www.pepysdiary.com/diary/1661/03/27/> [accessed 28 Sept. 2021]; for Doll see Pepys, *Diary*, 5 April 1669 <https://www.pepysdiary.com/diary/1669/04/05/> [accessed 28 Sept. 2021].

[6] Hollar's portrait appears to have been created in Antwerp, but he spent most of the period between 1637 and his death 40 years later in London, and his artistic representations of the London cityscape suggest a deep familiarity with the city and presumably its inhabitants, including bound people of colour. See R. Godfrey, *Wenceslaus Hollar: a Bohemian Artist in England* (New Haven, Conn., 1994).

Figure 20. Wenceslaus Hollar, 'Head of a Black woman with a lace kerchief hat' (1645), no. 46, plate opposite p. 88 in Folger Shakespeare Library. The woman is wearing quite expensive, albeit relatively plain, lace (in an age of incredibly opulent elite clothing), which may suggest that she was a domestic servant or attendant.

Two of the thirteen female freedom seekers had metal collars fixed around their throats when they eloped, clearly marking them as enslaved and property. Both were young and neither was named in the advertisement or on the collars that restricted them. Both sought escape from the dockside communities on the banks of the Thames, and the first eloped from Captain John Bowers in Rotherhithe on 18 September 1690. Bowers's advertisement appeared four days later, in which he described the freedom seeker with just seven words as 'AN Indian black girl, aged about 15'. He preferred to focus the advertisement not on the individual but on the clothes and collar that shaped her appearance, describing her apparel as 'a Drugget Gown and a Painted-Callico Petticoat'. The heavy woollen gown may not have offered much protection against the elements over quite possibly a thin South Asian cotton garment that she may have brought with her from the East Indies.[7]

Bowers had made a voyage to Bantam in Java and Surat in India in 1682–3, another to Madras and Bengal in 1684–7 and quite possibly other voyages for which records have not survived. He was clearly well connected to East India Company captains and officials who regularly travelled between England and India. Indeed, Captain John Hyde, the president of the East India Company, had been a passenger on Bowers's voyage in the *Persia* in 1681–2.[8]

Given that she was only fifteen years old and quite possibly wearing an identifiably South Asian cotton garment, it is possible that this girl had arrived in London quite recently in a ship captained by Bowers or by one of his associates. The 'Brass Collar about her Neck' clearly marked this girl as enslaved property and may indicate that she had attempted escape before. Seventeen years later Bowers left sizeable bequests to his wife and grandsons; that he had a family suggests that this unnamed enslaved girl was a household domestic servant but does not preclude the possibility of her having suffered sexual assault on the voyage to London or following her arrival in the city.[9] Was she in a sexual relationship with Bowers or another male member of his household? The power imbalance meant that she enjoyed little power or agency, and the collar she wore objectified and

[7] 'An Indian black Girl', *London Gazette*, 22 Sept. 1690.

[8] Bowers's logbook for the *Persia's* 1681–2 voyage still exists. See J. Bowers, 'Commander of the merchant ship *Persia*, Journal of voyage from England to Surat, in the merchant ship *Persia*: 1682–1683', India Office Records and Private Papers, Marine Department Records, Ships' Journals (1605–1705), British Library, IOR/L/MAR/A/LXXVII. See also the *Persia Merchant*: Receipt Book, British Library, India Office Records and Private Papers, Marine Department Records, Ships' Journals (1605–1705), British Library, IOR/L/MAR/A/LXXXV. For the reference to Hyde's presence on the first voyage see S. A. Khan, *Sources for the History of British India in the Seventeenth Century* (London, [1926] 2017), p. 78.

[9] Will of John Bowers, Mariner of Rotherhithe, Surrey, 24 May 1707, National Archives, PROB 11/494/386.

attempted to subdue her. If there was a sexual relationship between them, how can we define it and what terms can we use to describe it? Coercion or consent suggest binary alternatives when the situation would have been far more complex: as Diana Paton has observed, terms such as 'concubine' or 'paramour' obscure too much of the nature of such relationships.[10] Samuel Pepys's diary makes clear that he regularly fondled and assaulted White female servants, and that, however much they resented his actions, it would appear that the young women in his house were not at all surprised by their master's behaviour. Young female servants of colour, particularly those who were regarded as property by the men who held them in bondage, were even more vulnerable. The power imbalance between Bowers and this isolated young girl would have made any consensual relationship impossible. We do not know if the unnamed young woman had been assaulted by Bowers, or what prompted her to elope, but we do know that such assault was possible and common and that, whether or not it had happened in this case, this girl and others like her lived with the knowledge that it could happen at any time. All that we know for sure is that she tried to free herself.

Two and a half years earlier, a twenty-eight-year-old 'Indian' man named Francisco or Bugge, who had probably come to London in May 1687 on Bowers's voyage back from Madras and Bengal, had eloped from Bowers (see pp. 81–3).[11] This man had already been free for almost a month when Bowers advertised for him, while the unnamed freedom-seeking girl had been absent for five days when he advertised for her, despite her flimsy clothes and the heavy brass collar designed to mark her as property. Perhaps she had been able to secure assistance in removing the collar and a change of clothes, but if she was newly arrived in London the chances of a successful escape appear remote.

A year later another female freedom seeker eloped from the riverside maritime community. About 1,000 yards north of Bowers's home, across the Thames and past the thicket of masts and rigging of the ocean-going ships at anchor lay the densely packed East End communities of Wapping, Shadwell and Ratcliff. At their heart and just a few steps from the river was the Ship Tavern at Ratcliff Cross, from which an unnamed girl attempted to escape in 1691. This runaway was also fifteen years old and described simply as 'A black Girl', who like her fellow freedom seeker south of the river was dressed simply in 'a black Cloth Gown and Petticoat'. The brass collar fitted around her neck

---

[10] D. Paton, 'Mary Williamson's letter; or seeing women and sisters in the archives of Atlantic slavery', *Transactions of the Royal Historical Society*, xxix (2019), 153–80, at p. 163. See also S. Hartman, *Scenes of Subjection: Terror, Slavery, and Self-Making in Nineteenth-Century America* (New York, 1997), pp. 80–2.

[11] 'An Indian … his Name Francisco, alias Bugge', *London Gazette*, 5 March 1688, repeated 8 March 1688.

was described in more detail than the girl herself, for its purpose was to mark her as property and make her escape from enslavement impossible. With a frankness that showed how normative he thought it was to manacle a girl he owned, her enslaver included in his runaway advertisement the words 'with a brass Collar about her Neck, with this Inscription, John Campion at the Ship-Tavern at Ratcliff Cross, his Negro'.[12]

The Ship Tavern was an important enough institution to be marked on maps, and Campion was a successful vintner, wine merchant and innkeeper. Upon his death seven years later, he left bequests of more than £2,000 to his wife and four children, evidence that he had been a sufficiently successful merchant and businessman to afford to purchase an enslaved girl, perhaps to help his wife with household work or to assist in the tavern that was his place of business.[13] During these years the wharves that lined the river a very short distance from Ratcliff Cross were some of the best landing spots east of the City of London. Long known as 'Sailor Town', Ratcliff was filled with sailors and ship captains, shipwrights, merchants and working men and women of all of the ancillary trades that supported the burgeoning ocean-going trade, and the Ship Tavern was a major community hub. People of colour must have regularly passed through, some of them accompanying the people who owned them, and it is conceivable that Campion had acquired this unnamed girl from a customer or business connection. When he advertised for her, this young girl had already been absent 'near 3 Weeks', so the collar around her neck had not restrained her actions as he had hoped. By the end of the seventeenth century there was a growing Black community in the East End, some enslaved or bound and others free; she may have found refuge there or work as a free woman, or the protection of a partner or friends, whether Black or White. The longer she was absent, presumably with the collar removed or at least obscured, the better her chance of remaining free.

These were not the only female runaways implicitly identified as enslaved in runaway advertisements. On 4 August 1691 'an East-India tawney Maid' eloped. Named Corney, she was described as 'aged about 20, short, and inclining to be fat, thick Lipp'd, long black hair by Nature, though at present cut short like a Boys'. Although not restricted by a collar, Corney was nonetheless defined in the advertisement by the short statement that she had been 'bought at Bantam in the East-Indies', a clear assertion of her status as purchased chattel property. It is not clear where or from whom she

[12] A black Girl', *London Gazette*, 5 Nov. 1691.

[13] Will of John Campion, Vintner of Stepney, Middlesex, National Archives, PROB 11/448/117.

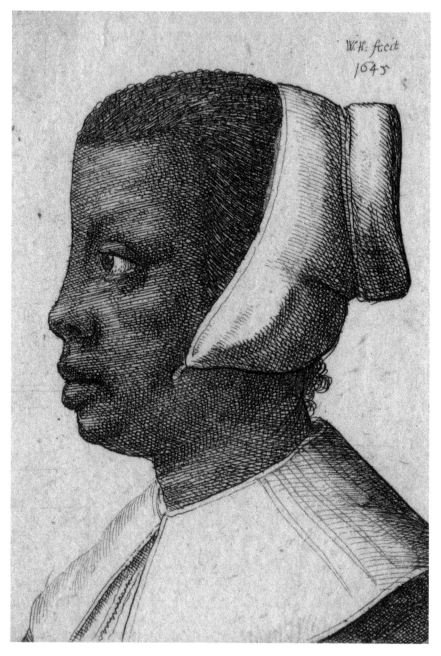

Figure 21. Wenceslaus Hollar, 'Head of a Black woman in profile to left' (1645), Folger Shakespeare Library. This young woman appears to be wearing the kind of clothing that many of London's domestic servants might have worn.

had escaped, and the advertisement simply promised a £1 reward to anyone who might give information leading to her recapture to a Mr Wilson in Litchfield Street near Soho. Wilson might have been the person who claimed ownership of Corney, or a contact and middleman.[14]

Three of the thirteen female runaways were identified as South Asian, and the proportions of female and male freedom seekers who were South Asians were almost identical. One was the first female freedom seeker for whom a runaway advertisement has been discovered. Named Sarah, she had disappeared 'from Mr. *Simon New's* house' on 16 January 1680, and the advertisement described her simply as 'an Indian Woman, about 40 years of Age, Tawney Complexion, long black hair, [and] a long cut down her forehead'. It is possible that Sarah had not run away but instead, as New's advertisement suggested, had 'Strayed or [been] spirited' away. However, the value of a forty-year-old woman would have been lower than that of a younger person, and a girl or young woman of colour was probably a more tempting target for those who sought to kidnap and sell such unfortunate women. New's house was in Vere Street, an increasingly well-developed area between the City and Westminster that lay south-west of Lincoln's Inn Fields.[15]

Bess eloped on 8 December 1702. Aged sixteen and described as 'A Negro Maid', she was wearing a striped 'stuff Wastcoat and Peticoat' and her dark complexion was 'much pitted with the Small Pox'. More than three weeks later Bess was still at liberty, and Benjamin Quelch readvertised for her in early 1703.[16] Quelch had been one of the men who had developed large-scale plantation slavery in Barbados and then helped transfer that system and the enslaved people who worked it to South Carolina. He was in London only temporarily, for he and his family had made their home in South Carolina where he became a major figure.[17] His years in Barbados and then South Carolina would have given him direct experience of early plantation slavery at its most brutal, a system that killed Africans almost as quickly as they were imported. Both of Quelch's newspaper advertisements for Bess mentioned that she was missing 'a piece of her Left Ear', possibly the result of an unusual injury but just as likely of the punitive clipping of

---

[14] 'RUN away … an East India tawney Maid', *London Gazette*, 6 Aug. 1691.

[15] 'Strayed or spirited … *Sarah*', *London Gazette*, 19 Jan. 1680.

[16] 'A Negro Maid', *The Flying Post; or, The Post Master*, 12 Dec. 1702; 'A Negro Maid … named Bess', *The Post Man and The Historical Account*, 2 Jan. 1703.

[17] R. Waterhouse, 'England, the Caribbean, and the Settlement of Carolina', *Journal of American Studies*, ix (1975), 259–81, at p. 277; J. P. Greene, 'Colonial South Carolina and the Caribbean connection', in *Imperatives, Behaviors, and Identities: Essays in American Cultural History*, ed. J. P. Greene (Charlottesville, Va., 1992), at p. 74; E. McCrady, *The History of South Carolina under the Proprietary Government, 1670–1719* (New York, 1897), p. 505.

an ear after one or more escape attempts. It is unclear why Quelch brought Bess to London. If he had travelled with his family, she may have been attending his wife and children, but if he had travelled alone he could not have employed her as he might an enslaved boy, as a personal attendant and messenger. A female attendant to a male travelling alone was unusual, and once again sexual exploitation could have been a factor.[18]

Quelch's advertisement specified that if anyone captured Bess they should return her to 'Mr Lloyd, at his Coffee House in Lombard street', making this hub of colonial commerce in the City a party to Quelch's attempts to reassert ownership of this freedom seeker. But twenty-five days after she 'ran away from her Master' Bess was still free. His advertisement had noted that 'she speaks English well', which may have enhanced her opportunities to create friendships or potential allies before seizing the chance of escape. Had Bess been recaptured by the time Quelch returned to Charleston, and did she then spend the rest of her life enslaved in South Carolina? Or did she become one more of the small but significant number of free women of colour in London?

---

[18] 'A Negro Maid … named Bess', *Post Man*.

7. *Caesar*: country marks

Run away from a Gentleman of Greenwich the 16th Instant, a Negro Youth, about 17 years of Age; Nose and Mouth formed like a White-man, yet of Colour very Black, small Cuts on each side of his Face, on the Temples; his Hair Cut about a Month since, he Beats a Drum well, and plays on the Flagelet, and Recorder, he goes by the name of Caesar, when he Ran away, he took several things of value; and had on an old Gray Cloath Coate Lin'd with Green Bazs, and Pewter Buttons to it, Coloured drouget Breeches and Gray Stockins, a greay Cap turn'd up with Furr, whosoever can bring Tydings of him unto Captain William Richardson, at the Star-Inn in Fish-streethill, near the Monument, so as he may be Returned to his Master shall have two Guinies Reward and all their Charges paid.

The Impartial Protestant Mercury, 20 December 1681

Runaway advertisements published in Restoration London newspapers tended to be less detailed than those that appeared in Caribbean and North American newspapers a century later. Colonial enslavers sought to identify particular freedom seekers who might attempt to disappear into large populations of enslaved and free people of colour. With a much smaller population of people of colour in London, it was far harder for freedom seekers to reach sanctuary or to hide in plain sight, and consequently the capital's earliest newspaper advertisements were often quite short and basic: advertisers did not believe that a great deal of descriptive detail was required to identify a freedom seeker.

On occasion advertisements described physical marks and scars on the bodies of escapees, and the physical restraints imposed upon them, presumably to aid identification. While these descriptions of markings and restraints were intended to help identify individual freedom seekers, the branded letters and markings on the shoulders, arms and breasts of some, together with the collars and chains fitted to others, show that these men, women and children had been subjected to violent assertions of ownership and control of their bodies. They were chilling evidence of the realities of enslavement in the English capital.

Some of the bound and enslaved people who were brought to seventeenth-century England also bore physical marks showing that they had been born in and had lived their early years in West Africa. There might be patterns of scars and inscribed marks on their foreheads, cheeks and perhaps upper arms and torsos, ritual bodily inscriptions that were often applied when they became young adults. This was a practice rooted in West African and Madagascan cultures and belief systems but it was not continued in the English colonies, and thus these markings served as inerasable evidence of African birth. By the mid eighteenth century Britons were labelling them 'country marks', assuming that particular patterns could reveal the bearer's 'country' of birth in West Africa. But in seventeenth-century London there was less knowledge about them and no fixed terminology as yet to describe the markings.[1]

One who bore such markings was Caesar, 'A Negro Youth about 17 years of age', who fled from 'a Gentleman of Greenwich' on 16 December 1681. Wearing a grey coat lined with green material and sporting pewter buttons, grey stockings, a fur cap and breeches, Caesar was a talented musician who could play the drum, the recorder and the flageolet (a type of flute) – the latter two popular instruments in early modern England. He thus appeared somewhat assimilated into English culture, yet his 'very handsome Face, with some small Scars or Cuts near his Eyes' forever marked him as African born.[2] A year later an unnamed 'Negro Man', about thirty years old and bearing 'three small scars in each cheek', escaped from Bell Wharf in Shadwell in the heart of the riverside East End.[3] And a year after that an unnamed 'Blackamoor', a 'lusty young Fellow, with Notches cross his Nose

---

[1] For example, a young Igbo boy who escaped from Heysham in Lancashire in 1765 was described in a Liverpool newspaper advertisement as having 'his Country Marks on his Temples', while in Jamaica a freedom seeker named Bob 'of the Chamba country, has his country marks in his face'. 'RUN away ... A NEGRO BOY of the Ebo Country', *Williamson's Liverpool Advertiser and Mercantile Register*, 30 Aug. 1765; 'RUN AWAY ... BOB', *Cornwall Chronicle, and Jamaica General Advertiser*, 15 Oct. 1785. Englishmen in West Africa noted and described the practice of ritual scarification: see eg Captain J. Adams who noted of the Hausa people that their 'country marks on the face consist of three short cuts, each about one and a half inch long, running obliquely on each side of the mouth' (J. Adams, *Remarks on the Country Extending from Cape Palmas to the River Congo* ... (London, 1823), p. 94). See P. E. Lovejoy, 'Scarification and the loss of history in the African diaspora', in *Activating the Past: History and Memory in the Black Atlantic World*, ed. A. Apter and L. Derby (Cambridge, 2010), pp. 99–138; M. A. Gomez, *Exchanging our Country Marks: the Transformation of African Identities in the Colonial and Antebellum South* (Chapel Hill, N.C., 1998), pp. 39–42, 97–8, 121–4, 140, 175; M. Vaughan, 'Scarification in Africa: re-reading colonial evidence', *Cultural and Social History*, iv (2007), 385–400. There are several essays focused on different West African traditions of scarification in *Marks of Civilization: Artistic Transformations of the Human Body*, ed. A. Rubin (Los Angeles, Calif., 1988).

[2] 'A Negro Youth ... his Name is Caesar', *The London Gazette*, 19 Dec. 1681. Different versions of this advertisement appeared in *The Impartial Protestant Mercury*, 20 Dec. 1681, and *The Loyal Protestant, and True Domestick Intelligence, Or, News both from City and Countrey*, 20 Dec. 1681, 22 Dec. 1681.

[3] 'On Friday the 28th of July last', *London Gazette*, 3 Aug. 1682.

and down his Forehead, ran away from his Master'.[4] All told, twenty-three (16 per cent) of the identifiably African freedom seekers had country marks (or other African bodily markings) upon them, and all but one of them were male. A further three advertisements included vague references to facial marks and scars, taking the possible total of those bearing country marks to approximately 18 per cent.

Country marks were so common that when Jack, 'A Guinea Negro Boy, about 8 years old … strayed away from Mr. Peter Paggens' in 1690, Paggens thought it worth mentioning that this African-born boy had 'no mark in his face'.[5] The absence of country marks was as noteworthy as their presence on the face of this young freedom seeker would have been. He had quite possibly come to Paggens on one of his ships bringing tobacco from the Chesapeake, and the very young boy surely served in this extremely wealthy family as a well-dressed and largely ornamental page boy. Captured while he was very young, Jack had not yet undergone the ritual scarification associated with passing from childhood.

One of those bearing African country marks was female, a young woman who eloped from Moses Cook on 17 March 1690. Cook did not bother to identify her by name in the advertisement he published three days later, instead describing her in disparaging terms as

> a thick, short, fat, Malagascow black Maid, aged about 20, with a round scar at the corner of each Eye near her Temples, and a scar in her Neck, her Hair about two Inches long, with a Cloth-coloured Man's Coat, a red Petticoat, a blue Shift, and a pair of Man's Shoes.[6]

Cook was a cordwainer and this young freedom seeker had escaped from his business and home in Great Turnstile Alley in Holborn, marked by the 'Sign of the Tobacco Roll'. Perhaps Cook believed that the country marks on her face would be more useful in identifying her than her name. Although it was not as common in Madagascar as in some areas of West Africa, ritual scarification did occur among the Malagasy people.[7]

Despite Cook's omission, we do know this woman's name, for three days later another record identified her as 'Anne (formerly Grace) a black of

---

[4] 'A Blackamoor', *London Gazette*, 30 Aug. 1683.

[5] 'A Guinea Negro Boy', *London Gazette*, 9 June 1690.

[6] 'RUN away … [a] Malagascow black Maid', *London Gazette*, 20 March 1690.

[7] R. Linton, 'Cultural areas in Madagascar', *American Anthropologist*, xxx (1928), 363–90, at p. 384. Cook is identified as a cordwainer in 'Nos 52–54 South Grove', in *Survey of London*: xvii, *The Parish of St Pancras*: part i: *The Village of Highgate*, ed. P. Lovell and W. McB. Marcham (London, 1936), pp. 95–102, *British History Online* <http://www.british-history.ac.uk/survey-london/vol17/pt1/pp95-102> [accessed 21 Jan. 2021].

Madagascar belonging to Moses Cook a shoemaker in Lincoln's Inn fields'.[8] On 20 March Anne was baptized at St Pancras Old Church on Euston Road. This church was at the northern edge of London (a few hundred yards from St Pancras Station today) and lay about two miles north of Cook's home and workplace in Turnstile Alley. Cook owned property in the vicinity of the church, so he and perhaps Anne may well have been familiar with the area. We cannot know what was going on, whether Anne had been recaptured or returned by choice, and her baptism was in some way a result of her escape attempt. Or might she still have been at liberty when she was baptized on the same day that Cook's runaway advertisement describing her was published? If so, what did the baptism mean to her? Was it an assertion of freedom, of independence and citizenship? Or could it have been a necessary precondition for marriage, perhaps a marriage forbidden by Cook or that she hoped would help enable her to remain free? We cannot know, for after appearing twice in records just three days apart, Anne disappeared from the archive.

Quite remarkably, another freedom seeker who appears to have had country marks can also be identified in London parish records. This young boy was described in a runaway advertisement as 'a Negro or Blackamore boy, by name Champion, about 14 years of Age, very black and handsome, with a scar in his forehead over his nose'. Champion had escaped from Madam Brooking, who may well have been Winifred Brooking, the widow of William Brooking. The will left by William Brooking in 1682 revealed him to be a wealthy 'gentleman', perhaps a merchant. Given that William Brooking provided instructions for burial according to whether he died in England or 'at Sea or in remote parts beyond the Sea', he appears to have travelled abroad quite regularly, and so may have acquired Champion on one such voyage. It is not clear where Winifred Brooking lived and from where Champion escaped, but he could be returned to Nicholas Hamburgh in Seething Lane a few hundred yards north-west of the Tower of London at the eastern edge of the City of London.[9]

Champion escaped on 17 September 1685, but six days later he was baptized at St Giles in the Fields, beyond the western edge of the City and some two and a half miles from Seething Lane. In the parish record he was

[8] Baptism of Anne (formerly Grace), 20 March 1690, Baptisms, Parish Register of Pancras, Euston Road. London Metropolitan Archives (LMA), London, England, P90/PAN1/001/1249/B. Digitized copy of original consulted at <https://www.ancestry.co.uk> [accessed 29 March 2021].

[9] 'Run away from Madam Brooking', *London Gazette*, 1 Oct. 1685; T. Sjölin, 'Madam Brooking', *Brooking Family Historian*, xiii (2009), at p. 239; Will of William Brooking, Gentleman of Saint Pauls Covent Garden, 9 Dec. 1682, National Archives, PROB 11/371/505.

described as 'William Champion a black aged about 14 years', but with no mention of his mistress or of any other White person.[10] The newspaper advertisement seeking his return or information about his whereabouts was published a week after his baptism of 1 October, a full two weeks after his escape. Therefore he was at liberty when he was baptized, and this must have been a decision of his own making. But we cannot know if there were any reasons beyond religious faith for William Champion's decision, or why he sought baptism at St Giles in the Fields, although it was a popular location for the capital's community of people of colour. Perhaps he sought comfort at a location where other Africans might support and protect him.

The years between 1650 and the turn of the eighteenth century were the earliest period of the English transatlantic slave trade and the newly developing slave-based plantation system. Consequently, African-born people outnumbered colonial- or English-born 'creolized' Africans, whether in the colonies or in England. Within a couple of generations White Britons in the colonies would have been inclined to assume that any younger person bearing country marks was enslaved, for locally born creoles – many of them of mixed-race ancestry – were more likely to benefit from emancipation, and thus would not have borne country marks. Yet in seventeenth-century London the status of people of colour was less clear and certainly less fixed, so why shouldn't Fortune, 'A Negro lately belonging to Capt. Joseph Smith Deceased', take advantage of Smith's death to seek freedom for himself? A 'short squat fellow', he bore 'cuts on each cheek' identifying him as African born but he clearly fancied his chances of achieving freedom.[11] Fortune had been in England for only a short while, arriving in London with Smith who was a wealthy merchant normally resident in Barbados. Smith had made his will before travelling from Barbados to London, in which he left sizeable sums of money to his siblings, nephews, nieces and friends, some of which was to be held in trust until the legatees came of age. Included in the legacies were one to his friend and fellow colonist William Flatt, who was to receive household goods 'and one Negro Man Scipio'.[12] Fortune was not mentioned, but Smith's will stipulated that after all financial bequests had been made the residue of his estate would pass on to the children of his brother Christopher, all of whom resided in Southampton, England. Had Fortune been returned to Barbados following Smith's death and the settlement of his estate, he would probably have been regarded as part of

[10] Baptism of William Champion, 23 Sept. 1685, St Giles in the Fields, Christenings, Parish Register of St Giles in the Fields, 1675–1719. LMA, London, England, P82/GIS/A/02.

[11] 'A Negro … goes by the Name of Fortune', *London Gazette*, 20 Nov. 1684.

[12] Will of Joseph Smith, Merchant of the Island of Barbados, 22 Oct. 1684, National Archives, PROB 11/379/186, 215.

Smith's estate, and he would probably have been sold to a sugar planter: escape in London must have seemed a much better alternative, however alien and threatening the English capital may have appeared. But, although Smith was no longer alive to pursue Fortune, his powerful mercantile friends did not hesitate to seek out the runaway, who could be returned to Edward Clarke under the sign of the hart and three pigeons in Shoe Lane on the western edge of the City. Clarke was a leading London merchant who was eventually a director of the Bank of England, was knighted and in 1696 became lord mayor.[13] A powerful and well-connected man, he was well positioned to preside over attempts to stymie Fortune's bid for freedom.

One of the first mentions of country marks in a newspaper advertisement appeared in December 1664 when an unnamed 'little Negro Boy of about 13 years of age' disappeared and was noted to have been either 'Lost or absented'. Wearing a grey livery, the boy bore 'a small Cross in his forehead'. Presumably he returned or was returned because four months later another advertisement appeared after the freedom seeker once again eloped. This time it is more likely that he had escaped, for he had already been absent for a month when the advertisement appeared. The advertisement included the fact that he spoke 'Spanish indifferently well, and good English'.[14]

Another African practice of bodily modification was the filing of their teeth – usually the front incisors – to sharp points.[15] This was more unusual in London than the country markings and thus more worthy of note in advertisements. When an unnamed twenty-three-year-old 'tall Negro Man' escaped in Bristol in 1701, an advertisement described his clothing in some detail, but the only physical description other than a vague reference to his height was mention of the fact that 'three of his upper Teeth sharp at the ends like a Dogs Teeth'.[16] The man who claimed this African was in all probability

[13] 'Clarke, Edward', in J. R. Woodhead, 'Cade–Cutler', in *The Rulers of London 1660–1689: a Biographical Record of the Aldermen and Common Councilmen of the City of London* (London, 1966), pp. 42–56, *British History Online* <https://www.british-history.ac.uk/no-series/london-rulers/1660-89/pp42-56#h3-0044> [accessed 14 April 2020].

[14] 'Lost or absented a little Negro Boy', *The Newes, Published for Satisfaction and Information of the People*, 8 Dec. 1664; 'Lost or absent a Negro Boy', *The Intelligencer, published for Satisfaction and Information of the People*, 1 May 1665.

[15] Europeans in West Africa regularly commented on those people they encountered with teeth 'as sharp as Awls' (W. Bosman, *A New and Accurate Description of the Coast of Guinea, Divided into the Gold, the Slave, and the Ivory Coasts …* (London, 1705), p. 487). See also J. S. Handler, R. S. Corruccini and R. J. Mutaw, 'Tooth mutilation in the Caribbean: evidence from a slave burial population in Barbados', *Journal of Human Evolution*, xi (1982), 297–304; J. S. Handler, 'Determining African birth from skeletal remains: a note on tooth mutilation', *Historical Archaeology*, xxviii (1994), 113–19.

[16] 'Run away from Mr Rogers of Bristol, a tall Negro Man', *The Post Man, and The Historical Account*, 30 Jan. 1701.

Francis Rogers, a member of a prominent family of Quaker merchants in Bristol. Heavily involved in the transatlantic slave trade, Rogers was the owner or co-owner of at least thirteen Bristol slave-trading ships voyaging between Africa and the colonies. The first of Rogers' slave-trading ships that we know of returned to Bristol some ten months after this freedom seeker had eloped, so he may well have come to the city aboard another merchant's ship or on an earlier voyage partially funded by Rogers for which no evidence of his involvement survives. Rogers' advertisement promised a sizeable three-guinea reward to anyone who captured the freedom seeker and returned him to either Rogers in Bristol or another merchant in the heart of the City of London, suggesting that Rogers thought this freedom seeker might have attempted the 120-mile journey to the capital, where he was more likely to be able to remain free or be able to join an ocean-going ship's crew.[17]

---

[17] The *Dispatch*, co-owned by Rogers and Joseph Martin, left Bristol in Oct. 1700 and returned in Oct. 1701, having transported 160 enslaved people to Jamaica. See Voyage 16006 in Slave Voyages: Trans-Atlantic Slave Trade – Database <https://www.slavevoyages.org/voyage/database> [accessed 15 April 2020]. For more on Rogers see Anonymous, 'Bristol Quaker merchants: some new seventeenth century evidence', *Bristol Record Society: Publications*, xvii (1951), 81–91, at p. 82; *Bristol, Africa and the Eighteenth-Century Slave Trade to America*: i, *The Years of Expansion, 1698–1729*, ed. D. Richardson (Bristol, 1986), pp. xxi–xxii; D. Richardson, *The Bristol Slave Traders: a Collective Portrait* (Bristol, 1985), p. 30.

8. *Benjamin*: branded

Benjamin, a Middle siz'd Negro, Aged about 20, both ears cut or clipped, and Branded on both Shoulders, went away on Saturday last from Theodore Palaologus. Whoever brings him to Doctor John Moiles in Ratcliff-Highway, shall have a Guinea's Reward and Charges.

The London Gazette, 13 October 1692

Country marks and filed teeth had meaning and significance for Europeans and most especially for the Africans thus marked. They were inerasable emblems of African nativity and upbringing, and thus assertions of an original cultural identity. As the years passed, a bound or enslaved African's memory of their family, of the geography, flora and fauna, and of the people, places, beliefs and traditions of their homeland might all fade, but their country marks and scarred teeth endured as abiding emblems of African identity. Sometimes, however, it was not these African emblems that marked the bodies of London's enslaved but rather the markings, mutilations or physical constraints violently imposed on enslaved bodies by enslavers. In March 1690 an unnamed 'Negro' eloped 'from on Board the Ship Loyal trade, from Bristol'. The Bristol merchant Abraham Birkin made no mention of this man's clothing, perhaps because readers would assume that the man was wearing seafaring garb, but he did describe his physical characteristics, noting 'all his Teeth before filed sharp, with two burnt Marks on his Shoulders'. These brands forever marked the man as enslaved, symbolically asserting the supremacy of White claims to his body over his membership in West African society demonstrated by his filed teeth.[1]

An unnamed man described by James Thomas as a 'Negro Man or Blackamore' was twenty-one years old when he escaped in 1695. The advertisement reported that 'Through his Nostrills have been holes', almost

---

[1] 'RUN away from on Board the Ship Loyal trade', *London Gazette*, 20 March 1690. Birkin was a Jewish merchant whose strong connections with Spanish colonies in the Americas enabled him to corner the Bristol-based trade in indigo. See N. García Fernández, 'Interacciones mercantiles entre los imperios del Atlántico: el comercio directo del añil colonial español hacia Bristol, vía Jamaica' ['Mercantile trade between Atlantic empires: the trade in Spanish indigo to Bristol via Jamaica'], *Caribbean Studies*, xxxiv (2006), 47–98. For a thoughtful discussion of branding in historical context see K. H. B. Keefer, 'Marked by fire: brands, slavery, and identity', *Slavery & Abolition*, xl (2019), 659–81.

certainly an African body modification, but the additional information that 'one of his Ears have been cut away' is something else entirely. The freedom seeker 'speaks good English' and 'formerly lived in Barbados', a colony in which attempted escape from enslavement could be punished by the mutilation of noses and ears, with even worse punishments for repeat offenders. The author of the advertisement may have been the James Thomas sent to Barbados in 1659 as an indentured servant, bound to labour for five years. If so, he had become one of a minority of such labourers who survived his period of servitude and then made enough money to acquire enslaved people. Thomas could afford to dress this unnamed man in 'a new Livery Coat and Wastcoat, a light Brown Cloath lin'd with Blew, a gilded flat Button, the Wastcoat Scarlit and blew small stript Callamanco with the same Button, and a stript and flowered Fustian Frock with a gilded flat Button'. The description of clothing was far more extensive than the description of the man wearing these garments, and Thomas's angry assertion that the freedom seeker 'pretends to be a Sea-man' implied that he had attempted escape before and that he might soon sell his valuable clothing, exchange it for the cheaper rough and tarred fabrics of the seafarer, and seek work aboard an ocean-going ship. Already absent for five weeks, this man may even have been at sea by the time Thomas wrote and published his advertisement.[2]

In June 1674 'a Blackamoor Man' escaped from John Seyntaubyn in Cornwall. Tall and slender and wearing loose-fitting old clothes, this freedom seeker 'names himself *John Angola*', an interesting identification with Africa in his surname. But it was the brand marks on his body –rather than his stature, his clothing or his name – that were most noticeable: a London newspaper advertisement described him as 'Iron-marked in his Brest with the sign of a Greyhound, and in his Left-side, with the sign of a Hawk flying'.[3] Nine years later 'a Blackamore Boy, about 14 or 15 Years old' eloped wearing black clothes and with 'a Ring in one of his Ears'. This unnamed boy was rendered more identifiable by the brand marks 'Imprest upon one of his Shoulders with an Iron, the Letters R.G.', almost certainly the initials of a past or present master.[4]

In the Caribbean and southern colonies brand marks of symbols and the initials of slave-owners were often visible on shoulders and breasts, for arduous

---

[2] 'Run away from James Thomas … a Negro Man or Blackamore', *The Post Boy, and Historical Account, &c. With Foreign and Domestick News*, 13 Aug. 1695; 'James Thomas of Llangover, Monmouth … bound to Joane Floyd, planter, to serve 5 years in Barbados', in P. W. Coldham, *The Complete Book of Emigrants, 1607–1660: a Comprehensive Listing Compiled from English Public Records …* (Baltimore, Md., 1987), p. 438.

[3] 'Run away … *John Angola*', *London Gazette*, 22 June 1674.

[4] 'These are to give notice … a Blackamore Boy', *London Gazette*, 19 April 1683.

plantation labour in a sultry climate meant that enslaved labourers wore relatively little or loose-fitting and open clothing while working. In London's colder climes these brand markings were generally covered by clothing, but descriptions of these markings in advertisements suggest that those who took up suspected freedom seekers would nonetheless seek to identify them by the marks of White ownership burned into their flesh. It would have been far more difficult for Peter to hide the 'mark burnt in his forehead and brest' when he eloped in 1662, or for the twenty-six-year-old man Johanna to hide the 'two Rings burnt in his Forehead', even though they were 'almost worn out'.[5] While the mark on his breast was probably a brand mark indicating the identity of his owner, it was unusual to burn a slave-holder's initials onto the forehead of an enslaved person. However, colonial legislatures by this time had begun to mandate both the mutilation of noses and ears and the branding of faces for the punishment of serious offences by the enslaved, including repeated attempts at escape. Thus, in July 1640 the Virginia General Court ordered that Emmanuel, an enslaved man who had eloped and been recaptured, 'receive thirty stripes and to be burnt in the cheek with the letter R and to work in shackles for one year or more'.[6] London freedom seekers with brands on their faces had almost certainly received these as punishment in the North American or Caribbean colonies.

Benjamin, 'Aged about 20' when he sought freedom in London in October 1692, appears to have been marked as property and then again as punishment for attempting escape. Theodore Palaeologus gave no description of Benjamin's stature and countenance other than the vague reference to his being 'Middle siz'd', but noted that the young man had 'both Ears cut or clipped, and [was] branded on both shoulders'.[7] While the latter were marks of ownership, the former were most likely the scars of punishment for resistance or escape. Palaeologus was an unusual English colonist. His grandfather, a descendant of Constantine XIII, the last reigning sovereign of the Byzantine empire, had arrived in England in 1628, and he and his three sons had all fought on the Royalist side during the Civil War. One of these sons, Ferdinand, then emigrated to Barbados where he became a planter in St John's parish, and by 1680 the estate he co-owned with Alexander Beale, clearly visible on Richard Ford's 1685 map of the island, was worked by

---

[5] 'AN East-Indian Tawney-black boy', *Mercurius Publicus, Comprising the Sum of all Affairs now in agitation in England, Scotland, and Ireland, Together with Forrain Intelligence; For Information of the People, and to prevent false News*, 25 Sept. 1662; 'RUN away … a Black named Johanna', *London Gazette*, 29 Jan. 1691.

[6] 'Decisions of the General Court' (22 July 1640), *Virginia Magazine of History and Biography*, v (1898), 233–41, at p. 237.

[7] 'Benjamin, a Middle siz'd Negro', *London Gazette*, 13 Oct. 1692.

seventy enslaved people.[8] Ferdinand Palaeologus died in Barbados in 1678, leaving half of his share of the 'plantation, with all profit, stock, and goods thereunto belonging' to his son Theodore, who would gain the remainder upon the death of his mother. Perhaps Theodore had brought Benjamin with him when he moved back to London and settled in Stepney in the East End. Benjamin's status was inscribed upon his body, and he was branded as property and mutilated, most probably as punishment for previous escape attempts. During these early years of plantation slavery in Barbados, White labour was being completely replaced by enslaved African labour, and as the sugar plantation system took hold, planters were destroying Black bodies almost as fast as they could import them. Any enslaved man who had been in Barbados during this period, with its violent horrors etched upon his body, would have had every reason to seek freedom.[9]

[8] Barbados Census, dated 1680, American and West Indies, Colonial Papers, January–May 1680, National Archives CO1/44, 230; R. Ford, *A New Map of the Island of Barbados* (London, 1685).

[9] F. Palaeologus's will is reprinted in R. H. Schumburgk, *The History of Barbados; comprising a Geographical and Statistical Description of the Island* ... (London, 1848), pp. 229–30. For more on the Palaeologus family in England and Barbados see D. M. Nicol, *The Immortal Emperor: the Life and Legend of Constantine Palaiologos, Last Emperor of the Romans* (Cambridge, 1992), p. 124; J. H. L. Archer, *Monumental Inscriptions of the British West Indies from the Earliest Date* (London, 1875), pp. 347–8; *Notes and Queries: a Medium of Intercommunication for Literary Men, General Readers* ..., 10th series, viii (1907), 335. For more on the situation of enslaved plantation labourers in late 17th-century Barbados, see S. P. Newman, *A New World of Labor: the Development of Plantation Slavery in the British Atlantic* (Philadelphia, Pa., 2013), pp. 189–242.

9. *Pompey*: shackled

RUN away from his Master the 14th instant, Pompey *a Black Boy about 15 years of Age, he had on a sad colour'd Frock, a blue Wastcoat and blue Stockings, with a brass Collar about his neck, without Cap or Hat. Whosoever secures him and brings him to his Master Mr.* William Stevens *a Merchant in* East-lane *on* Rotherheth-Wall*; or to Mr.* Howard's *the Crown Coffee-House behind the Royal Exchange, shall have Twenty Shillings Reward.*

The Daily Courant, 22 May 1703

The bodies of people of colour in and around Restoration London were sometimes constrained as well as marked, and some were forced to wear metal collars and even chains that marked them as enslaved property. During this period transatlantic slave voyages originating in London carried thousands of tons of chains and manacles, most of which had been manufactured in the capital, the hub of English manufacturing (see Figure 22). Between 1651 and 1700 more than 600 slave voyages originated in London which transported more than 190,000 enslaved men, women and children from West Africa to the Americas.[1] The punishment of convicts and prisoners in England included branding, mutilation, whipping and on occasion the use of iron collars, chains and restraints, and so it may have been only the scale of production of these metallic restraints that appeared remarkable. Londoners did not see shiploads of Africans shackled together; virtually all the people fitted with coarse iron collars and chains in Restoration London were White convicts and prisoners.[2]

The collars forced on enslaved people in London were strikingly different. Individually crafted from silver, brass and sometimes steel, these were intended to complement the smart liveries and clothing of enslaved personal attendants, and to reflect the wealth of those who claimed ownership of them. Fifteen (7 per cent) of Restoration London's freedom seekers were manacled in this way. On slave ships and in the colonies rough cast-iron restraints were brutally functional and abrasive, darkened and oxidized by sweat and

---

[1] Data on 635 slave voyages originating from London drawn from Slave Voyages: Trans-Atlantic Slave Trade – Database <https://www.slavevoyages.org/voyage/database> [accessed 24 May 2021].

[2] See eg J. M. Beattie, *Policing and Punishment in London, 1660–1750: Urban Crime and the Limits of Terror* (Oxford, 2001), pp. 277–312.

Figure 22. Iron shackles, Collection of the Smithsonian National Museum of African American History and Culture, Gift from the Liljenquist Family Collection. These coarse iron shackles may well have been used on a transatlantic slave ship, and they are typical of the mass-produced coarse iron restraints made for strength and utility.

blood. A century later a newly arrived African who escaped in Jamaica was, according to a newspaper advertisement, identifiable by the brand marks on his shoulder and the 'iron collar around his neck'. He was but one of the millions of West Africans and their descendants in the Caribbean and North America who felt the weight of such restraints on their own bodies.[3]

In seventeenth-century London collars were less abrasively functional, although they still signalled to all who wore or saw them that those restrained by them were enslaved property. The city's runaway advertisements often specified the metals from which these collars were fashioned, and five were made of brass, seven of silver and one of steel (see Figure 23). Although steel was cheaper than silver and brass, it was – when freshly forged with a muted shine and a blueish tinge – individually handcrafted, and it would have looked far more attractive and expensive than the coarse iron restraints of the colonies. Only two of these English freedom seekers had iron collars, and one was worn by a boy who had escaped a year earlier wearing a brass collar which he may have had removed and either sold or discarded. Perhaps the master had chosen to replace a lost and quite expensive brass collar with a cheaper one made of iron. Whatever they were made of, these collars were

[3] 'TAKEN UP … a New Negro Man', *Royal Gazette*, 17 Nov. 1781. For further discussion of iron collars, see D. Thompson, 'Circuits of containment: iron collars, incarceration and the infrastructure of slavery' (unpublished Cornell University PhD thesis, 2014).

still severe restraints, both psychologically and physically, a constant and unforgettable reminder to the wearer that they were property. But they had a dual function, for not only did these collars constrain the wearers and mark them as property but they also ostentatiously advertised the success, power and wealth of the person who claimed ownership of the collar wearer. This explains why so many of the enslaved attendants portrayed in the portraits of wealthy men and their families were not only dressed in stylish and expensive livery but also sported shiny silver or brass collars.

Figure 23. Steel ankle iron and key, inscribed 'Deverall Corn street Bristol, 1733'. Reproduced with permission of Bryan Collection, Crab Tree Farm Foundation, Lake Bluff, Ill. Photograph by Jamie Stukenberg, Professional Graphics Inc.[4]

[4] The parts of this ankle iron and key that are less tarnished give a sense of how shiny this would have appeared when it was freshly forged more than 250 years ago. John Deverall was a Bristol-based slave ship captain. See *Bristol, Africa and the Eighteenth-Century Slave Trade to America*: iii, *The Years of Decline, 1746–1769*, ed. D. Richardson (Bristol, 1991), p. 41; *The Trade of Bristol in the Eighteenth Century*, ed. W. E. Minchinton (Bristol, 1957), p. 152.

These ostentatious collars probably had little direct relationship to the cast-iron manacles of the slave trade and the plantations. It is more likely that the shiny collars fitted to enslaved Londoners were inspired by the brass and silver collars that elite English owners traditionally had made for their favourite dogs. Today it is challenging to consider that the collars used for pet animals were the inspiration for the collars made for and locked around the necks of enslaved Londoners, but the similarities between these dog and slave collars are remarkable. Surviving fifteenth-, sixteenth- and seventeenth-century English dog collars look almost identical to those around the necks of enslaved people in portraits from this era. Often the name of the dog's master was engraved on the collar, as in 'S. Thomas Cave of Stanford', 'John Green Farmbury' or 'Thomas North Dulcut near Wells', a practice copied by enslavers who had their own names engraved on the collars worn by the enslaved people they claimed.[5] Surviving portraits of Queen Anne, and of Charles I's five children, show dogs with silver and brass collars respectively, as do numerous other seventeenth- and eighteenth-century English portraits. Most striking of all are portraits like that of an unnamed young girl created around 1725, which displays her being attended by both an enslaved boy and a dog: both the boy and the dog wear collars and are portrayed gazing admiringly up at their fabulously dressed young mistress (Figure 24). It is hard to imagine a more striking representation of the ways in which elite English families' attitudes towards highly favoured pets informed their understanding and treatment of enslaved boys as accoutrements and as property.[6]

Elite Londoners placed advertisements for highly prized and favourite dogs that were lost, some of them wearing collars. One of James II's dogs escaped in 1687, 'a brown and white Spaniel Dog, the King's Collar about his Neck, Written, The King's Dog', while 'a little Dog' lost from the duchess of Richmond's house wore a collar 'with the Duke of Buckingham's name Engraven on it'.[7] The advertisements for dogs with collars are strikingly

---

[5] Brass collar inscribed 'S. Thomas Cave of Stanford', 17th century; brass collar inscribed 'John Green Farmbury'; brass collar inscribed 'Thomas North Dulcut near Wells', in Anonymous, *Four Centuries of Dog Collars at Leeds Castle: a Collection of Dog Collars Presented by Gertrude Hunt in Memory of her Husband John Hunt* (London, 1979), nos. 9, 12 and 29. Images from the collection may be seen at see <https://www.leeds-castle.com/Visit/Attractions/The+Dog+Collar+Museum> [accessed 24 May 2021].

[6] P. van Somer, *Anne of Denmark* (1617), Royal Collection Trust <https://www.rct.uk/collection/405813/anne-of-denmark-1574-1619> and A. Van Dyck, *The Five Eldest Children of Charles I* (1637), Royal Collection Trust <https://www.rct.uk/collection/404405/the-five-eldest-children-of-charles-i>; B. Dandridge, *A Young Girl* (*c.*1725), Yale Center for British Art <https://collections.britishart.yale.edu/catalog/tms:715> [accessed 16 Sept. 2021].

[7] 'Lost the 19th Instant at Kingston, a brown and white Spaniel', *The London Gazette*, 22 Sept. 1687; 'Lost on Saturday last from the Dutchess of Richmond's House', *London Gazette*,

Figure 24. Bartholomew Dandridge, *A Young Girl with an Enslaved Servant and a Dog* (*c.*1725), Yale Center for British Art.

23 Aug. 1683. For other examples see 'Lost on Monday the 11th Instant, out of *Ax-yard*, a large Spaniel dog ... a Brass Collar about his neck', *London Gazette*, 14 Oct. 1680; 'Lost on Friday ... a Spaniel Dog ... a Brass Collar about his Neck, whereon is Engraven, This Dog belongs to the Marquis de Sessack', *London Gazette*, 31 Aug. 1685; 'Lost from Arlington-House a black and white Spaniel ... with a brass Collar about his neck, written the Duke of Grafton's Dog', *London Gazette*, 8 April 1689; 'Lost on Midsummer-Day last, in or about Drury Lane, a small Brindled Dog ... with a Brass Collar', *London Gazette*, 7 July 1692; 'Lost last Sunday ... a Black Greyhound Dog ... He has a Brass Collar with the Owners name, and the Inner Temple engraved on't', *The Flying Post; or, The Post-Master*, 20 July 1697; 'Lost or stoln ... a black Danish Dog ... a Brass Collar [with] the inscription Captain Ferrers', *The Post Man: and The Historical Account*, 9 June 1702.

similar to those for enslaved young people wearing collars: they often included physical descriptions of dogs' markings and colourings similar to descriptions of enslaved people's physical attributes, scars and bodily markings; accounts of where they had been lost; descriptions of the collars and the names engraved upon them; and information about where and to whom they might be returned for a reward. For example:

> A Very large white Spaniel Dog with a short Tail, his Cheeks and Ears red, a Star in his Forehead, two red Spots joining on the Nether side, and a small one upon his Rump, with a brass Collar, and John Turner of Richmond in Surrey, Engrav'd thereon, lost on Monday last, between Foster lane and Noble-street. Whosoever brings tydings of him first to Mr. Weelys Apothecary at the Union in Fleet Street, shall have Two Guinea's Reward. (*London Gazette*, 31 December 1685)

Expensive and fashioned by skilled craftsmen, both dog and slave collars were clearly intended to show off the wealth of the men and women who could afford brass and silverware. A half-century later, when jewellers' newspaper advertisements had become quite common, the Westminster goldsmith Matthew Dyer announced his willingness to make '*Silver Padlocks for Blacks or Dogs*, Collars ... &c'.[8] But however shiny or expensive these brass and silver collars may have been, to the enslaved they remained demeaning physical restraints and emblems of bondage, the markers of animals held as property.

The London enslaved who were restrained in this way tended to be very young. Only one of the collar-wearing freedom seekers was described as an adult man, while the remainder were all aged between ten and seventeen, and 13 were sixteen or younger. Two were female, the remainder male, and three were South Asian. Young and fresh-faced boys and girls made attractive adornments to wealthy Englishmen and women, and a shared aesthetic enhanced these human emblems of success with flashy restraints. On 14 May 1703 fifteen-year-old Pompey eloped wearing 'a sad colour'd Frock, a blue Wastcoat and blue stockings, with a brass Collar about his neck, without Cap or Hat'.[9] It is revealing that the collar was described in this advertisement as part of the smart clothing and bodily adornment with which William Stevens had dressed and presented Pompey, all the better to display Stevens' own wealth and prestige. To Pompey the collar must have felt altogether different.

---

[8] Advertisement from *London Advertiser* in 1756, reproduced in E. F. Rimbault, 'Slavery in England', *Notes and Queries: a Medium of Intercommunication for Literary Men, Artists, Antiquaries, Genealogists, etc.*, 2nd series, xxxvi (6 Sept. 1856), 187. For some examples of these collars from the 17th and 18th centuries see Anonymous, *Four Centuries of Dog Collars at Leeds Castle*.

[9] 'RUN away from his Master ... Pompey', *The Daily Courant*, 22 May 1703.

Stevens was a merchant in East Lane in Rotherhithe, a small lane south of the Thames leading to East Stairs surrounded by the docks, trading warehouses homes and businesses of south-east London. Almost eight months later Pompey tried again, but this time Stevens advertised in search of 'a Black Boy about 16 Years of Age' wearing 'a Blue Wastcoat, a pair of light colour'd Cloth Breeches, and Iron Coller about his Neck'.[10] This was the only occasion on which a freedom seeker escaped wearing a collar made of anything other than silver, brass or newly forged steel. Why had Stevens replaced the brass collar with an iron one? Had Pompey succeeded in ridding himself of the hated brass collar during his first escape attempt, discarding the broken restraint so that it could never again torment and demean him? Once Pompey was recaptured, Stevens might well have objected to paying for a craftsman to fashion another brass collar, choosing instead to replace it with a cheaper coarse iron collar fashioned by a local blacksmith rather than a jeweller.

The use of silver collars on enslaved children suggests that they were closely supervised by those who commanded them. These soft metal collars would have been a tempting target for thieves who could easily remove them from a child's neck and have them melted down by one of the city's many silversmiths. At the same time, silver collars might become part of an escape attempt, used as currency by the wearer who might exchange a silver collar for refuge, food or clothing. Such collars thus had many potential functions, both for those who had them made and placed on the enslaved and for those who were forced to wear them. Moreover, in addition to reflecting the wealth of those who claimed ownership of enslaved people, silver and brass collars softened slavery in the eyes of Englishmen and women who saw the liveried children of colour with shiny and valuable collars attending and working for those who dressed and presented enslaved servants in a fashion that obscured their legal status. Numerous portraits from the seventeenth and eighteenth centuries reflect this, showing beautiful and well-dressed enslaved children in the context of sumptuously dressed families in idyllic surroundings. In Catherine Molineux's memorable phrase, enslaved children became 'a form of social currency, consumed and displayed in a semiotic system of status'. Enslaved children were often given as gifts, and in portraits their dark skins and beautiful clothing both contrasted with and complemented the pale skin and ornate clothing of those they attended. The display of beautifully dressed enslaved children attending elite Londoners made real both racial slavery and the imperial

---

[10] 'POmpe a Black Boy', *Daily Courant*, 8 Jan. 1704. An almost identical advertisement appeared in a second newspaper two days later: 'POmpe, a Black Boy', *The English Post: with News Foreign and Domestick*, 10 Jan. 1704.

Figure 25. Detail showing unnamed enslaved attendant wearing a locked collar in *Elihu Yale; Dudley North; Lord James Cavendish; David Yale; and an Enslaved Servant* by an unknown artist (*c.*1708), oil on canvas, Yale Center for British Art, Gift of Andrew Cavendish, 11th duke of Devonshire. The boy is serving those present, and his turban and elaborately braided coat are in contrast to the somewhat more sedate clothing of the men pictured. The lock holding the collar around his neck emphasizes that he was almost certainly enslaved and the property of one of those present, perhaps the duke of Devonshire.

endeavours on which it was based. But it did so in a way that made slavery appear relatively benign (Figure 25).[11]

This was slavery as most Londoners saw it, and in an age of incredible poverty and high mortality rates in the capital few Londoners appear to

---

[11] For a thorough analysis of liveried young Black servants as supporting characters in late 17th-century English portraiture see C. Molineux, *Faces of Perfect Ebony: Encountering Atlantic Slavery in Imperial Britain* (Cambridge, Mass., 2012), pp. 20–53, at p. 31.

Figure 26. Snuff-box or tobacco box made by Jean Obrisset, early 1700s.
© The Trustees of the British Museum. The African is identified as such
by his facial features, his hair and most especially the collar marking him
as enslaved. That this image graced a box intended for slave-produced
tobacco shows that the owner felt no shame in using slave-produced
commodities, and presumably had no problem with slave-ownership.

have been distressed by the enslavement of well-dressed Black children
sporting silver and brass collars. That enslavers continued using such collars
and displaying them in portraits well into the eighteenth century suggests
a lack of any sense of such behaviour being unseemly or offensive: it was
entirely normative. A snuff or tobacco box made by the London-based
Huguenot craftsman Jean Obrisset confirms the point (Figure 26). Skilfully
fashioned from pressed horn, the box was an everyday item for a wealthier
man, containing the tobacco he consumed that had been produced by
enslaved labourers in the colonies. The top of the box features the head
of an enslaved African, his stylized nose, lips and hair reflecting English
stereotypes. But it is the collar around his neck that marks him as enslaved,
visible on an item used, displayed and perhaps shared with other Londoners
on a daily basis. In seventeenth-century London an enslaved person wearing

a collar, whether a real person or a symbolic representation of one, was an unremarkable motif or emblem of wealth and success.[12]

While sailors, planters and merchants who had sailed on slave-trading ships or spent time in the plantation colonies had some experience of just how violent racial slavery could be, those who lived in Restoration London would have known very little of these realities. The small group of Londoners who had the most direct experience of the reality of slave ships and plantation slavery were the enslaved or bound servants brought to the city. For the African- and South Asian-born children who had been ripped from their families and forced to labour in an alien city, the collars some were forced to wear were constant and harsh physical reminders of their situation, affirmations of their lack of individuality expressed in the words often inscribed upon these shackles.

The enslaved who eloped while wearing collars generally belonged to members of the elite in London's fashionable areas, or to wealthy merchants and craftsmen in or near the city's maritime communities. One such shackled freedom seeker was a 'Black Boy of about 14 years of Age'. Wearing 'a Green Jacket, and Drawers' and speaking 'very little English', this freedom seeker was most noticeable for 'a Silver Collar about his neck, if not taken off'.[13] While brass and steel collars were thick and would probably require a blacksmith or other metal worker or a locksmith to remove them, silver collars were thin and might be cut easily or even bitten through by a third party. This particular freedom seeker was the property of Jonas Shish, who like his father was a successful shipbuilder in Rotherhithe. Both father and son specialized in building ships for the Royal Navy, and these ships could have brought back enslaved people from South Asia, West Africa or the American and Caribbean colonies.[14]

---

[12] For more on Jean (or John) Obrisset see T. V. Murdoch, 'Huguenot artists, designers and craftsmen in Great Britain and Ireland, 1680–1760' (unpublished Queen Mary University of London PhD thesis, 1982), pp. 178–9. For the use of collars in 18th-century Britain see S. P. Newman, 'Freedom-seeking slaves in England and Scotland, 1700–1780', *English Historical Review*, cxxxiv (2019), 1160–3.

[13] 'A Black Boy', *London Gazette*, 29 Nov. 1683.

[14] Samuel Pepys recorded that on 3 March 1668, along with Charles II and his court, he attended the launch of 'the new ship built by Mr. Shish, called 'The Charles'' (*The Diary of Samuel Pepys: Daily Entries from the 17th Century London Diary*, 3 March 1668 <https://www.pepysdiary.com/diary> [accessed 17 April 2020]). See also J. P. Hemingway, 'The work of the surveyors of the Navy during the period of the establishments: a comparative study of naval architecture between 1672 and 1755' (unpublished University of Bristol PhD thesis, 2002); *The Voyage of Captain John Narborough to the Strait of Magellan and the South Sea in His Majesty's Ship Sweepstakes, 1669–1671*, ed. R. J. Campbell, P. T. Bradley and J. Lorimer (London, 2018), p. 24.

Also attempting to escape from a London maritime community was an unnamed 'black Girl, aged about 15 years', who eloped wearing 'a black Cloth Gown and Petticoat, with a brass Collar about her Neck, with this Inscription, John Campion at the Ship-Tavern at Ratcliff-Cross, his Negro'.[15] Several of the collars described in these runaway advertisements were inscribed with wording of this kind, and not one of them named the enslaved person wearing this metal band. The writing was outward facing, invisible to a wearer who was probably unable to read the English words they could trace with their fingers but not see. The script was intended to convey information to the White English people who saw the enslaved child wearing the collar. Campion was a successful vintner, wine importer and innkeeper at Ratcliff, a block north of the Thames in the East End. His willingness to have his own name and the words 'his Negro' engraved on this collar speaks volumes about his acceptance of racial slavery, and his belief that fellow Londoners in the East End and beyond would see nothing untoward in this girl, her collar and his ownership of her. Yet the words tell us nothing about her, or how she felt with her throat bound by a heavy metal collar that obscured her own identity while proclaiming that of the enslaver who claimed her. While she could not see or read the words, she could feel their meaning: whatever the nature of her work for Campion, this unnamed girl sought liberty from the slavery symbolized by the collar she was wearing when she eloped.

Other collars were similarly engraved with information about the enslavers rather than those who wore them. One was a steel collar worn by an 'Indian black Boy' who eloped in Chelsea in 1690 and bore the words 'Mr. Rob. Goldesborough of Chelsea in the County of Middlesex near London', and the collar was linked to a steel cuff around his wrist by an iron chain.[16] Toney, a sixteen-year-old 'Negro boy', eloped in 1690 with 'a Brass Collar on, which directs where he lived', while in 1664 an unnamed 'little Blackamoor Boy' escaped despite wearing 'a Silver Collar about his neck, inscribed Mrs. Manby's blackamoor in Warwick Lane'.[17] This short road ran northwards past Newgate Market, just north-west of St Paul's cathedral, but it is unclear whether Mrs Manby was a householder or a businesswoman: either way, the collar clearly identified this boy as her property. Another 'Black Boy, an Indian, about 13 years old' eloped wearing a collar inscribed with the words 'The Lady Bromfield's Black in Lincolns-Inn Fields'.[18] However privileged his position in this household might have been, especially compared to the poverty and work

[15] 'A black Girl', *London Gazette*, 5 Nov. 1691.
[16] 'Run away … an Indian black Boy', *London Gazette*, 17 April 1690.
[17] 'A Negro Boy, named Toney', *London Gazette*, 30 Oct. 1690; 'Lost … a little Blackamoor Boy', *The Intelligencer, Published for Satisfaction and Information of the People*, 16 May 1664.
[18] 'A Black Boy, an Indian', *London Gazette*, 10 Sept. 1694.

regimes of bound labourers in South Asia and the Americas, this young boy sought escape from a status that defined him by colour as an object, a status symbolized by the collar that marked his body as property.

Similarly, in 1685 a seventeen- or eighteen-year-old 'Taunymore with short bushy Hair, very well shaped, in a gray Livery lined with yellow' eloped. The freedom seeker was identified in the runaway advertisement only by the 'Directions' engraved upon 'a Silver Collar about his Neck'. These 'directions' consisted of the words 'Captain George Hasting's Boy, Brigadier in the King's Horse Guards'. The wearer of this silver collar was thus rendered a non-person in the eyes of White people, while the power of the person who claimed ownership of this enslaved boy was flamboyantly affirmed in the recitation of his name and rank in an elite military unit.[19] Likewise, when a fifteen-year-old 'Black Boy' named John White eloped from Colonel Percy Kirke in March 1686, his clothes were undistinguished but he could be identified by 'a Silver Collar about his Neck, upon which is the Colonel's Coat of Arms and Cipher': on this occasion it was not even a slave-holder's name but his crest that marked this boy as the property of an elite White man.[20]

A collar fashioned out of a valuable metal and engraved with words that celebrated the rank and power of an enslaver simultaneously celebrated an enslaving master while objectifying the wearer. Few other items so perfectly epitomize the loss of identity inherent in what Orlando Patterson termed the 'social death' of the enslaved, in which the enslaved were isolated from fellow Africans and from the 'social heritage' of their communities. Historians have suggested the attempts by enslavers to deny the enslaved these comforts were less successful than Patterson imagined, but in Restoration London a young person torn from Africa and marked by a collar must surely have felt extremely isolated.[21] Even today such collars continue to accomplish

---

[19] 'A Taunymore', *London Gazette*, 26 March 1685.

[20] 'A Black Boy ... named John White', *London Gazette*, 22 March 1686. Kirke's father, George, had been a member of the court of Charles II, and Percy married Lady Mary Howard, daughter of the earl of Suffolk. For two years during the early 1680s he commanded the English forces stationed in Tangier and may have brought John White back with him when he returned to London and his home near the Palace of Whitehall. See P. Wauchope, 'Percy Kirke', *Oxford Dictionary of National Biography* <https://doi.org/10.1093/ref:odnb/15664> [accessed 18 April 2020]; 'Houses in the Bowling Green', in *Survey of London: xiii, St Margaret, Westminster: part ii, Whitehall I*, ed. M. H. Cox and P. Norman (London, 1930), pp. 236–48, *British History Online* <http://www.british-history.ac.uk/survey-london/vol13/pt2/pp236-248> [accessed 2 May 2019].

[21] O. Patterson, *Slavery and Social Death: a Comparative Study* (Cambridge, Mass., 1982), pp. 5–6. For a powerful critique of Patterson's thesis as it applied to the enslaved on slave ships and in the colonies, see V. Brown, 'Social death and political life in the study of slavery', *American Historical Review*, cxiv (2009), 1231–49.

what slave-holders intended more than three centuries ago: we know the names and can learn about the people who owned both the collars and the people forced to wear them, while the identities of the enslaved remain invisible. More than 350 years later, the violence against these enslaved children is reimagined and symbolically re-enacted every time we read an advertisement and the engraved wording inscribed upon each collar, and even more so when we see surviving collars and restraints.

The desperation of young people torn from home, enslaved and then manacled in this way comes alive in the actions of Edward Francis. Restrained by a silver collar, he failed in his attempt to free himself and appears to have attempted a more desperate and violent bid for freedom. In December 1687 Francis had attempted to 'Run away from Mr. Thomas Dymock at the Lyon Office in the Tower' of London. Dymock was 'Keeper of His Majesties Lyons in the Tower', a sinecure that allowed Dymock a home in the Tower and the income from displaying the exotic animals in his care, including lions, tigers, leopards and other creatures. Just under twenty years later John Strype recorded that this royal menagerie included six lions, two tigers, three eagles, two mountain lions, a jackal and numerous other wild beasts. Dymock regularly used London's newspapers to advertise a 'convenient place' for viewing these exotic animals and to warn others that he alone enjoyed the royal licence to publicly show and profit from such exhibitions. Caring for these animals was both difficult and dangerous, and just a year before Francis eloped Mary Jenkinson – a member of the household of 'the Person who keeps the Lyons *in the* Tower' – was fatally mauled by the largest lion.[22]

---

[22] 'ON the 30th of December last, Run away ... a black Boy', *London Gazette*, 5 Jan. 1688; J. Strype, *A Survey of the Cities of London and Westminster ... written at first in the year MDXCVIII by John Stow ...* (London, 1720), i. 119. For Dymock's advertisements see 'ALL Persons whom it may concern are desired to take notice, that the Master-Keeper of His Majesty's Lyon-Office ...', *The Protestant Mercury. Occurrences, Foreign and Domestick*, 21 May 1697, and 'His Majesty has been pleased ... To prohibit and forbid all Persons whatsoever except Thomas Dymock ...', *London Gazette*, 7 July 1687. For Mary Jenkinson's death see *A True Relation of Mary Jenkinson, Who Was Killed by One of the Lyons in the Tower, on Munday the 8th of February 1686* (London, 1686), and C. Grigson, *Menagerie: the History of Exotic Animals in England, 1100–1837* (Oxford, 2016), p. 43. Bears, lions, tigers and other animals were often restrained by chains affixed to collars or ankle cuffs: see eg the chain restraining a rhinoceros brought to England in 1684 in the anonymous engraving 'The Exact Draught of that Famous Beast the Rhinoscerus' (1684), Glasgow University Library, Special Collections. Dymock appears as the holder of the Lion Office in the Tower of London in various official documents: see eg 'Petition of Tho. Dimock for repairs and building conveniences in the lion office', 26 April 1687, 'Entry Book: April 1687, 21–30', p. 67, in *Calendar of Treasury Books*: viii, *1685–1689*, ed. W. A. Shaw (London, 1923), pp. 1318–38, *British History Online* <http://www.british-history.ac.uk/cal-treasury-books/vol8/pp1318-1338> [accessed 17 May 2021].

It was not only the wild animals that were restrained by collars and chains, for the sixteen-year-old 'black Boy' who eloped from Dymock – unnamed in this advertisement – wore 'a Silver Collar about his Neck, Engraven, Thomas Dimock at the Lyon Office'. Wearing three coats and grey stockings, this sixteen-year-old appears to have been clothed to work outside in December, perhaps to help feed, clean and care for the animals. If so, how might this collar have felt to a young adult made to work with caged, chained and manacled animals in the Lion Tower? He was probably African born for he 'speaks but bad English' and had 'holes in both his Ears' that were perhaps his last physical connection to an African childhood.[23]

Dymock offered two guineas reward to any person who would apprehend and return the young African. We can assume the freedom seeker was recaptured because, just over four years later, Edward Francis, now an adult and described in court records as a 'blackamoor serv[an]t' in Dymock's household, once again acted to free himself.[24] This time, however, Francis did more than simply escape, for in February 1692 he was arrested and interrogated on suspicion of having attempted the murder of his master's family. Dymock testified that a year earlier he and his first wife had become very ill, and 'after some time Languishing' the latter had died. Following his own recovery Dymock remarried, taking Rebecca Way as his second wife in October 1691. Dymock and his new wife later testified that on Sunday 10 January 1692 he had 'Bid his Servant the Black to warme him Some Ale', but after drinking the ale he became very ill. Rebecca, her stepdaughter Ann and the maid Johanna Lickfield then ate some watery gruel intended for Thomas and also became seriously ill; after eating the remains of the gruel, the family's cat died. Rebecca ordered remedies from an apothecary but these were of little benefit to Lickfield, who vomited up everything she ingested, and several weeks later sadly concluded that 'I shall never be well now as I was Before'. Lickfield believed that the gruel had made her sick and on first tasting it she had asked Francis if it contained pepper, for the dish 'seemed to be Hott and Burning in my Mouth'.[25]

---

[23] 'ON the 30th of December last, Run away … a black Boy'.

[24] While we cannot be certain that the freedom seeker and Edward Francis were the same person, the short time span between these incidents and Dymock's references to earlier offences by Francis make it very likely.

[25] 'The Examination & Confession of Edw: Francis blackamon servt. To Mr, Tho: Dymock in the Tower Keeper of the Lyons taken before the Right Honorable the Lord Lucas Chief Governour of the Tower', 16 Jan. 1692, London Metropolitan Archives (LMA), LMSLPS150030020; 'The Examinacon of Mr. Thomas Dymock taken bef upon Oath before the Rt. Honoble. Robt. Lord Lucas Chief Governour of their Maties. Tower of London', 16 Jan. 1692, City of London Sessions: Sessions Papers – Justices' Working Papers, LMA,

His suspicions raised, Dymock became convinced that Francis was responsible for poisoning the Dymock household. With his wife Rebecca present, Dymock summoned Francis and berated him for past offences but then softened his tone and told Francis that because of his past practice of 'Confessing the Truth he [Francis] had noe punishment'. Having made it clear that honesty was the best policy, Dymock urged Francis to once again 'Confesse the Truth' and admit to attempting to poison the family. According to Dymock, 'The Blacke then told his Master it was Ratts Bane that he did put in and that he bought two pippeing worths of that Ratt Killer which his master had Formerly Imployed to kill the Ratts'. After further questioning Francis admitted to his master that he was also responsible for the poisoning of Dymock and his first wife a year earlier. Clearly taken aback, Dymock asked if Francis had placed 'the poison into his Victualls to kill him', to which Francis replied in the affirmative. With no apparent sense of irony, Dymock asked 'what hurt have I don to you that you should be soe bloody to me to kill me', and for the first time Francis did not respond to a question the answer to which – to him at least – may have appeared self-evident. Then Francis's motivation dawned on Dymock who asked him the most important question of all – did 'you thinke to geet your Liberty by Killing me' – to which 'The Black said yes'.[26]

Dymock 'sent For a Constable' and had Francis taken before Robert Lucas, the third Baron Lucas of Shenfield and constable of the Tower of London. Thomas and Rebecca Dymock, their servant Johanna Lickfield and Edward Francis himself were each interrogated by Baron Lucas, and it is his records of their testimony that survive. Francis confirmed that he was indeed responsible for the two separate instances of poisoning members of the Dymock household. He testified that he had secured rat poison after learning from 'another Black called Tom living at the Corner of Mincing Lane ... [that it] would make people sick & vomit'. Throughout the court record Francis was referred to by witnesses as Dymock's 'Servant the Black', 'blackamoor servt' or simply 'the Black'. If he had been a free man and an employee of Dymock, Edward Francis could have left his employment with

LMSLPS150030015; Rebekah Dymorke testimony, Feb. 1692, LMA, LMSLPS150030018, LMSLPS150030019; Johanna Lickfield testimony, Feb. 1692, LMA, LMSLPS150030017.

[26] 'Examinacon of Mr. Thomas Dymock'. Thomas and Rebecca had married a few months earlier in the church of All Hallows London Wall: see Marriage of Thomas Dimock & Rebekkah Way, 10 Oct. 1691, Marriages, 1675–1729, All Hallows London Wall. LMA, London, England, P69/ALH5/A/004/MS05086. More than a decade later Dymock's will mentioned his widow Rebecca and his now married daughters Ann and Elizabeth but, perhaps not surprisingly, Edward Francis does not appear. See Will of Thomas Dymock, 1 July 1704, National Archives PROB 11/477/103.

little or no risk and there would have been no need for him to kill to secure his liberty. It thus appears highly likely that Francis remained enslaved, and that he was probably the same person who, as a sixteen-year-old enslaved boy four years earlier, had been forced to wear a collar while working for his master. If so, he appears to have reached the conclusion that he could not be free while his master was alive.[27]

Four months after his arrest Francis was released, and perhaps there was more to this case than the surviving records suggest. Whatever the truth of this case, the testimony of Edward Francis himself and of Thomas and Rebecca Dymock and their maid Johanna Lickfield all make clear that it was readily conceivable to seventeenth-century White Londoners that enslaved Black servants who could not achieve freedom by escaping might resort to violence to free themselves. Self-liberation through escape was only one of the means of resistance by which the enslaved might make themselves free and, while violent resistance was unusual in the metropolis, it was just as possible as it was in the colonies. More than anything else, this case illustrates how real slavery must have felt to those who endured it in seventeenth-century London. The collars worn by some of the enslaved, which probably originated in the collars elite English people commissioned for their prized dogs, must have reinforced a feeling among the enslaved that they were chattel and akin to the animals owned by their masters. Little wonder, then, that when his attempt to escape failed, Edward Francis resorted to violence, for he could imagine no other way to become free.[28]

---

[27] 'The Examination & Confession of Edw: Francis'.

[28] The release of 'Edward Francis the Black' is recorded in *The Proceedings on the King and Queens Commissions of the Peace, and Oyer and Terminer, and Goal-Delivery of Newgate, Held for the City of London and County of Middlesex, at Justice Hall in the Old-Baily, the 29th, and 30th days of June, and 1st of July, 1692* (London, 1692), p. 6. The Old Bailey Proceedings for Feb. and March 1692 are missing and there is no record of what transpired in the court case.

10. *Quoshey*: escaping from ships and their captains

*A Negro, named Quoshey, aged about 16 years, belonging to Capt.
Edward Archer, run away from Bell-Wharf the 25th Instant, having
on a Plush Cap with black fur, a dark Wastcoat, a speckled Shirt, old
Callamanca Breeches, branded on his left Breast with E.A. but not plain,
and shaved round his Head. Whoever brings him to Mr. Rowland Tryon
in Lime-Street, or to Mr. Richard Clearke at Bell-Wharf in Shadwell,
shah have a Guinea Reward, and Charges.*

The London Gazette, 30 December 1700

At least forty-two male freedom seekers escaped from ships or from ship
captains who were in London, a number that represents almost one quarter
(22 per cent) of all male runaways. Although a few of them were very
young and probably worked as cabin boys and personal attendants for ship
captains and officers, most were old enough to work as seamen aboard
these ships. The ages of thirty-four are known, and they were on average
just under twenty-two years old when they eloped. A half-century later
Olaudah Equiano began his life aboard ship at about the age of eleven as the
enslaved property of Naval Officer Michael Pascal; he was to live through
his teenage years and enter adulthood working on naval and merchant ships
before securing his freedom at about the age of twenty-one. This pattern
of development from enslaved cabin boy to enslaved seaman suggests that
bound seafarers were one of the most visible groups of bound people of
colour in London, particularly in dockland areas of the city. These boys
and men could be seen between the City of London and Greenwich, and
perhaps as far out as Gravesend and the mouth of the Thames.[1]

During these years at least some of the enslaved seamen had their first
experience of life at sea as enslaved cargo aboard the Middle Passage ships
taking enslaved people from West Africa to the colonies. One of these seamen
was Quoshey (*sic*), whose Akan day name Quashey tells us that he was born
on a Sunday on the Gold Coast of West Africa. On Christmas Day 1700
Quoshey was a frightened teenager who was very far from home.[2] The
seventy-eight words of the newspaper advertisement that appeared when he

---

[1] Olaudah Equiano, *The Interesting Narrative and Other Writings*, ed. V. Carretta (New York, 2003), pp. 62–137.
[2] 'A Negro, named Quoshey', *London Gazette*, 30 Dec. 1700.

eloped identified him as an object rather than an individual, the enslaved property of another man. Other than his name, age, rough clothing and the initials of his owner branded on his breast, we know nothing about him.

We can, however, make some tentative assumptions based on what we can learn of Edward Archer. Quoshey resisted his enslavement by eloping from Archer on Christmas Day. When this newspaper advertisement appeared five days later Quoshey was still at liberty. The very existence of this advertisement suggests the agency and individuality of a teenaged boy who was willing to assert his right to control over his own body by stealing himself away. Captain Edward Archer claimed ownership of Quoshey and painfully branded his initials onto the teenager's breast, imposing his identity on the sixteen-year-old. Archer lived (or had lived) by Bell Wharf on the eastern edge of Shadwell in London's East End. This fast-growing suburb was defined by the ocean-going ships moored on the Thames and was filled with the homes of seafarers and their families, all the industries associated with building and outfitting ships, and the taverns and businesses that supported this community. Within a few blocks were taverns such as the King of Denmark and the King of Sweden, as well as Blackamoor Alley, Parrot Alley, Sugar House Yard and Tobacco Alley, all testifying to the cosmopolitan nature of the area, its inhabitants and the goods and people they transported.[3]

For at least some of his career Archer was a slave-ship captain. Quoshey's name suggests that in late 1696 or early 1697 he had been taken from a Gold Coast trading post such as Cape Coast Castle and loaded onto Archer's ironically named ship, the *Happy Return*. It was a relatively small slave ship of under 100 tons, into which 122 enslaved souls were packed tightly between the decks.[4] Of these only ninety-eight survived the Middle Passage, a mortality rate of almost one fifth. Most of the survivors were sold to Barbados planters, but Quoshey, if he was indeed aboard, was probably retained as a favourite by Archer, for as a slave-ship captain Archer was entitled to ship and either sell or keep one or several enslaved people on his own account.

The newspaper advertisement of December 1700 did not, as was common, state that Quoshey had run away from Archer but instead that the teenager 'belonging to Capt. Edw. Archer' had 'run away from Bell-Wharf'. The wording makes more sense given that Archer had sailed from

---

[3] D. Morris and K. Cozens, 'The Shadwell waterfront in the eighteenth century', *Mariner's Mirror: the International Quarterly Journal of the Society for Nautical Research*, xcix (2013), 88–9.

[4] Voyage of the *Happy Return*, Voyage 20137 in Slave Voyages: Trans-Atlantic Slave Trade database <https://www.slavevoyages.org/voyage/database> [accessed 21 April 2020].

London on 29 November on another slave ship, the *Mayflower*, which like the *Happy Return* was destined for West Africa and then Barbados.[5] Why did Quoshey not accompany Archer? Did the captain not trust the young boy or think him sufficiently capable to serve him? Or did Archer want to protect him from the diseases and the horrors of this deadly voyage? Or did Archer perhaps not want to use valuable space and provisions for Quoshey, instead availing himself of the opportunity to gain another enslaved person as his perquisite, to be sold in the colonies to increase his profits from the voyage or, like Quoshey, brought back to London? With whom did Quoshey reside after Archer left, and what work was he doing?

We cannot answer these questions but we can surmise that the teenager was sufficiently motivated to escape, perhaps seeking to take advantage of Archer's absence. He may have been treated poorly by those who ruled him, or maybe Archer had denied him the opportunity to sail back to West Africa. He may have known or feared that he might be sold and transported to the colonies or he may simply have missed the captain. It is quite possible that Quoshey had developed a bond of affection with Archer, and Olaudah Equiano's autobiography shows that enslaved boys and young men could become very close to the ships' officers who enslaved them. Indeed, having sailed on a Middle Passage ship and seen the horrors below decks as well as the terror of arrival in the Caribbean, Quoshey may, perhaps out of numbing terror, have experienced some strangely positive emotions towards the man who had preserved him from the worst of all this. If Quoshey did feel anything like affection for Archer, we would today interpret it as a form of Stockholm Syndrome, a condition in which captives develop a deep psychological link with and dependence upon their captors.[6] Enslavement and sale in West Africa, the Middle Passage and exposure to Caribbean plantation slavery must have had a deeply traumatic effect on boys such as Quoshey, and if his escape was motivated by affection for Archer this may have been symptomatic of such trauma.

Since Archer was absent and unable to receive Quoshey from any person who might recapture him, the advertisement gave two names and locations to which Quoshey might be returned in expectation of the significant

---

[5] Voyages of the *Mayflower*, Voyage 15150 in Slave Voyages: Trans-Atlantic Slave Trade database.

[6] For the possible application of Stockholm Syndrome to the enslaved and their captors see M. R. Cheatham, 'Hannah: Andrew Jackson's slave and Stockholm Syndrome', *Brewminate*, 10 April 2020 <https://brewminate.com/hannah-andrew-jacksons-slave-and-stockholm-syndrome> [accessed 17 Sept. 2021]; B. A. Huddleston-Mattai and P. R. Mattai, 'The Sambo mentality and the Stockhom Syndrome revisited: another dimension of the plight of the African American', *Journal of Black Studies*, xxiii (1993), 344–57.

reward of one guinea. One of the contacts named in the advertisement was Richard Clearke (or Clarke) on Bell Wharf in Shadwell, who was quite possibly responsible for Quoshey during Archer's absence. Given that Quoshey was reported to have escaped from Bell Wharf, he had probably been living and working in Clearke's home.[7]

The second contact to whom Quoshey might be returned was Rowland Tryon on Lime Street in Aldgate ward of the City of London. The Tryons were a well-known mercantile family in the City of London with connections to the Caribbean. In the mid-1690s, six or seven years before Quoshey's escape, Rowland Tryon appeared in the lists of tax-paying property owners in Stepney. Adjacent to Shadwell, this proximity may have been a factor in a relationship between Archer and Clearke or Tryon. But a few years later Tryon was listed as a church warden for St Dionis Backchurch on Lime Street, the address mentioned in the advertisement. Tryon was a director of the Royal African Company, a transatlantic slave trader and a merchant, and his uncle Thomas had spent five years as a merchant in Barbados. Rowland Tryon served as the colonial agent representing South Carolina, and was in Barbados when he died in 1720. The trade in enslaved people and what they produced enabled Tryon, a wealthy and successful man, to indulge himself by subscribing to the first octavo edition of the *Tatler*, among other things.[8]

Archer, Tryon and maybe Clearke illustrate how deeply racial slavery had permeated London, and how it connected a ship captain in the East End, and other businessmen and residents of the East End's maritime community with

---

[7] Richard Clark or Clarke is a relatively common name, and this individual cannot be identified definitively. At least two wills exist for mariners named Richard Clarke whose home was in this general area: see Will of Richard Clarke, Mariner of St Paul Shadwell, 6 Dec. 1721, National Archives, PROB 11/582/383; Will of Richard Clarke, Mariner now belonging to His Majesty's Ship Newark of Stepney, 12 Jan. 1704, National Archives, PROB 11/474/174.

[8] D. Keene, P. Earle, C. Spence and J. Barnes, 'Middlesex, St Dunstan Stepney, The Hamlet of Spittlefields, Fossan Street North Side', in *Four Shillings in the Pound Aid 1693/4: the City of London, the City of Westminster, Middlesex* (London, 1992), *British History Online* <http://www.british-history.ac.uk/no-series/london-4s-pound/1693-4/middlesex-fossan-street-north-side> [accessed 22 April 2020]; St Dionis Backchurch Parish: Minutes of Parish Vestries, Vestry held 1 April 1714, London Metropolitan Archives, digital version accessed at <https://www.londonlives.org/browse.jsp?id=GLDBMV30501_n169–8&div=GLDBMV30501MV305010023#highlight> [accessed 22 April 2020]; W. A. Pettigrew, *Freedom's Debt: the Royal African Company and the Politics of the Atlantic Slave Trade, 1672–1752* (Chapel Hill, N.C., 2013), pp. 233, 239; J. D. Alsop, 'New light on Richard Steele', *British Library Journal*, xxv (1999), 26–7; Will of Rowland Tryon of Frognal, Kent, 8 July 1720, National Archives, PROB 11/573/73. When Tryon died in Barbados he was listed as being of 'Fragnall, Co. Kent'. See J. McRee Sanders, *Barbados Records: Wills, 1639–1725* (Baltimore, Md., 1981), iii. 344.

the wealthy merchants and investors of the City of London and the colonies. Similar networks of connections can be seen in the advertisements for other freedom seekers associated with slave-trading ships and their captains. One such advertisement was for twenty-five-year-old Joseph, 'a Malegasco [Madagascar] Negro Man' who had eloped from Captain Thomas Edwards in October 1688.[9] The Royal African Company's monopoly of West African slave trading encouraged interlopers – those slave-trading ships owned by non-company groups and individuals – to trade in Madagascar. Between 1664 and 1687, for example, at least twenty-eight English ships carried nearly 5,000 enslaved people from Madagascar to Barbados and Jamaica; many more such enslaved people were transported across the Indian Ocean; and a few Madagascans were brought back to England.[10]

Edwards had captained at least one slave-trading voyage to Madagascar a decade earlier and may at that time have purchased Joseph, then a young teenager. At the turn of the eighteenth century Edwards would twice captain the *James and Francis* on voyages from West Africa to Jamaica. The ship was owned by Sir Bartholomew Gracedieu, a leading slave-trader and Jamaica merchant who eventually became the agent representing the colony in London. Gracedieu appeared in several London runaway advertisements as a contact to whom recaptured freedom seekers might be returned.[11] One of these was Tony, a 'Black-Moor Fellow' who had 'RUN away from Capt. Wadlow, from on Board the Ship St. Jago' in August 1696.[12] The advertisement promised a sizeable two-guinea reward to 'Whoever secures him and brings him to Col. Bartholomew Gracedieu, at the Flying Hose in Thames Street'. Archer, Tryon, Edwards, Wadlow and Gracedieu were all part of London's great web of aristocrats, gentlemen, merchants, craftsmen, ship captains and others who both made possible and profited from the

---

[9] 'RUN away from Captain Thomas Edwards of New England … Joseph', *London Gazette*, 8 Oct. 1688.

[10] Details of these 28 voyages can be found in Slave Voyages: Trans-Atlantic Slave Trade database. For more on the Madagascan slave trade see J. C. Armstrong, 'Madagascar and the slave trade in the seventeenth century', *Omaly sy Anio*, xvii–xx (1983–4), 211–33; V. B. Platt, 'The East India Company and the Madagascar slave trade', *William and Mary Quarterly*, 3rd series, xxvi (1969), 548–77.

[11] Voyage of the *Society*, Voyage 21510; Voyages of the *James and Francis*, Voyages 20234 and 21278, in Slave Voyages: Trans-Atlantic Slave Trade database. For another advertisement mentioning Sir Bartholomew Gracedieu see 'A Negro Woman', *London Gazette*, 14 July 1684. For more on Gracedieu see K. G. Davies, 'The origins of the commission system in the West India trade', *Transactions of the Royal Historical Society*, ii (1952), 89–107, at p. 105; Pettigrew, *Freedom's Debt*, pp. 55, 73–4; P. Gauci, 'Sir Bartholomew Gracedieu' (2004), *Oxford Dictionary of National Biography* <https://doi.org/10.1093/ref:odnb/49752> [accessed 24 April 2020].

[12] 'RUN away from Capt. Robert Wadlow … Tony', *London Gazette*, 6 Aug. 1696.

trade in enslaved people and the goods they produced. In London these people were efficiently networked, and when enslaved people escaped from ships or ship captains the network went into action.

For the enslaved boys and young men plucked from the holds of slave-trading ships and then selected to serve the men who captained them, the prospect of another hellish Middle Passage voyage may have been sufficient motive for escape. Working on deck would have done little to diminish the horror of such voyages. A 'Negro Man-servant nam'd Peter, aged about 31 Years' was described in an advertisement as 'a lusty well-set man, of a stern Countenance'.[13] His dour countenance may have been shaped in part by the seafaring life implied by the fact that he was described as 'belonging to the Sloop, the New Content of Jamaica, Francis Morgan Commander, lying at Lime-House Hole' on the Thames. Two days after this advertisement appeared, the *New Content* sailed for the Gold Coast of West Africa where the ship took on 139 enslaved people, 120 of whom would survive this hell only to enter another when they disembarked in Jamaica.[14] The advertisement specified that if Peter was recaptured he was to be returned to Francis Morgan, the captain of the *New Content*, or to Charles Kent in Old-Change in Cheapside. Kent was the owner or co-owner of ships engaged in at least seven early eighteenth-century slave-trading voyages.[15] Was Peter aboard the *New Content* when it sailed or had he remained free long enough to avoid months of witnessing and sharing the immiseration of the enslaved aboard ship? We shall never know.

Enslaved people who worked aboard ships trading between London, West Africa, the Americas and beyond may have seen London as one of the best venues for an escape. It was the largest city many freedom seekers had ever encountered, and its cosmopolitan population presented a better opportunity for establishing a new life and identity than the dangerous trading posts of West Africa or the small ports of the new English colonies, all of them locations in which a person of colour faced the danger of re-enslavement, probably on far worse terms. In January 1700 Joseph Kidd escaped 'from on board the *Providence* of *London, John Hendricx* Commander'.[16] A twenty-

---

[13] 'Ran away ... a Negro Man-servant nam'd Peter', *The London Post. With Intelligence Foreign and Domestick*, 29 Aug. 1701.

[14] Voyage of the *New Content*, Voyage 21333 in Slave Voyages: Trans-Atlantic Slave Trade database.

[15] Voyages of the *Valentine and Elizabeth*, Voyage 20893; the *Kent*, a ship Charles Kent named for himself, Voyage 16040; the *Dolphin*, Voyage 15212; the *Charles Galley*, Voyages 16045 and 15228; the *Sarah Gally*, Voyage 20586; and the *John Gally*, Voyage 24063, in Slave Voyages: Trans-Atlantic Slave Trade database. Kent is listed as an independent slave trader in the appendix of Pettigrew, *Freedom's Debt*, p. 231.

[16] 'Run away ... *Joseph Kidd*', *The Flying Post; or, The Post-Master*, 4 Jan. 1700.

eight-year-old 'Negro' speaking 'indifferent good *English* and *Portuguise*', Kidd escaped from a slave-trading ship soon to leave for West Africa, Antigua and Virginia, perhaps a voyage he hoped to avoid.[17] Similarly, an unnamed 'Negro Man aged about 20' eloped 'from on board the Sussex Sloop. W. Rhett Commander' in August 1694; two months later, when the newspaper advertisement appeared, this man still had not been recaptured.[18] William Rhett had been a merchant ship captain earlier in life before moving with his young family to South Carolina, where he held senior offices under the lords proprietor of Carolina, including comptroller of customs for that colony and for the Bahamas. A wealthy man who almost certainly owned enslaved people, he appears to have brought this enslaved man to London. When Rhett returned to the heart of the South Carolina plantation complex, this enslaved man with 'a stern countenance' perhaps managed to avoid a return to South Carolina slavery. The sizeable home Rhett built on Point Plantation on the outskirts of Charleston survives to this day as one of the city's oldest homes, this building and a surviving portrait of Rhett providing tangible evidence of the man and his success even today. Little survives in the historical records – beyond this one newspaper advertisement – of the man who escaped from Rhett's ship in London.[19]

Like Equiano a few decades later, some enslaved people in London were the property of officers of the Royal Navy. In 1692 an unnamed 'tall slender Negro' was reported to have 'RUN away from Their Majesties Ship the

[17] The *Providence* had undertaken at least one slave-trading voyage in 1697–8: see Voyage of the *Providence*, Voyage 20142 in Slave Voyages: Trans-Atlantic Slave Trade database. Apparently the ship undertook another voyage in 1700 that does not yet appear in the Slave Voyages database: a letter from Virginia in August 1700 mentions the arrival of 'Capt. John Hendrix, Commander of the *Providence*, who came from Antego'. See Governor F. Nicholson to Council of Trade and Plantations, James City, Virginia, 27 Aug. 1700, in 'America and West Indies: August 1700, 26–29', in *Calendar of State Papers Colonial, America and West Indies: xviii, 1700*, ed. C. Headlam (London, 1910), pp. 494–505, *British History Online* <http://www.british-history.ac.uk/cal-state-papers/colonial/america-west-indies/vol18/pp494-505> [accessed 24 Feb. 2020].

[18] 'Went from on board the Sussex Sloop … a Negro Man', *London Gazette*, 22 Oct. 1694.

[19] 'Colonel William Rhett', in C. K. Bolton, *Portrait of Persons Born Abroad Who Came to the Colonies in North America before the Year 1701* (Boston, 1919), i. 57–9. For an account of the Colonel W. Rhett House in Charleston see A. Whaley, '54 Hassell Street – Colonel William Rhett House' <https://charleston.com/charleston-insider/diary-of-a-charleston-tour-guide/54-hasell-street-colonel-william-rhett-house> [accessed 24 April 2020], and 'Col. William Rhett House', Historical Marker Project <https://historicalmarkerproject.com/markers/HMLAG_col-william-rhett-house_Charleston-SC.html> [accessed 24 April 2020]. Henrietta de Beaulieu Dering Johnston's portrait of William Rhett, dated *c.*1710, is held by the Gibbes Museum of Art in Charleston, S.C.

Dragon'.[20] Recently rebuilt and re-outfitted at a Deptford shipping yard, the *Dragon* was commanded by William Vickars, who may have owned this unnamed freedom seeker.[21] But the advertisement did not mention Vickars as owner or a contact person for the one-guinea reward, instead suggesting that if recaptured this man could be brought to 'Mr. Guy's at the Swan Tavern over against the Royal Exchange'. This may have been Thomas Guy, a major London bookseller who made a fortune by printing English bibles for Oxford University, investing in South Sea Company stock and then selling before that company's crash, and profiting from the purchase of discounted tickets for the outstanding pay of sailors. If this was indeed the man who would pay one guinea to the person who brought him a runaway man of colour, how ironic it seems to us that at his death the bulk of Guy's fortune would establish the London hospital named in his honour.[22] But in Restoration London the ownership of enslaved Black people and humanitarianism towards White Londoners were not seen as incompatible.

Another enslaved deserter from the Royal Navy was a nineteen-year-old 'Tall Negro Black' who was reported to have 'Run away from Captain Joseph Waters, on Board Their Majesties Ship the Charles Galley at Portsmouth' in August 1692.[23] Portsmouth was the home base of the Royal Navy, but advertising in a London newspaper made sense both because of its wide circulation and because an escapee might relatively easily travel the seventy miles from England's south coast to the capital. The *Charles Galley* had been built by Phineas Pett in his Woolwich shipyards some two decades earlier, and just three months earlier the ship had been engaged in the battle of Barfleur off the French coast, after the French fleet had been deployed by Louis XIV to restore James II to the English throne. Perhaps this freedom seeker had seen enough of battle for the country that had enslaved him.[24] John Symonds, the captain of HMS *Tiger*, did not hesitate to state that the 'Mollatta Boy about Eleven Years of Age, yellow Complexion, wooly Hair like a Negro' who had escaped in April 1701 'belongs to Capt. John

[20] 'RUN away from Their Majesties Ship', *London Gazette*, 7 Jan. 1692.

[21] I. Schomberg, *Naval Chronology; or, An Historical Summary of Naval and Maritime Events …* (London, 1802), p. 289; D. F. Marley, *Wars of the Americas: a Chronology of Armed Conflict in the New World 1492 to the Present* (Santa Barbara, Calif., 1998), pp. 208–9.

[22] N. Hervey, 'Thomas Guy' (2008), *ODNB* <https://doi.org/10.1093/ref:odnb/11800> [accessed 24 April 2020]; M. Dresser, 'Set in stone: statues and slavery in London', *History Workshop Journal*, lxiv (2007), 173, 194–5.

[23] 'Run away from Captain Joseph Waters', *London Gazette*, 4 Aug. 1692.

[24] P. Aubrey, *The Defeat of James Stuart's Armada, 1692* (Leicester, 1979); 'British Fifth Rate galley-frigate "Charles Galley" (1676)' <https://threedecks.org/index.php?display_type=show_ship&id=3562#BWAS-1603> [accessed 24 April 2020].

Symonds of his Majesty's Navy'.[25] It is a statement of ownership, an affirmation of enslaved status made during an age when monarchs led the way in chartering and investing in the very companies that made the slave trade and plantation colonies possible. Owning enslaved people and serving the Crown were intimately aligned, and the Royal African Company was royal in much more than name alone.

Others ran from merchant ships of various kinds, or from the captains who commanded them. A 'Tall Slender Negro' eloped from John Gandy at Poplar, located in the East End just above the Isle of Dogs.[26] The freedom seeker 'speaks some English, [and] came from the East Indies in the Loyal Merchant', an East India Company ship that had only recently returned from a two-year voyage to Bombay and Surat.[27] If captured, the runaway could be returned to Gandy in Poplar or to the Virginia Coffee House, a focal point of colonial trade on Threadneedle Street behind the Royal Exchange.[28] Another runaway who might be returned to the Virginia Coffee House was 'a negro man of middle stature, well set, full face, [who] speaks very broken English'.[29] He had escaped 'from the Ship Maryland Merchant' anchored on the Thames just off Deptford in late September 1701. At least one of those who escaped from ships and their captains was South Asian. An unnamed 'Indian Black Boy, aged about 14 or 15, middle statured, short Neck'd, pretty full Bodied, full Eyed, has no Hat, pretty long Legg'd, but somewhat small with blue Stockins, and an old mix'd grey Coat' had eloped from John Daniel in October 1691.[30] A decade earlier Daniel had undertaken a voyage to Bantam and beyond, becoming one of the first English sailors to see the western shores of Australia.[31]

It was far from uncommon for boys and men of colour to serve on the ships that sailed between London, West Africa, South Asia and the colonies in North America and the Caribbean. Consequently, such boys and men were a familiar sight in the maritime communities east of the City of London, working on or around ships anchored on the Thames, walking on the docks and stairs leading to the river or taking their places in the area's taverns and

---

[25] 'A Mollatta Boy', *The Post Boy*, 7 June 1701. See also R. Winfield, *British Warships in the Age of Sail, 1603–1714: Design, Construction, Careers and Fates* (Barnsley, 2009), pp. 118–19.
[26] 'A Tall Slender Negro', *The Post Man: And The Historical Account*, 30 Sept. 1701.
[27] J. Bruce, *Annals of the East India Company ...* (London, 1810), iii. 295.
[28] A. G. Olson, 'The Virginia merchants of London: a study in eighteenth-century interest-group politics', *William and Mary Quarterly* 3rd series, xl (1983), 363–88, at p. 367.
[29] 'A Negro man', *The Post Man: And The Historical Account*, 2 Oct. 1701.
[30] 'AN Indian Black Boy', *London Gazette*, 15 Oct. 1691.
[31] I. Lee, 'The first sighting of Australia by the English', *Geographical Journal*, lxxxiii (1934), at p. 317.

inns.[32] It is no surprise that the earliest fixed Black communities in London sprang up in these places. For some the rough equality of seafaring may have appealed, for although this was a dangerous and poorly paid profession, sailors were required to live and work cooperatively at sea, and close bonds formed between people of different races during times of danger at sea. While some who were enslaved or bound to ship captains may have eloped, they and others may then have sought to serve on other ships as free men, engaging in 'maritime marronage'.[33] Despite his own enslavement and experience of the Middle Passage, Equiano nonetheless made clear in his autobiography that, even while enslaved, there were times when 'I was very happy, for I was extremely well treated by all on board'.[34] But not all enslaved or even free Black sailors were thus situated, and the voyages that took these boys and men back to South Asia and West Africa may have been psychologically as well as physically uncomfortable, requiring these sailors of colour to live and work on the ships of the White British empire. Such service could be dangerous too, for unscrupulous captains might easily sell an enslaved or even a free man of colour in the Caribbean or North America, where a healthy and 'seasoned' individual could command a hefty price. It is not surprising that so many of the boys and men identified in newspaper advertisements in Restoration London were associated with ships and ship captains. Nor is it surprising that so many chose to attempt escape.

[32] R. Costello, *Black Salt: Seafarers of African Descent on British Ships* (Liverpool, 2012), pp. 3–22.
[33] N. A. T. Hall, 'Maritime Maroons: "grand marronage" from the Danish West Indies', *William and Mary Quarterly*, 3rd series, xlii (1985), 476–98.
[34] Equiano, *The Interesting Narrative*, p. 84.

11. *Goude*: Thames-side maritime communities

*A Negro Boy named Goude, aged about 17, speaks no English, Run away
on Sunday last at Six in the Evening, had on an old sad-coloured serge
Coat, a pair of sad-coloured cotton Breeches, and an old black Tarry Hat
on his head. Whoever brings him to Lyme-house, to Mr. John Woodfine,
shall have Forty shillings reward.*

The London Gazette, 23 December 1686

A significant number of freedom seekers escaped from homes and workplaces in
the bustling riverside communities to the east and south of the City of London.
Just over 14 per cent of London's freedom seekers escaped from the communities
on the southern banks of the Thames, and a further 32 per cent from the East
End communities across the river, making a total of 46 per cent of the total of
126 who escaped from named places in London. These riverside communities
were predominantly working class, filled with the homes, boarding houses and
workplaces of the labourers, workers and craftsmen associated with shipbuilding
and ocean-going trade, as well as the taverns and businesses that serviced such
communities. If the City of London funded empire, these were the areas that
worked it. Wealthier merchants, shipbuilders and businessmen emerged from
these communities, some staying within them but others moving to larger
houses and estates beyond their borders in Hackney, Bow and elsewhere.

A contemporary rendering of the area immediately east of the Tower of
London, while highly inaccurate, is nonetheless suggestive of the significance
of the maritime communities of the East End to the city's economic life and
growth (Figure 27). Hugging the northern banks of the Thames east of the
Tower of London, the riverside includes St Katherine's Stairs, Hermitage
Stairs, Wapping Stairs and Shadwell Dock: to the north of Shadwell Dock
the tower of St Dunstan's in Stepney rises above the surrounding homes and
businesses. This map compresses longer distances, as well as straightening
out a considerable curve in the river, thereby including as much of the
fast-growing East End as possible. This area of the East End looks to be
no more than a few hundred yards from the Tower, but Wapping Stairs is
nearly three quarters of a mile distant and Wapping invisible to a person
standing on the edge of Tower Wharf. Shadwell Docks was more than a
mile along the river from the Tower, and Stepney church a good mile and
a half distant. Morden and Lea, the creators of this visual representation,

Figure 27. Detail from Rob. Morden and Phil. Lea, 'A Prospect of London and Westminster', in *London &c. Actually Surveyed, by Wm. Morgan* (London, 1682), Library of Congress.

saw the rising commerce and maritime of the area as essential to London's growth, and showing the ships on the river and one wharf, one dock and several sets of stairs communicated to viewers the avenues along which people and trade goods were funnelled into and out of London. Although the riverside communities of the East End were spreading ever further from central London, the connections between the mercantile financial hub within the City and these maritime communities remained as tangible and as significant as this fanciful representation suggests.

Some freedom seekers eloped from the homes and workplaces of shipbuilders: there were a growing number of shipyards to the east of Shadwell on both banks of the Thames. In 1684 'AN East-India Mallatto' escaped from James Yeames, a shipwright in Ratcliff in the East End.[1] At thirty years, this man was unlikely to have been a household servant and probably worked in the shipyard to which – the advertisement stated – he might be returned. He wore clothing suited to such work: 'a sad coloured Cloth Serge Coat and Breeches (his Coat daubed with Pitch) a blew Shirt and no Hat'. Yeames built ships for both the navy and commercial clients, and at his death in 1706 he left land and money to his wife, his daughters, his grandchildren and his sister.[2] Yeames's advertisement specified that if the freedom seeker was captured he could be returned for a one guinea reward either to 'James Yemes at his Yard at Ratcliff Cross' or 'to Mr Cary at the Virginia Coffee House in St. Miles Alley in Cornhill'. The identity of Cary is uncertain: he might have been a major London merchant of that name who was heavily engaged in trade with the Chesapeake and Carolina colonies, or the similarly named captain of the London slave-trade ship *Oxford*, which in 1683 had brought 200 enslaved people from Madagascar to Barbados.[3] Given that the Cary specified in Yeames's advertisement was operating out of the Virginia Coffee House just south of the Royal Exchange, it is more likely that he was the merchant rather than a rather more transient ship captain, although men of both professions could be found in coffee houses. But, whatever Cary's

[1] 'AN East-India Mallatto', *London Gazette*, 19 May 1684.

[2] For example, surviving records include documents such as a petition from Yeames stating that he was contracted to build two sloops for the navy, in which he requested that 12 of his workers be exempted from being pressed into the Royal Navy. See James Yeames, March 1693, Navy Board: Records, Records of the Admiralty, National Archives, ADM 106/428/97.

[3] For the merchant Thomas Cary see Will of Thomas Cary, Merchant of London, National Archives, PROB 11/554/162, and A. G. Olson, 'The Virginia merchants of London: a study in eighteenth-century interest-group politics', *William and Mary Quarterly*, 3rd series, xl (1983), 363–88, at pp. 371–2. For Thomas Cary the ship captain see Will of Thomas Cary, Mariner, National Archives, PROB 11/392/348, and Voyage of the *Oxford*, Voyage 20105 in Slave Voyages: Trans-Atlantic Slave Trade – Database <https://www.slavevoyages.org/voyage/database> [accessed 20 April 2020].

profession, it is clear that a successful shipwright such as Yeames might easily acquire an enslaved or bound person from a ship captain or merchant and be able to call on the cooperation of a professional man in the City to aid in the recovery of his enslaved property.

Three years later eighteen-year-old Andrew, 'a Negro Black', escaped 'from his Master, Mr. Francis Johnson in Old Gravel Lane, Wapping'.[4] Francis Johnson appears to have been a ship captain and related to the extremely wealthy Johnson shipbuilding family.[5] Francis Johnson and Sir Henry Johnson both hailed from and maintained homes in the small Suffolk coastal town of Aldeburgh, as well as living and working in London's East End. Sir Henry Johnson was in turn connected to another of the great shipbuilding families of east London. His mother Mary was the daughter of Peter Pett, a leading shipwright and commissioner of Chatham dockyard, who in turn was the son of Sir Phineas Pett, shipbuilder and surveyor general of the Royal Navy. Sir Henry Johnson was a major shipbuilder in his own right and ran the Blackwall shipyard his father had purchased from the East India Company.[6] What did all of this mean for Andrew when he eloped on Christmas Eve 1686? Johnson was a ship captain living near the river, and a member of a familial network of shipbuilders with large workforces and connections to merchants and investors in the City of London, all of which meant that Andrew would surely have found it extremely difficult to remain at liberty. Joining the crew of an outgoing ship or finding employment in another shipyard or elsewhere in and around London would not have been easy, for Andrew was attempting to escape not just from a man but from an entire system, a network of people engaged in the practical side of empire, colonization and slavery, the people who built and

---

[4] 'THE 24th of December Last, a Negro Black, named Andrew', *London Gazette*, 6 Jan. 1687.

[5] The 1690 will of Francis Johnson, a ship captain living in Wapping, included bequests of properties in Aldeburgh, Suffolk. Sir Henry Johnson Jr's family home was also in Aldeburgh, including Aldeburgh Manor, and like his father he represented the area in parliament. See Will of Francis Johnson of Wapping, Stepney, Middlesex, 8 Jan. 1690, National Archives, PROB 11/398/35; 'Henry Johnson (1661–1719)', The History of Parliament <http://www. histparl.ac.uk/volume/1715–1754/member/johnson-sir-henry-1661-1719> [accessed 20 April 2020]. Since both Francis and Henry Johnson Jr were in close proximity to each other in the East End of London and from the same small coastal town in Suffolk, a familial relationship is highly probable.

[6] R. McCaughey, 'Phineas Pett' (2008), *Oxford Dictionary of National Biography* <https://doi. org/10.1093/ref:odnb/22060> [accessed 20 April 2020]. See also W. F. Prideaux, 'Eastern men of mark: the Johnsons of Blackwall', in *East London Antiquities: Some Records of East London in the Days of Old* (London, 1902), at p. 121; J. Burke and J. B. Burke, *A Genealogical and Heraldic Dictionary of the Landed Gentry of Great Britain and Ireland*, 3 vols (London, 1850), iii. 181; 'Blackwall Yard: Development, to c.1819', in *Survey of London*: xliii and xliv, *Poplar, Blackwall and Isle of Dogs*, ed. H. Hobhouse (London, 1994), pp. 553–65, *British History Online* <http://www. british-history.ac.uk/survey-london/vols43–4/pp553-565> [accessed 20 April 2020].

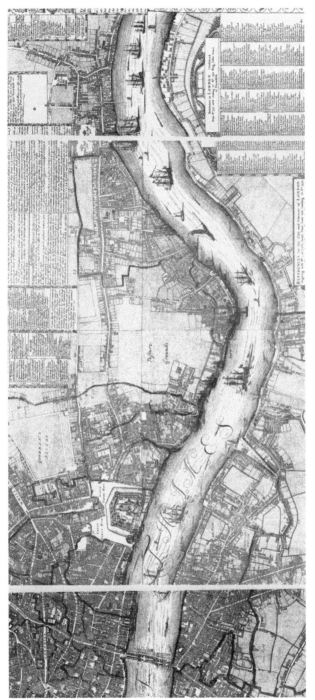

Figure 28. Riverside locations for the return of freedom seekers, 1659–1704. Detail from William Morgan, *London &c. Actually Surveyed by William Morgan, his maᶫjesᶦties cosmogr.* (London, 1681–2), Library of Congress. Graphic by the author.

maintained the ships that made possible both plantation slavery and the trade between West Africa, the colonies and London.

Others in the maritime communities who owned enslaved people were less prominent than Yeames or Johnson. In October 1687 the *London Gazette* included an advertisement for an unnamed 'Black Negro about 5 Foot 10 Inches high'.[7] The freedom seeker 'speaks pretty good English' and was wearing a 'Sea Coat' and 'a close bodied Cloth coat underneath'. He had escaped 'from Mr. Barret in Wapping, Sail Maker', and could be returned either to Barret or to Vernon's Coffee House on the northern side of the Royal Exchange.[8] Others escaped from these riverside communities but the advertisements for them did not reveal much about the work they had done or the households they had lived in. For example, 'Zebulon, for shortness Zeb', seventeen years old and wearing 'Canvas Clothes, a Furr Cap, black Stockings, [and] plain soled Shoes', eloped from Christopher Newham in Love Lane, Ratcliff.[9] We cannot tell much about either Zebulon or Newham other than that Newham was listed as a property holder in the tax records for Ratcliff.[10] Similarly 'A tall Gold Coast Negro, [who] goes by the Name of Sam. Hind' and 'speaks English very well' escaped from a Mrs. Hall in Poplar in July 1681.[11] There is no indication either of the work that the African-born Samuel Hind performed nor of the nature of Mrs Hall's home and work, but Poplar was home to many who worked in or provided ancillary services for the neighbouring shipbuilding yards. Indeed, Poplar was the site of a hospital and almshouse for disabled East India Company seamen, and the Blackwall yard had originally belonged to the company.[12] South of the river

[7] 'Went away from Mr. Barret … a Black Negro', *London Gazette*, 31 Oct. 1687.

[8] Barret was identified in church marriage records as a sailmaker in Whitechapel and regularly appeared in the local real estate tax assessments. See marriage record of Nicholas Barrett and Margaret Stanlake, 5 Sept. 1679, in *Allegations for Marriage Licences Issued by the Vicar General of the Archbishop of Canterbury, July 1679 to June 1687*, ed. G. J. Armytage (London, 1890), p. 5. For an example of Barrett being assessed taxes for his property in Fleece Lane, Wapping, see D. Keene, P. Earle, C. Spence and J. Barnes, 'Middlesex, St Mary Whitechapel, Wapping Whitechapel, Fleece Alley', in *Four Shillings in the Pound Aid 1693/4: the City of London, the City of Westminster, Middlesex* (London, 1992), *British History Online* <http://www.british-history.ac.uk/no-series/london-4s-pound/1693-4/middlesex-fleece-alley> [accessed 25 Jan. 2019].

[9] 'A Negro Boy', *London Gazette*, 11 Oct. 1683.

[10] D. Keene, P. Earle, C. Spence and J. Barnes, 'Middlesex, St Dunstan Stepney, The Hamlet of Ratcliffe, Cutthroate Lane', in *Four Shillings in the Pound Aid 1693/4, British History Online* <http://www.british-history.ac.uk/no-series/london-4s-pound/1693–4/middlesex-cutthroate-lane> [accessed 21 April 2020].

[11] 'A tall Gold Coast Negro', *The Loyal Protestant, and True Domestick Intelligence, Or, News both from City and Countrey*, 26 July 1681.

[12] 'Poplar High Street: the East India Company almshouses', in *Survey of London: xliii and xliv, Poplar, Blackwall and Isle of Dogs*, pp. 107–10, *British History Online*

a nine-year-old 'Negro Boy' escaped from Mrs Davis in East Greenwich. Since this was another leading shipbuilding area, this unnamed boy may have been in a household directly connected to the maritime industries, but that he was wearing silver earrings and 'a grey Livery' suggests he may have been a personal attendant in a more affluent household, and Greenwich was perhaps the most affluent of these riverside communities.[13]

Most runaway advertisements specified at least one location to which a recaptured runaway or information about their whereabouts might be taken. Often the first was the home or business location from which the freedom seeker had eloped, but generally another location was also specified, representing a person and place the master trusted to protect his interest in the bound or enslaved servant. As Figure 28 illustrates, from 1681 onwards a great many of London's freedom seekers could be returned to people and locations in London's maritime communities, illustrating the extent to which racial slavery and the bound labour of people of colour had become normative in these places.

More and more people of colour were living and working in the capital's maritime communities. Although it is difficult to learn anything about them and their lives, their place in communities tied to ocean-going shipbuilding and imperial trade is clear. Occasionally the surviving records enable us to learn a little more and to speculate about the individuals who resisted. One such was 'A Negro Boy named Goude, aged about 17, [who] speaks no English, [and who] Run away, on Sunday last, at Six in the Evening'.[14] These sparse words chronicling Goude's attempt to escape from John Woodfine reveal very little about the freedom seeker. What experiences, what suffering, what hopes, pride, fears and desperation are hidden behind these words? The fifty-seven words of this advertisement – as ever, probably the only surviving record of this person – are those of an enslaver asserting legal control of Goude and defying his agency by defining the teenager by his clothing, his single name and his subordinate status.

How much suffering had seventeen-year-old Goude endured by the time he escaped into London in December 1686? It is quite possible that, as little as a year earlier, he had been living free and with his family in the Kingdom of Dahomey in the northern section of present-day Benin, a world away from London and England. We cannot know how or when he was enslaved, but like many others Goude might have been transported to the Kingdom of Allada (Ardra) on the infamous Slave Coast. During the 1670s and 1680s

---

<http://www.british-history.ac.uk/survey-london/vols43-4/pp107-110> [accessed 21 April 2020].

[13] 'A Negro Boy', *London Gazette*, 22 Aug. 1687.

[14] 'A Negro Boy', *London Gazette*, 23 Dec. 1686.

a rapidly growing number of enslaved people were transported from the Slave Coast to the Americas, and most had been brought to Allada by canoe through the region's coastal lagoons, often by merchants from Lagos. Many had come from great internal slave markets deep in the interior, often from Dahomey in the north. The name Goude, or very similar names, were common in this region, including Goodie, Ogoodoo, Agoddy, Ahdagood.[15]

Perhaps Goude had never seen the ocean before. What must enslaved Africans have thought as they came to the trading posts and saw many more manacled people like themselves, and the European traders and their ships? Olaudah Equiano memorably described a similar experience of first seeing the ocean and slave ships at anchor, recalling that these sights 'filled me with astonishment, which was soon converted into terror, which I am yet at a loss to describe, nor the then feelings of my mind'.[16] In one of the coastal trading ports, one of the largest being Ouidah, Goude would have been sold to agents of the Royal African Company and then loaded onto John Woodfine's ship the *John Bonadventure*. Woodfine worked for England's Royal African Company, as did his slave-trading brother Thomas, captain of the sister ship *Sarah Bonadventure*. John Woodfine took the *John Bonadventure* to West Africa in 1678, 1680, 1684, 1686 and 1689, and the *Sarah Bonadventure* in 1682, and a total of 2,816 enslaved Africans disembarked from these voyages that he oversaw. John Woodfine and John Carter, the Royal African Company agent at Ouidah, served the company well, and on this particular voyage Carter recorded on 1 March 1686 that Woodfine's ship 'is about halfe slaved, and [I] doubt not that he will be compleated in less than ten days more'. The *John Bonadventure* sailed from Africa with 582 enslaved people on board, half of them adult men, a third adult women and the remainder children like Goude.[17]

---

[15] Between 1650 and 1675 at least 7,500 enslaved people were taken in English ships from this area of the West African coast, rising to 53,700 in the years 1676–1700 (Slave Voyages: Trans-Atlantic Slave Trade database). For the slave trade of this region see R. Law, 'The slave trade in seventeenth-century Allada: a revision', *African Economic History*, xxii (1994), 59–92; R. Law, 'Trade and politics behind the Slave Coast: the lagoon traffic and the rise of Lagos, 1500–1800', *Journal of African History*, xxiv (1983), 321–48; R. Law, *The Slave Coast of West Africa, 1550–1750: the Impact of the Atlantic Slave Trade on an African Society* (Oxford, 1991). For names see Slave Voyages: African Names – Database <https://www.slavevoyages.org/resources/names-database> [accessed 12 March 2021]. As *goud* is the Dutch word for gold, it is possible he had been purchased by Dutch slave traders on the Gold Coast, but this is unlikely because he almost certainly arrived in London on an English slave ship from the Slave Coast.

[16] O. Equiano, *The Interesting Narrative and Other Writings*, ed. V. Carretta (New York, 2003), p. 55.

[17] J. Carter, Whidah [*sic*], 1 March 1686, in *The Local Correspondence of the Royal African Company of England, 1681–1699*: ii, *The English in West Africa, 1685–1688*, ed. R. Law (Oxford, 1991), p. 330. The Slave Voyages: Trans-Atlantic Slave Trade database lists six ships

Try as we might, we can never recapture the physical and psychological trauma of the Middle Passage. Equiano believed that those who died and were thrown overboard were better off than those who survived: 'Often did I think many of the inhabitants of the deep much more happy than myself; I envied them the freedom they enjoyed, and as often wished I could change my condition for theirs.'[18] One hundred and forty of those on the *John Bonadventure*, a horrifying 24 per cent, died before arrival in Jamaica. Woodfine's employers were always concerned about 'any mortallity [that] should happen among yo'r negroes in yo'r voyage', a concern that they had communicated in their written instructions to his brother Thomas in 1685, signing their letter to him with the cheery and affectionate salutation 'Your loving Friends'. But their concern was financial rather than humanitarian, and Thomas Woodfine had been enjoined by his supervisors to have completed 'a Certificate under yo'r Mates and Chirugeons hands testifying the Time of the Death of such as shall happen to dye, for Wee shall allow of none, but what are so certifyed to be dead'.[19]

'As shall happen to dye': these words imply that such mortality was natural, an act of God, an unfortunate and unavoidable weakening of profit margins. The enslaved such as Goude had an altogether different experience of the deaths of men, women and children chained together and mired in human filth. These voyages are the stuff of nightmares, but for Goude and millions like him the Middle Passage was a real-life experience that probably never left him, forever shaping his understanding of White people and the society into which he had been violently drawn. Goude's experiences may have been mediated by Woodfine selecting him from the mass of humanity below decks to serve him as a cabin boy. Consequently, instead of being sold to the sugar planters of Jamaica, he remained aboard the *John Bonadventure* and accompanied Woodfine back to London and his home in Limehouse, almost certainly as Woodfine's personal property.[20]

---

captained by John Woodfine and three by his brother Thomas. The 1685–6 voyage of the *John Bonadventure* is Voyage 9858.

[18] Equiano, *The Interesting Narrative*, p. 58.

[19] Royal African Company, Instructions to Captain T. Woodfine, London, 10 Dec. 1685, in *Documents Illustrative of the History of the Slave Trade to America*, i, *1441–1700*, ed. E. Donnan (Washington, D.C., 1930), p. 353.

[20] It was common for the captains and senior officers of slave ships to be allowed to buy and transport one or two enslaved people and then to either sell them in the colonies or perhaps bring at least one back to Britain as an enslaved personal servant. For example, in their 1725 contract with W. Barry, the captain of the *Dispatch*, the ship owners I. Hobhouse, N. Ruddock and W. Baker specified that 'The captain is to have four per cent. Commission on the net proceeds of the live cargo, and is allowed to buy two slaves on his own account. The chief mate may also have two slaves, but is to pay for their food' (I. Hobhouse, N. Ruddock

We do not know exactly when Goude and Woodfine arrived in Limehouse, which is where Goude made his escape. The *John Bonadventure* had left Jamaica on 7 August 1686, so the ship probably arrived in London between October and December.[21] By the end of 1686 Goude had been under the control of White men for about nine or ten months, yet according to Woodfine he 'speaks no English'. Perhaps he was struggling to learn this strange new language of absolute domination and horrible violence, a language of power and subordination. Or perhaps this traumatized teenager had retreated into himself, hiding behind his own silence. Indeed, he may have known English better than he revealed. Woodfine had dressed him for work on board ship and as his personal servant on land, and Goude had exchanged the loose-fitting and brightly coloured thin fabrics of West Africa for an old tarred hat, and an equally old coat and breeches, the latter described as 'sad' or sombre coloured. It is hard not to imagine the drab, sad colouring matching the mental state of the boy who wore these clothes.

But the very existence of this short advertisement suggests more than sad subordination: perhaps absolute desperation, quiet courage or angry resistance. While he would have been one of the many anonymous souls who had been incarcerated on the *John Bonadventure*, the only surviving record that names and identifies him simultaneously testifies to the fact that Goude resisted his enslavement. As London prepared for Christmas, a festival that surely meant nothing to him in a place he could hardly comprehend, Goude ran away from Woodfine. To resist enslavement by seeking freedom in Barbados or Jamaica or South Carolina took courage enough: the penalties for such resistance were harsh and the opportunities for success few. But at least in these colonies there were many enslaved people of colour who might harbour or assist runaways. For a teenage boy torn from family and community in West Africa and traumatized by the death and suffering of a Middle Passage voyage, the courage to elope into the alien environment of an overwhelmingly White London is astonishing.

As with all the advertisements for people of colour who escaped into seventeenth-century London, we can learn far more about those who advertised for them and the people to whom they might be returned. As the

---

and W. Baker, instructions to William Barry, quoted in J. Latimer, *The Annals of Bristol in the Eighteenth Century* (Bristol, 1893), p. 144). Thus when J. Chapman, first mate of the slave ship *Daniel and Henry* died at sea in 1700, his goods, which were inventoried, included, in addition to various trade goods, '1 man Slave 1 girl ditto m'rked J:C.' (N. Tattersfield, *The Forgotten Trade: Comprising the Log of the Daniel and Henry of 1700 and Accounts of the Slave Trade from the Minor Ports of England, 1698–1725* (London, [1991] 1998), p. 164).

[21] Voyage of the *John Bonadventure*, Voyage 9858 in Slave Voyages: Trans-Atlantic Slave Trade database.

captain of at least six successful slave-trading voyages for the Royal African Company, John Woodfine had become a relatively wealthy and successful man who would take possession of the Manor House in the countryside north of Ratcliff, complete with a park filled with deer. When he died in 1693 Captain John Woodfine was not even fifty years old, yet he left parcels of land in Middlesex and Essex to each of his five children as well as £100 to his mother. The trade in Africans had made Woodfine wealthy, and he could well afford an enslaved cabin boy or personal attendant.

Goude was not the first of these, for Woodfine had published another advertisement five and a half years earlier.[22] The earlier notice specified that an unnamed 'Negro Boy' who had escaped was aged between 14 and 16 and 'speaks very bad English', which means that this was not Goude (who more than five years later was described by Woodfine as being seventeen years old and speaking no English at all). This unnamed boy had probably come from the Gold Coast of West Africa, where Woodfine and the *John Bonadventure* had recently taken on board 560 enslaved people, half of them being men, 40 per cent women and 5 per cent each boys and girls. Only 401 were alive when the ship docked in Barbados, a crippling but far from exceptional mortality rate of 28 per cent.[23] The Royal African Company agents in Barbados reported that Woodfine had taken possession of his 'Commiss'n Negroes', one of whom in all likelihood was this young boy whom Woodfine had chosen to retain and bring back to London's East End rather than sell.[24]

We do not know precisely when the *John Bonadventure* sailed back up the Thames but it was probably late in 1680 or early in 1681, and this unnamed boy attempted to escape in June of the latter year. As a person who advertised for two runaways, Woodfine clearly was one of the growing number of aristocrats, gentlemen, merchants and sea captains who could afford the personal benefits of enslaved labour, and who enjoyed advertising his success through the ownership of such boys. Had the first unnamed boy died, or had Woodfine sold him in London, West Africa or the Caribbean on a subsequent voyage, later replacing him with Goude and perhaps others? Or had the escape attempt of either or both of the unnamed first boy and Goude perhaps succeeded? We cannot know, and in the end all these records tell us for sure is that these two enslaved boys who had endured the Middle Passage had the audacity and courage to resist their bondage in London by attempting to escape. And that is no small thing.

---

[22] 'A Negro Boy', *London Gazette*, 2 June 1681.

[23] Voyage of the *John Bonadventure*, Voyage 9932 in Slave Voyages: Trans-Atlantic Slave Trade database.

[24] E. Stede and S. Gascoigne to the Royal African Company, Barbados, 4 Sept. 1680, in *Documents Illustrative of the History of the Slave Trade*, ed. Donnan, p. 264.

12. *Quamy*: merchants, bankers, printers and coffee houses

A Black Boy run away from Mr. Richard Tudway, Merchant, on the 15th past, he is about 10 year old, named Quamy, in a dark coloured Coat lin'd with blue, with large Brass Buttons, a striped pair of Breeches, blue Stockins, a light coloured Cap lined with blue. Whoever gives notice of him to Mrs. Racheil Tudway at her house in Distaff Lane, or to Mr. Joseph Whitfield in the New Exchange at the Strand, shall have 20 s. Reward.

The London Gazette, 2 March 1693

The financial heart of England's colonial empire was in the eastern section of the City of London. Radiating out from the Royal Exchange on Cornhill were the headquarters of the East India Company on Leadenhall Street, and the Royal African Company which began operations at Wanford Court just north of the exchange, before moving to Leadenhall Street, not far from East India House.[1] The incorporation of the Bank of England towards the end of the seventeenth century, with a building located no more than 250 yards west of the Royal Exchange, consolidated the institutional base of this imperial mercantile hub which linked London and England to India, West Africa, the Caribbean and North America. It is hardly surprising that the merchants and bankers helping to develop England's empire were among those who owned enslaved people in London, often putting them to work in their households and businesses and using them as living emblems of the foundations and riches of the trade in human beings and the goods they produced.

The Royal African Company itself owned enslaved people both in West Africa and in London. In the eighteenth century at least one enslaved person 'belonging to the Royal African Company' escaped, in this case 'a black Lad, nam'd Quashy' who was apprenticed to a cooper named Negus in Wapping.[2] For decades the company had been sending enslaved boys to London, often to be trained in the trades and skills needed by company officials on the West African coast, and perhaps at other times as gifts

---

[1] The two offices of the Royal African Company (and its predecessor companies) are referenced in J. Strype, *A Survey of the Cities of London and Westminster ... written at first in the year MDXCVIII by John Stow ...* (London, 1720), i. 132. For the East India Company offices see book ii. 88.

[2] 'WHEREAS a black Lad, nam'd Quashy', *Daily Advertiser*, 20 April 1763.

for company directors, investors and supporters. In 1698, for example, company officials in London instructed their agents at Cape Coast Castle on the Gold Coast to dispatch 'Ten good healthy Young Negroes' back to London. For as long as the company existed, officials sent enslaved boys to London 'to be made Bricklayers, Carpenters, Smiths & Coopers'.[3] Company officials in West Africa and in the Caribbean also sent enslaved boys to company officials, directors, investors and personal friends to serve as enslaved personal attendants. Ship captains and Royal African Company officials were thus a major source of the enslaved children, mostly boys, who served merchants, officials and other elite Londoners.[4]

From the mid seventeenth century onwards, leading merchants were prominent among the Londoners who acquired enslaved boys. In August 1659 an unnamed 'Negro boy about nine years of age' disappeared from St Nicholas Lane, which lay a few hundred feet northeast of London Bridge, within the neighbourhood filled with the new financial institutions of empire.[5] A half-century or so later, John Stow reported that this street continued to be 'inhabited by Merchants and wholesale Dealers'. In 1659 one of these was Thomas Barker and the runaway advertisement he paid for recorded that his business premises were 'at the Sugar Loaf in that lane'.[6] Barker appears to have been a London shipper and merchant who invested in the East India Company as well as in privateering voyages, and during the mid-1650s he had spent time in Tunis.[7] Barker might have acquired this

---

[3] Royal African Company to Merchants at Cape Coast Castle, London, 6 Sept. 1698, Letter Books, Letters Sent to Africa, 1698–1703, Company of Royal Adventurers of England Trading with Africa and Successors (hereafter RAC), National Archives, T70/51, p. 6 verso; Nathaniel Senior to Royal African Company, Cape Coast Castle, 10 May 1764, Inward Letter Books, 1753–1762, RAC, National Archives, T70/30, p. 271. For more on the training of African boys in England see S. P. Newman, *A New World of Labor: the Development of Plantation Slavery in the British Atlantic* (Philadelphia, Pa., 2013), pp. 148–9.

[4] See eg John Pery's acknowledgement of receipt of an enslaved boy in a letter to Dalby Thomas, governor of Cape Coast Castle and superintendent of all of Britain's West African slave-trading forts, in John Pery to Dalby Thomas, London, 6 July 1705, Letter Books, Letters Sent to Africa, 1703–1715, RAC, National Archives, T70/52, p. 47 verso.

[5] 'A Negro Boy', *Mercurius Politicus, Comprising the Sum of Foreign Intelligence, with the Affairs now on foot in the Three Nations of England, Scotland, & Ireland. For Information of the People*, 11 Aug. 1659.

[6] J. Strype, *A Survey of the Cities of London and Westminster*, i. 163.

[7] T. K. Rabb, *Enterprise and Empire: Merchant and Gentry Investment in the Expansion of England, 1575–1630* (Cambridge, Mass., 2013), p. 240; R. Davis, *The Rise of the English Shipping Industry in the Seventeenth and Eighteenth Centuries* (London, 1962); C. R. Pennell, *Piracy and Diplomacy in Seventeenth-Century North Africa: the Journal of Thomas Barker, English Consul in Tripoli, 1677–1685* (London, 1989), pp. 54–5. See also I. Habib, *Black Lives in the English Archives, 1500–1677* (Aldershot, 2008), p. 182.

young boy in North Africa or he might have been aboard a ship captured by one of the privateers in which Barker invested. The advertisement that Barker placed in the *Mercurius Politicus* suggested that the boy 'was lost'. While this may be true, particularly if the young boy had only recently arrived at Barker's home, he had disappeared from the street in which Barker lived. St Nicholas Lane was no more than 500 feet in length, so it is very possible that this boy had eloped rather than become lost.

One merchant advertising for a freedom seeker began his notice with 'A Black Boy run away from Mr. Richard Tudway, Merchant', a simple sentence that encapsulates the connections between London's mercantile elite and racial slavery.[8] The ten-year-old freedom seeker was identified by Tudway as Quamy, probably an anglicized version of the West African Akan name Kwame. He was one of very few of the London freedom seekers who were known by African names. Quamy was dressed in a livery reflecting Tudway's wealth and success, including 'a dark coloured Coat lin'd with blue, … large Brass Buttons, a striped pair of Breeches, blue Stockins, [and] a light coloured Cap lined with blue'. Tudway was one of the many merchants deeply invested in the trade in enslaved people and the goods they produced. He was the co-owner of at least five slave-trading ships, three of which travelled to Antigua where he owned the Parham Hill plantation. When slavery finally ended a century and a half later Tudway's family still owned Parham Lodge, Parham Old Work and Parham New Work plantations in Antigua.[9] Slavery made Tudway a very wealthy man and his will included bequests of well over £1,000 in cash, the granting of his Antigua plantation to his widowed sister-in-law and her son, and the bequest of the presumably quite large residue of his estate in England to his daughter Elizabeth.[10] During his lifetime a beautifully liveried enslaved African boy embodied Tudway's wealth, success and standing. Tudway's advertisement specified that Quamy could be returned to the merchant's wife Rachel Tudway at their house in Distaff Lane, where no doubt the young boy had spent much of his time. How must Quamy have experienced his life with the Tudways? His African name may have been an important link to the people and the life he had lost but would have appeared appearing incongruous and exotic in his daily life and work in London; it was

---

[8] 'A Black Boy … Quamy', *London Gazette*, 2 March 1693.

[9] Voyages of the *Prosperous*, Voyage 15085 and Voyage 21262; the *Champion*, Voyage 15147; *Codrington*, Voyage 21225; and the *London*, Voyage 15121 in Slave Voyages: Trans-Atlantic Slave Trade – Database <https://www.slavevoyages.org/voyage/database> [accessed 6 May 2020]. For the ownership of the Parham plantations at the time of abolition see the estate record for Parham, Antigua, in the Legacies of British Slavery database <https://www.ucl.ac.uk/lbs/estates> [accessed 6 May 2020].

[10] Will of Richard Tudway, Merchant, 11 Jan. 1707, National Archives, PROB 11/500/5.

yet another way of othering a boy whose status was entirely different from that of the White domestic servants and employees of the Tudway family. At the age of ten years, could he have fully appreciated the deep involvement of Tudway in the slave trade and plantation slavery? What, if anything, had Quamy experienced of those institutions? And what was it that caused this terribly young boy to run away?

Like Tudway, Theodore Johnson identified himself as a merchant in the advertisement he placed for Ben, 'A Blackamoor Boy' aged about seventeen who had 'Run away' in March 1686.[11] Similarly, '*William Steavens* Merchant in *East Lane* on *Rotherheth-wall*' advertised for 'POmpe a Black Boy' who had escaped from Steavens in May 1703 and again in January 1704.[12] Other advertisers were so well known in the merchant and banking communities as to need no such identification as merchants or financial leaders, and many newspaper readers would have recognized their names. One such was John Johnson, a goldsmith and banker who would go on to be knighted and to become lord mayor of London.[13] In March 1690 'Joseph Moore, a young Negro Boy', eloped from Johnson's premises in Cheapside. Described as 'straight and well-favoured', Moore was about fifteen or sixteen years old when he ran from a household that in 1693 included his master John Johnson, Lady Johnson, their three children, a journeyman, two lodgers, two servants and a coachman.[14]

While merchants regularly advertised for enslaved or bound people of colour who had escaped, the business premises of booksellers, printers and coffee houses were often cited in runaway advertisements as the venues within the City's financial district to which recaptured freedom seekers might be returned. Coffee houses were important venues for merchants, businessmen and ship owners and captains who often had no offices as such, where they

---

[11] 'A Blackamoor Boy, call'd Ben', *London Gazette*, 15 March 1686.

[12] 'RUN away … Pompey', *Daily Courant*, 22 May 1703; 'POmpe a Black Boy', *The Daily Courant*, 8 Jan. 1704; 'POmpe, a Black Boy', *The English Post: With News Foreign and Domestick*, 10 Jan. 1704.

[13] F. G. H. Price, *A Handbook of London Bankers, with Some Account of their Predecessors the Early Goldsmiths* (London, 1890–1), p. 94; J. Noorthouck, 'Addenda: the succession of aldermen from 1689', in *A New History of London including Westminster and Southwark* (London, 1773), pp. 894–7, British History Online <http://www.british-history.ac.uk/no-series/new-history-london/pp894-897> [accessed 4 Dec. 2018]; F. G. H. Price, 'Signs of old London', *London Topographical Record Illustrated*, ed. T. Fairman Ordish (London, 1907), iv. 60; S. Davidson, 'Goldsmiths that keep running cashes: seventeenth century commissioning agents for obtaining and retailing plate', *Silver Society*, xxvii (2011), at p. 99.

[14] 'Missing since Tuesday last, one Joseph Moore, a young Negro', *London Gazette*, 24 March 1690; see also J. Lane, *Apprenticeship in England, 1600–1914* (London, 1996), p. 143.

imbibed the coffee and chocolate that were the fruit of enslaved labour in the colonies. Printers, most especially those who printed early newspapers, broadsheets and other advertising materials, were also significant in the distribution of information and knowledge, including notices advertising runaways or serving as agents to whom information about or even recaptured runaways themselves might be taken. Lloyd's coffee house was a popular venue among those who owned enslaved people at home or in the colonies, for they knew it was frequented by those connected to the plantations, the Royal African and the East India companies, and to racial slavery more generally: these coffee houses were places of business as well as sociability, and Lloyd's was the focal point of business and sociability for many involved in the slave trade and the plantations. Just three years after Edward Lloyd opened his establishment Captain John Braddyl advertised that a freedom-seeking twenty-year-old 'Tawny Moor' might be returned to 'Mr. Lloyd's Coffee-house in Tower Street', and two years later anyone who secured 'a Negro Man named Will' was invited by Braddyl to give 'notice to Mr. Lloyd at his Coffee-house'. By the time Captain Davy Breholt advertised for 'William Peter, a Negro Man, aged about 26', Lloyd had moved to the premises on Lombard Street that his coffee house would occupy for the next century, and Breholt suggested that any person who took William Peter into custody should return the runaway either to Breholt or to 'Mr. Edward Lloyd at his Coffee-House in Lombard street'.[15] All three of these freedom seekers had eloped from ships or from ship captains; this suggested that from its earliest days Lloyd's was a meeting places for ship owners and captains. Lloyd's and most of the City's coffee houses were concentrated within a short walk of the Royal Exchange, and business with regard to commerce and shipping was regularly conducted both on the floor of the exchange and in these nearby coffee houses. In February 1665, for example, Samuel Pepys had left his office for 'the 'Change, and at the Coffee-house with Gifford, Hubland, the Master of the ship … I read over and approved a charter-party for carrying goods to Tangier'.[16] Given that enslaved people and the crops they produced were becoming an essential part of English shipping, returning freedom-seeking runaways to Lloyd's made perfect sense.

Masters also made use of other coffee houses close to the exchange as venues for the return of runaways. When fourteen-year-old Calib escaped, Charles Pope offered a one-pound reward to anybody who 'gives notice of him… at the

---

[15] 'Run away … a Tawny Moor', *London Gazette*, 10 Oct. 1689; 'RUN away … a Negro Man named Will', *London Gazette*, 9 March 1691; 'William Peter, a Negro Man', *London Gazette*, 4 Feb. 1695.

[16] *The Diary of Samuel Pepys: Daily Entries from the 17th Century London Diary*, 2 Feb. 1665 <https://www.pepysdiary.com/diary> [accessed 7 May 2020].

Royal Coffee-house over against the Royal Exchange'.[17] Pope was a merchant in Bristol, and for enslavers like him who were based outside London, coffee houses were particularly useful business venues. When a young 'Black Boy' disappeared from Lady Broughton's home Marchwhiel Hall in Wales, she suggested that anyone with notice of the unnamed boy inform her or 'Mr. John Elmore at Exeter-Change Coffee-house in the Strand' in London.[18] The coffee houses were just as useful to people in London but beyond the City's financial district. When the East End shipbuilder James Yeames advertised for a runaway 'East-India Mallatto' in May 1684, he suggested that anyone with information about the freedom seeker could either contact him in Ratcliff or notify 'Mr Cary at the Virginia Coffee House' in the heart of the City, some two and a half miles west of Yemes's East End shipyard.[19] Smithy's in Thames Street, Elford's in Lombard Street, Man's in Charing Cross, the Garter in Threadneedle Street, Garraway's in Exchange Alley and the Carolina in Birchin Lane were just some of the coffee houses in the financial centre of the City employed by advertisers for freedom seekers.[20]

Enslavers also made use of the offices of printers and booksellers as venues to which freedom seekers might be returned. When seventeen-year-old Zebulon escaped in October 1683, Christopher Newham placed an advertisement promising a guinea reward to anyone who gave information about 'the said Negro, so as he may be restored again to his Master'.[21] This information could be delivered to Newham at his premises in Love Lane in Ratcliff in the East End, 'or to John Bringhurst, Bookseller in Gracechurch-street' in the City. Operating under a sign showing a book, Bringhurst was a Quaker printer operating just north of London Bridge, at the southern end of the City's financial district.[22] Similarly, following Humphry's escape from John Brooke in August 1696 a newspaper advertisement specified that the London-based contact to whom Humphry might be returned was 'Mr Brabazon Aylmer at

[17] 'Run away ... Calib', *London Gazette*, 12 Nov. 1685.

[18] 'A Black Boy', *London Gazette*, 28 Oct. 1686.

[19] 'AN East-India Mallatto', *London Gazette*, 19 May 1684.

[20] 'RUN away ... a Negro Man ... Smithy's Coffee-house', *London Gazette*, 24 May 1686; 'RUN away ... a Negro man ... to Mr. Elford at his Coffee-house', *London Gazette*, 6 Dec. 1688; 'A Negro Boy ... to Mr. *Man's* Coffee-house', *London Gazette*, 21 Nov. 1681; 'A Negro Boy ... to Mr. Dines at the Garter Coffee house', *London Gazette*, 22 Aug. 1687; 'AN Indian Boy', *London Gazette*, 30 Nov. 1682; 'These are to give Notice ... run away a lusty young Black,,, any one can give Notice of him at the Carolina Coffee-house', *The Flying Post; or, The Post-Master*, 8 April 1701.

[21] 'A Negro Boy ... whose Name is Zebulon', *London Gazette*, 11 Oct. 1683.

[22] H. R. Plomer, *A Dictionary of the Printers and Booksellers who Were at Work in England, Scotland and Ireland from 1668 to 1725* (Oxford, 1922), pp. 49–50; J. W. Jordan, *Colonial Families of Philadelphia* (New York, 1911), ii. 1142.

the Three Pigeons in Cornhill'.[23] Set against the Royal Exchange, Brabazon's printing business was centrally located, and like other such establishments it was a place where people met and exchanged news and information.[24] When a ten-year-old 'Black Boy' who had been born in Maryland 'Ran away from his Master Captain Richard Pery' in London in May 1682, the only contact named in the newspaper advertisement was 'Mr. *Robert Horne*, Book-seller, at the South Entrance of the Royal-Exchange, London'.[25] On occasion the printers mentioned as contacts in runaway advertisements were the publishers of newspapers, as when 'Mr. Crouches Bookseller at the corner of Popes-Head-Alley, London' was the first-named contact for information concerning the escape of a twenty-one-year-old unnamed 'Negro' man in August 1684.[26] Opposite the Royal Exchange and operating under the sign of the Prince's Arms, Samuel Crouch supplemented the publication of books with the newspaper the *True Protestant Domestic Intelligence*.[27] Similarly, one of the contacts for information concerning Fortune who eloped in November 1684 was 'Thomas Howkins Stationer'.[28] Situated just south of the Royal Exchange in George Yard (between Lombard Street and Cornhill), Howkins or Hawkins published books and for a while the *City Mercury*.[29] Seven years earlier, an advertisement for 'A Negro Man, by name *Anthony*' had named two contacts, one of them 'Mr. *Thomas Vyle* at the Office of the *City Mercury* at the Northwest corner of the *Royal Exchange*'.[30] Newspapers and coffee houses were central pillars of London's emerging public sphere, and were integral to the maintenance of racial slavery through runaway advertisements and the mechanisms for capture and reward initiated by these notices.

---

[23] 'RUN away … a … Negro Man, named Humphry', *London Gazette*, 10 Sept. 1696.

[24] Plomer, *Dictionary of the Printers and Booksellers*, p. 11; M. Smolenaars, 'Brabazon Aylmer' (2004), *Oxford Dictionary of National Biography* <https://doi.org/10.1093/ref:odnb/32019> [accessed 11 May 2020]. Like Bringhurst and indeed most printers of this era, the majority of works published by Brabazon were religious, and he briefly held the copyright for John Milton's *Paradise Lost*.

[25] 'ON Thursday … a Black Boy', *London Gazette*, 18 May 1682.

[26] 'A Negro … about 21 years of age', *London Gazette*, 8 Sept. 1684.

[27] Plomer, *Dictionary of the Printers and Booksellers*, p. 89.

[28] 'A Negro … goes by the Name of Fortune', *London Gazette*, 20 Nov. 1684.

[29] Plomer, *Dictionary of the Printers and Booksellers*, p. 163.

[30] 'A Negro Man, by name Anthony', *London Gazette*, 30 Aug. 1677. Thomas Vyle was one of a number of people who in 1682 were indicted for printing illegal materials, but his connection with this newspaper is unclear, and perhaps it was simply that the publisher would pass information to him. At this time the news sheet *The City Mercury: Or, Advertisements concerning Trade* was printed by Andrew Clark at the Royal Exchange. See D. F. McKenzine and M. Bell, *A Chronology and Calendar of Documents relating to the London Book Trade, 1641–1700*: ii, *1671–1685* (Oxford, 2005), p. 351; Plomer, *Dictionary of the Printers and Booksellers*, pp. 70–1.

Enslavers also depended on goldsmiths and bankers to serve as contacts for those who might have information on the whereabouts of freedom seekers. Stephen Evance was a goldsmith whose premises on Lombard Street, immediately south of the Royal Exchange, could be identified by the sign above the doorway depicting a young Black boy. A major figure in the international bullion markets, Evance was as much a banker as a goldsmith, and he invested in the Royal African and East India companies and made substantial loans to the crown. In March 1687 Captain John Bowers named Evance as his contact in the City of London for information regarding Francisco, a twenty-eight-year-old South Asian man who had escaped.[31]

A great deal of gold was mined and circulated in West Africa, where gold jewellery was relatively common and where gold and gold dust functioned as a primary medium of trade. The desire for trade in this gold had been one of the primary attractions for the first English traders travelling to the Gold Coast, and by the late seventeenth and early eighteenth centuries a significant proportion of the gold in circulation in England had come from West Africa. Occasionally gold featured in runaway advertisements, as when seventeen-year-old Caesar escaped from 'a Gentleman in Greenwich' in December 1681. The newspaper advertisement described Caesar as bearing 'small Cuts on each side of his Face, [and] on the Temples', country marks that identified him as having been born in West Africa. Caesar was a talented musician, and his enduring connection to West African culture included 'a Gold Ring in one Ear, with a Gold Nob to it'.[32]

But if West African gold enabled Caesar to retain something of his African heritage and culture, it also enabled an attractive reward to anybody who might help in the recapture of this freedom-seeking boy. How ironic that the price of his freedom was measured out in coins named for the gold taken from his West African homeland, and bearing the Royal African Company's emblem of a castle and a West African elephant below the head of the monarch. The newspaper advertisement seeking out Caesar promised 'two Guinies Reward'. The guinea was a new coin, first minted in 1663, and produced largely from West African gold. Fluctuations in the value of gold meant that its actual worth, originally twenty shillings or one pound, increased to as much as twenty-five shillings before eventually settling to an accepted value of twenty-one shillings.

---

[31] 'An Indian … his Name Francisco', *London Gazette*, 8 March 1688. For Evance see S. Quinn, 'Gold, silver and the Glorious Revolution: international bullion arbitrage and the origins of the English gold standard', *Economic History Review*, xlix (1996), 473–90; H. Lancaster, 'Sir Stephen Evance' (2004), *ODNB* <https://doi-org.ezproxy.lib.gla. ac.uk/10.1093/ref:odnb/49172> [accessed 11 May 2020].

[32] 'Run away from a Gentleman of Greenwich … Caesar', *The Impartial Protestant Mercury*, 20 Dec. 1681.

Between 1674 and 1714 the Royal African Company minted 548,327 guinea coins from West African gold.[33] The obverse of many guinea coins featured a small elephant or sometimes an elephant and a castle, symbols of the Royal African Company, which was responsible for both the English transatlantic slave trade and the importation of the gold from which the coins were minted.

The seventeen-year-old 'Negro Boy' named Zebulon who ran away in October 1683, a 'Negro Man' named Pall who escaped from a ship moored off Ratcliff in 1686, and an unnamed sixteen-year-old 'Negro Maid' who eloped in 1702 and could be returned to Lloyd's coffee house were all considered worthy of a one-guinea reward for any person who either recaptured them or provided information leading to their recapture.[34] Humphry, 'a middle-sized negro Man' aged about thirty, was worth a three-guinea reward, while Stephen was worth five guineas. A twenty-year-old 'Native of the Leeward Islands', well dressed in a grey livery lined with red and speaking good English, Stephen eloped in November 1701, three months after his arrival from the Caribbean. His value to William Mead was made clear by the latter's offer of '5 Guineas Reward' for information leading to his capture.[35] One guinea was a significant amount: during the second half of the seventeenth century a day's labour might earn an unskilled Englishman about 10*d* and an unskilled woman between 3*d* and 4*d*.[36] If a guinea were worth 21 shillings, it would take an unskilled man twenty-five days and an unskilled woman two months to earn one guinea.

A total of 151 of the runaway advertisements specified the value of a reward for the location or recapture of a freedom seeker, and the guinea was ubiquitous. Two offered a reward of half a guinea, seventy-five offered one guinea, thirteen offered two guineas, five offered three guineas and two promised five guineas (Figures 29 and 30). All told, ninety-seven (64 per cent) of the advertisements specified a financial reward measured in guineas. African gold had drawn English traders to the West African coast where European trade goods were exchanged for gold, some of which was then used to purchase enslaved people. Then, back in London, this same gold was used to reward anyone who recaptured an escaped enslaved person.[37]

[33] K. G. Davies, *The Royal African Company* (London, 1957), p. 181.

[34] 'A Negro Boy … whose Name is Zebulon', *London Gazette*, 11 Oct. 1683; 'RUN away … a Negro Man, named Pall', *London Gazette*, 24 May 1686; 'A black Girl', *London Gazette*, 5 Nov. 1691.

[35] 'RUN away … [a] Negro Man named Humphry', *London Gazette*, 10 Sept. 1696; 'A Negro Man, named Stephen', *London Gazette*, 24 Nov. 1701, 2.

[36] Jane Humphries and Jacob Weisdorf, 'The wages of women in England, 1260–1850', *Journal of Economic History*, lxxv (2015), 432, table A1.

[37] For more on the West African gold trade see R. Bean, 'A note on the relative importance of slaves and gold in West African exports', *Journal of African History*, xv (1974), 351–6; K. Y. Daaku, *Trade and Politics on the Gold Coast, 1600–1720* (Oxford, 1970), 21–4; C. R.

Figure 29. Five-guinea coin, Charles II, 1668,
Cleveland Museum of Art, Norweb Collection.

The Royal Exchange, the headquarters of both the Royal African Company and the East India Company; the workplaces of printers and of publishers of newspapers; the premises and homes of merchants, goldsmiths and bankers; and the coffee houses in which such people met combined to create an imperial and commercial network within the City of London. The newspaper advertisements seeking out freedom-seeking enslaved people regularly highlighted these locations and the people who operated within and between them as the key people to whom those with information concerning runaways should turn. What did this mean for the freedom seekers themselves? When Francisco escaped from Captain John Bowers in February 1688, remaining free posed a substantial challenge.[38] Not only did Francisco need to evade Bowers and his friends in Rotherhithe, but he also had to do his best to avoid being noticed by any who might report him to Stephen Evance in the heart of the City of London. To Francisco and other freedom seekers in London, the sign depicting a Black boy that hung above Evance's business premises was anything but a symbolic abstraction, for Evance and the owners of a variety of businesses in the City were deeply enmeshed in the transatlantic slave trade and in the colonial ventures built upon enslaved labour. They were committed to both the maintenance of racial slavery as it existed in London and the preservation of the property rights of enslavers within the city. Perhaps the sign of the

---

DeCorse, *An Archaeology of Elmina: Africans and Europeans on the Gold Coast, 1400–1900* (Washington, D.C., 2001), 32–6.

[38] 'AN Indian … his Name Francisco', *London Gazette*, 5 March 1688.

Figure 30. Five-guinea coin, William and Mary, 1691,
Cleveland Museum of Art, Norweb Collection.

Black boy meant little to many Londoners, existing as it did among the forest of signs identifying homes and businesses in London in the period before buildings were identified by numbers. But it surely meant much more to enslaved and bound people of colour, who knew that although they had been removed from slave ships, plantations and trading outposts they nonetheless remained subject to a society committed to their subordination. Yet some found freedom, whether for short periods or permanently. By the time Bowers placed his advertisement Francisco had been free for more than three weeks, and perhaps this newspaper advertisement was the final resort for an enslaver who feared he had lost this bound servant for good.

The City of London was the second key area for the return of recaptured freedom-seeking runaways, or for information pertaining to their whereabouts (Figure 31), the first being the riverside maritime communities to the east. Many newspaper advertisements specified that information or runaways themselves might be relayed to coffee houses and the places of business of printers, merchants and tradesmen in this section of the City. The Royal Exchange, the headquarters of the East India Company and of the Royal African Company, and eventually the Bank of England itself provided the rough boundaries of this area of imperial and colonial business, an area so thoroughly invested in and so deeply attuned to the slavery on which England's colonies depended that the public display of enslaved personal attendants and then the return of those who attempted escape were part and parcel of daily business.

Figure 31. City of London locations for the return of freedom seekers, 1659–1704. Detail from *London &c. actually surveyed by William Morgan, his ma[jes]ties cosmogr.* (London, 1681–2), Library of Congress. Graphic by the author. Also marked on the map are the East India Company, at EIC from 1638 onwards; the Royal African Company at RAC1 between the 1660s and 1677, and at RAC2 from 1677 onwards; and the Bank of England at BANK from 1694. Key coffee houses around the Royal Exchange were Jamaica (J1); Garraway's (G1); Jonathan's (J2); Lloyd's (L); Maryland (M1); Virginia (V1); Carolina (C1); Bowman's (B1); Cole's (C2); Elford's (E); Batson's (B2); Marine (M2); Royal (R); Garter (G2); Vernon's (V2).

13. *David Sugarr* and *Henry Mundy*: escaping from colonial planters in London

TWO Negroe Servants, David Sugarr *and* Henry Mundy *went away from their Master Colonel* Drax, *from his house in* Hatton-Garden, *on the 27th instant, with several of his Goods; being young men both, Pock-broken;* Mundy *hath Gold Ear-rings and is very black, the other Tauney, their Liveries are black, with grey Campain Coats and Swords. Whoever gives notice of them to their Master, so that they may be apprehended, shall have a Guinea reward for each.*

The London Gazette, 1 December 1679

What may well have been the very first newspaper advertisement for a freedom seeker in London appeared in the *Mercurius Politicus* in September 1655. Six years after the execution of Charles I and just four months after the fleet dispatched by Lord Protector Oliver Cromwell had captured Jamaica, an unnamed fourteen-year-old 'Negro Boy' in a blue livery, who ingeniously 'wears a Perriwig for disguise', eloped in London.[1] He was the first of a number of London freedom seekers who had spent part of their lives in the colonies. But this runaway was unusual in that he was 'A Negro Boy of the Lord Willoughbyes of Parham': he had escaped from Willoughby when the latter was incarcerated in the Tower of London, where the unnamed freedom seeker had resided with and served him. Willoughby was deeply involved in England's New World colonies and their developing use of enslaved Africans, and later appointed a deputy to take control of his colonial interests in Surinam. This deputy's family included the young Aphra Behn, whose experiences of racial slavery would inspire her to write *Oroonoko; or, The Royal Slave*, one of the first English-language works of prose fiction about enslaved Africans.[2] The very, very little we know of this boy who

---

[1] 'A Negro Boy', *Mercurius Politicus, Comprising the Sum of All Intelligence, with the Affairs and Designs now on foot in the three Nations of England, Scotland, & Ireland, In defence of the Commonwealth, and for Information of the People*, 20 Sept. 1655.

[2] Aphra Behn, *Oroonoko; or, The Royal Slave* (London, 1688). For Willoughby's release and his appointment of a deputy, and the likelihood of this deputy's family party including Behn, see J. Rodway, *Chronological History of the Discovery and Settlement of Guiana, 1493–1668* (Georgetown, Guyana, 1888), p. 138; L. Brown, 'The romance of empire: *Oroonoko* and the trade in slaves', in *Ends of Empire: Women and Ideology in Early Eighteenth-Century Literature*, ed. L. Brown (Ithaca, N.Y., 1993), at pp. 26–7.

escaped into a city wearied by Civil War and half-way through the Cromwellian Protectorate contrasts with the huge archival impression made by Willoughby. However, the records of Willoughby's colonial ventures may suggest something about the young freedom seeker's background, and they reveal a great deal about the ways in which elite colonial adventurers began developing and profiting from colonies built upon plantation agriculture and racial slavery, and how some of these colonists would bring enslaved people with them on their return to England.

Francis, the fifth Baron Willoughby of Parham, acceded to his title following the death of his elder brother in about 1618 (Figure 32). During the 1630s he opposed the autocratic policies of Charles I and began the Civil War as a Parliamentarian, commanding their forces in his native Lincolnshire. But in September 1647 his disagreements with Cromwell and other army commanders led to his arrest and impeachment for treason. Following his release on bail and the confiscation of his ancestral lands in Lincolnshire, Willoughby fled to Holland and declared his allegiance to Charles I. In 1647 the earl of Carlisle leased his claim to Barbados and the West Indies to Willoughby for twenty-one years. After securing Charles II's confirmation of this lease and a commission as lieutenant general of the West Indies, Willoughby sailed for Barbados in early 1650. His tenure was short-lived for in January 1652 a Parliamentary fleet with support from some Parliamentarian colonists removed Willoughby from power. Willoughby's surrender of Barbados to Sir George Ayscue included a guarantee that his own lands, plantations and property in Antigua, Barbados and Surinam would 'be to him entirely preserved'. Willoughby may have been displaced from the governorship but his control of the enslaved Africans he owned remained secure. Having been relieved of his command, Willoughby travelled back to England via the nascent colony of Surinam. While attempting to regain control of his sequestered family lands in Lincolnshire, he gave his support to a planned Royalist uprising in the spring of 1655, and it was this failed rebellion that resulted in his imprisonment in the Tower of London between June 1655 and September 1657.[3]

[3] 'Patent from Jas. Earl of Carlisle to Fras. Lord Willoughby of Parham, constituting him Lieut.-general of the Caribbee Islands, "for the batter settling and securing" of them for 21 years from Michalmas 1646', 26 Feb. 1647, 'America and West Indies: February 1647', in *Calendar of State Papers Colonial, America and West Indies*: i, *1574–1660*, ed. W. N. Sainsbury (London, 1860), p. 327, *British History Online* <http://www.british-history.ac.uk/cal-state-papers/colonial/america-west-indies/vol1/p327c> [accessed 27 April 2020]; 'Articles agreed on by Lord Willoughby of Parham and Sir Geo. Ayscue, Daniel Searle, and Capt. Michael Packe for the rendition of Barbadoes to Sir Geo. Ayscue, General of the State's fleet before said island, for the use and behoof of the Parliament of the Commonwealth of England', 'America and West Indies: Addenda 1652', in *Calendar of State Papers Colonial, America and West Indies*: ix, *1675–1676 and Addenda 1574–1674*, ed. W. N. Sainsbury (London, 1893), pp. 85–7, *British History Online* <http://www.british-history.ac.uk/cal-state-papers/colonial/america-west-indies/vol9/pp85-87> [accessed 27

VERITÉ SANS PAIR

NOBILISS: DŪS FRANCISCUS WILLUGHBYE
BARO DE PARHAM etc.

Pub.ᵈ March 1.1798 by Edw.ᵈ Harding Nᵒ 98 Pall Mall.

Figure 32. 'Francis Willoughby, 5th Baron Willoughby of Parham', published
by Edward Harding (1798), National Portrait Gallery, London.

April 2020]; 'To receive into the Tower Lord Newport, And. Newport, his brother, Francis Lord Willoughby of Parham … and keep them in safe custody till delivered in course of law', 9 June 1655, in *Calendar of State Papers, Domestic Series, [Commonwealth] 1649–1660, preserved in the State Paper Department of Her Majesty's Public Record Office*, viii: *January–October 1655*, ed. M. A. Everett Green (London, 1881), p. 164. For biographical details of Willoughby see S. Barber, 'Power in the English Caribbean: the proprietorship of Lord Willoughby of Parham', in *Constructing Early Modern Empires: Proprietary Ventures in the Atlantic World, 1500–1750*, ed. L. H. Roper and B. Van Ruymbeke (Leiden, 2007), pp. 189–212; M. A. LaCombe, 'Francis, fifth Baron Willoughby of Parham' (2004), *Oxford Dictionary of National Biography* <https://doi.org/10.1093/ref:odnb/29597> [accessed 27 April 2020]; M. Parker, *Willoughbyland: England's Lost Colony* (London, 2015).

After his first arrival in Barbados in 1650 Willoughby had written a long letter to his wife Elizabeth: 'since all is gone at home it is time to provide elsewhere for a being.' He described Barbados enthusiastically as 'one of the best and sweetest islands in the English possession' and Surinam as 'the sweetest place that ever was seen', and promised to send sugar to her as a valuable commodity with which she might compensate unnamed third parties who had loaned her money. But what was only implicit in this letter was that Willoughby's hope of a restoration of his own fortune and property rested on the importation and exploitation of enslaved Africans. His only mention of such people in this correspondence was an aside about the utility of 'negroes, which are the best servants in these countries, if well tutored'.[4] It was during the 1650s, with the English Civil War little more than an inconvenient distraction, that Royalists and Parliamentarians in Barbados were transitioning from White bound and indentured servants to enslaved Africans, and Willoughby believed that a constant supply of enslaved labour was essential to the success of the colonial endeavour and the production of sugar. In about 1655 Willoughby proposed a series of incentives for all 'Such as are able & willing to transport themselves at their own charge' to Surinam. In addition to fifty acres of land per adult and thirty acres per child, Willoughby promised to advance provisions and tools as well as enslaved 'Negroes'.[5]

Some seven years later, following the Restoration and Willoughby's resumption of his governorship of Barbados and Surinam, and with sugar production generating tremendous profits, Willoughby and the Barbados Council sought assurances that the Royal African Company would furnish a sufficient number of enslaved Africans at reasonable prices. The duke of York, the company's governor, responded to Willoughby by promising to supply at least 3,000 Africans annually.[6] Although Willoughby's estate in England had been restored to him, it was his plantations in Barbados, Surinam and Antigua that significantly increased his wealth. When Willoughby was lost with his ship in a hurricane in 1666 his will left his plantations in Surinam, Barbados and Antigua to his children and grandchildren, as well as numerous bequests, including a grant of 100,000 pounds of sugar annually

---

[4] Lord Willoughby to Lady Willoughby, *c.*1651, in *Memorials of the Great Civil War in England from 1646 to 1652, edited from the Original Letters in the Bodleian Library*, ed. H. Cary (London, 1842), ii. 317, 314, 316, 312.

[5] 'Certain Overtures Made by Ye Lord Willoughby of Parham Unto All Such As Shall Incline to Plant in Ye Colonye of Saranam on ye Continent of Guiaiana', British Library, Sloane MS. 159, fol. 21.

[6] G. F. Zook, 'The Company of Royal Adventurers trading into Africa' (unpublished Cornell University PhD thesis, 1919), p. 74.

to his nephew Henry Willoughby, 50,000 pounds of Muscovado sugar to Peter La Rouse 'for his constant care', 20,000 pounds of sugar to Jane Frith 'for her faithful care in the government' of his family, and 20,000 pounds of sugar to each of his five executors. Sugar was as significant a currency in his will as land or money, an object of enormous value. Yet the enslaved who produced it were not mentioned, an invisible yet essential part of the wealth that Willoughby bequeathed to his heirs.[7]

Willoughby had spent only two months in 1652 in Surinam – which he called Willoughbyland – before returning to England. Quite possibly he had brought the enslaved young boy who would escape from him in London from Barbados via Surinam, for, like Willoughby himself, a good number of the early Surinam settlers had come from Barbados, bringing with them enslaved workers, and the first English ship bringing enslaved Africans directly from Africa to Surinam did not arrive until 1664. The arrival of that ship, the *Swallow*, was referred to in a letter that mentions 'The Ladeyes' who 'live at St Johnes hill', quite possibly Behn and her mother and sisters; perhaps this was the slave ship that at least partially inspired Behn's later description of the Middle Passage in *Oroonoko*.[8]

In 1652, more than a decade earlier, Willoughby had sailed back to England, probably with an enslaved boy as his personal attendant, and three years later this boy took advantage of Willoughby's incarceration to escape. The freedom seeker was part of an unknown number of enslaved people owned by the aristocrat, most if not all of whom had been born in Africa. Over the eleven years between the arrival of the first slave ship in Barbados in 1641 and Willoughby's departure in 1652 records survive for thirty of these ships depositing more than 6,600 enslaved Africans on the island. The African regions from which twenty-one of these ships sailed are known, and of these 67 per cent came from Calabar and the Bight of Benin, so this was the most likely point of origin for the young runaway.[9] This

---

[7] Will of Francis Lord Willoughby of Parham, 17 July 1666 (proved 10 May 1678), National Archives, PROB 11/356/511.

[8] 'Letters to Sir Robert Harley from the Stewards of his Plantation in Surinam, 1663–1664', repr. in *Colonising Expeditions to the West Indies and Guiana, 1623–1667*, ed. V. T. Harlow, 2nd series, no. 56 (London, 1925), p. 90. This first transatlantic slave ship to arrive in Surinam was the *Swallow*, which landed 130 enslaved Africans in Feb. 1664. See Voyage of the *Swallow*, Voyage 9587 in Slave Voyages: Trans-Atlantic Slave Trade – Database <https://www.slavevoyages.org/voyage/database> [accessed 27 April 2020]. See also J. Roberts, 'Surrendering Surinam: the Barbadian diaspora and the expansion of the English sugar frontier, 1650–75', *William and Mary Quarterly*, 3rd series, lxxviii (2016), 225–56; Parker, *Willoughbyland*, p. 166.

[9] It is very likely that there were more voyages but that records of these have not survived or have not yet been added to the Slaves Voyages database, but these 30 (and the 20 for

region was home to various political and ethno-linguistic groups, and the boy might have come from the Igbo, Ibibio, Duala or any of a number of such communities.[10]

While it is tempting to wonder if this young African met Aphra Behn and perhaps influenced *Oroonoko*, it is impossible given that when he escaped she was fifteen and living in Canterbury. She would not meet Willoughby until the 1660s, and her story was probably shaped by the people she met during her own visit to Surinam.[11] Behn described Oroonoko as a native of 'Coramantien' on the Gold Coast, a different people from a different region some 800 miles to the east of the probable home region of the freedom seeker who had eloped from Willoughby. Yet some of what Behn described, presumably gleaned from her own observations and perhaps from discussions with the enslaved themselves and with the Whites who trafficked and enslaved them, might easily have applied to the Africans who sought liberty in London. Thus, for example, she described the country marks inscribed on the bodies of some West Africans as 'so delicately Cut and Rac'd all over the fore-part of the Trunk of their Bodies, that it looks as if it were Japan'd; the Works being raised like high Poynt round the Edges of the Flowers. Some are only Carv'd ... at the Sides of the Temples'.[12] Today most historians believe that Behn visited Surinam, but whether or not she did, it is entirely possible that the enslaved and free Africans she encountered in London may very well have helped inspire and shape *Oroonoko*.

Elite and aristocratic prisoners held in the Tower of London were sometimes afforded relatively comfortable apartments in which they might be attended by personal servants and to which food and other goods were brought in. These servants could come and go, perhaps running errands and delivering or receiving messages and goods for those they served, making escape for this particular young African a real possibility. And perhaps he had attempted escape before, given that Willoughby's advertisement noted that 'he wears a Perriwig for disguise'. It seems unlikely that a highly stylized English wig could have disguised a fourteen-year-old African boy, so this may indicate a broader contemporary usage of the word 'disguise' meaning to dress, cover or conceal,

---

which no point of origin is recorded) provide an indication of where many of the first generation of enslaved Africans in Barbados had originated.

[10] Map 83, 'Political and ethnolinguistic boundaries along the Bight of Biafra during the slave-trade era', in D. Eltis and D. Richardson, *Atlas of the Transatlantic Slave Trade* (New Haven, Conn., 2010), p. 125.

[11] J. Todd, *The Secret Life of Aphra Behn* (London, 1996), pp. 14–15. See also E. Campbell, 'Aphra Behn's Surinam interlude', *Kunapipi*, vii (1985), 25–35; Brown, 'The romance of empire'; K. M. Rogers, 'Fact and fiction in Aphra Behn's '"Oroonoko"', *Studies in the Novel*, xx (1988), 1–15.

[12] Behn, *Oroonoko*, p. 139.

in this case covering the boy's own hair. Whatever Willoughby meant, he was clearly indicating a knowledge of the ability of this young boy to at least partially conceal his identity as the enslaved property of another man, and to travel unhindered around London. The young freedom seeker escaped into Cromwell's London, the metropolitan hub of a fast-expanding commercial empire. An English naval force had captured Jamaica a few months before this young freedom seeker eloped from Willoughby: whatever the domestic situation, and regardless of whether parliament or the king ruled, England's slave empire was rapidly expanding.

Willoughby was one of a significant number of colonial governors, planters, merchants and others who brought enslaved people back to London. While Willoughby spent only a relatively short period of time in Barbados and Surinam, other Englishmen settled in the colonies and in some cases established large and successful plantations built upon enslaved labour. One of these was Henry Drax, who established one of the first Barbados plantations to grow and process sugar. He built Drax Hall on the plantation in the 1650s, a mighty English country house that is owned to this day by his descendants and that continues to dominate St George parish as one of two surviving Jacobean plantation houses on the island. By the time of the Barbados census of 1680, Drax was one of the island's largest and wealthiest planters, owning more than 700 acres and 327 enslaved Africans, and shipped £5,000 worth of sugar to England annually.[13] But a year earlier, and by then fabulously wealthy, Drax had sailed to London never to return to his Barbados plantations again. He took with him at least two enslaved 'Negroe Servants, *David Sugarr* and *Henry Mundy*', both of whom eloped from Drax some four months after their arrival in the capital. They were dressed as befitted their role as servants to a very wealthy man who was living in a fashionable house in Hatton Garden, 'very gracefully built, and well inhabited by Gentry'. The freedom seekers' 'Liveries are black, with grey Campain Coats and Swords' and '*Mundy* hath Gold Ear-rings'.[14]

Before leaving Barbados Drax had written detailed instructions for Richard Harwood, the man he employed to manage his plantation in his absence. These provide the most detailed guide to the lives and working conditions for enslaved Africans during the early years of English sugar plantations. An arduous agricultural regimen was matched by several months of

---

[13] Barbados Census, Sir J. Atkins to Mr Blathwayt, 1 April 1680, CO 1/44, item 47, 173; R. S. Dunn, 'The Barbados census of 1680: profile of the richest colony in English America', *William and Mary Quarterly*, xxvi (1969), 3–30, at p. 4.

[14] 'Two Negroe Servants', *London Gazette*, 1 Dec. 1679. 'Hatton Garden', in J. Strype, *A Survey of the Cities of London and Westminster ... written at first in the year MDXCVIII by John Stow ...* (London, 1720), i. 255–6.

semi-industrialized processing of the crop, so that semi-refined sugar, molasses and rum could be exported to England. Decades of intensive agriculture had exhausted the island's soil, and the work regime described by Drax and designed by him and others to extract sugar and profit from people and the land involved an almost unimaginable amount of back-breaking labour. With blithe indifference, Drax told Harwood that to keep sugar agriculture and production on track it would be necessary 'to supply the places of those who shall be deseased or Dy' by annually purchasing fifteen or so 'Choyce Young Negros', implying that all members of the sizeable original workforce he left to Harwood would have died within little more than twenty years.[15]

Drax was right and enslaved Africans died in astonishing numbers in mid- to late seventeenth-century Barbados. The 1680 census recorded a total of 38,782 enslaved people on the island, even though an estimated 116,000 had been brought to Barbados between 1626 and 1675.[16] Few people had been born, but many had died. One might assume that for Sugarr and Mundy, the former named for the crop that had made Drax so wealthy, life in London would have been infinitely preferable to the harsh working conditions and early death facing them on the Drax Hall plantation. We cannot know the circumstances of their escape shortly after arriving in London: perhaps Drax was a cruel master, and maybe he had threatened to return them to plantation slavery. These men had probably experienced the Middle Passage and then plantation slavery: even if their working lives in London were dramatically better than they would have been in Barbados, Sugarr and Mundy knew what White Englishmen were capable of doing to enslaved Africans, and that a return to the horrors of the Caribbean was always possible. Whatever the immediate cause, these young men chose to take their chances. Escape in London may have been somewhat easier and less dangerous than it would have been in Barbados, and perhaps the opportunity to seek out a new life was too tempting.

Henry Drax died in 1682, some three years after David Sugarr and Henry Mundy had eloped. His will detailed the disposal of extensive land and property holdings but contained no direct mention of the enslaved people he owned in the colonies or perhaps in England. Drax allowed his wife £400 per annum 'to be paid her out of the yearly produce of my Plantation in Barbados', as well as bequests to others 'out of the profits of my Barbados estate'. Drax's male heir would receive a life interest in 'All my Manors, Lands Tenements Plantations … whatsoever with their appurtenances

---

[15] P. Thompson, 'Henry Drax's instructions on the management of a seventeenth-century Barbadian sugar plantation', *William and Mary Quarterly*, 3rd series, lxvi (2009), 565–604, at p. 585.

[16] Estimates function, Slave Voyages: Trans-Atlantic Slave Trade database.

whatsoever in England and Barbados'.[17] The enslaved who had generated all this wealth were no more than 'appurtenances', and neither those in Barbados nor any in England were identified. David Sugarr and Henry Mundy may have been returned to Barbados, or perhaps they were still in England and either bound in service to the Drax household or free.

Nine years later, on 25 October 1691, Hannah Sophia Drax was baptized at St Martin in the Fields, which lay about one and a half miles south-west of Drax's home in Hatton Garden. The parish register recorded that Hannah was the daughter 'of Henry Drax a Negroe & Sarah'.[18] Was Henry Drax the same Henry Mundy who as a young man had eloped from Drax in 1679? If so, why had he taken the name Drax? Perhaps it was a mark of gratitude for having his freedom recognized by Drax, or perhaps for his position as a nominally free servant: London's parish records suggest that at least some people of colour took on English last names, especially when seeking baptism or marriage. The name Drax was synonymous with colonial wealth and power and may have helped Henry Drax make his way in London. If Henry Drax's wife Sarah had been Black, this would almost certainly have been registered in the parish record, as for her husband, so the absence of any indication means that she was probably White. If Henry Drax was indeed the man who had attempted to escape from the planter Henry Drax over a decade earlier, this simple baptismal record suggests that at least some of London's runaways ended up free, whether through their own agency or because their actions encouraged enslavers in England to make provision for these bound workers' freedom.

Just a couple of years before Hannah's baptism, another bound servant of a colonial planter escaped in London. Born in Barbados, Anthony was described in an advertisement as 'a black above 20 years old … tall, and well set' and with 'a broad full Visage'. Speaking 'very good English', he wore 'his hair longer and fuller than Ginney blacks' from West Africa.[19] The advertisement began with the formulaic statement 'RUN away from Mr. William Bird', who was almost certainly William Byrd I, the owner of Westover, one of Virginia's largest plantations. The son of a London goldsmith named John Bird, William Byrd I had travelled to Virginia in 1670 at the invitation of his maternal uncle Thomas Stegge, and a year later

---

[17] Will of Henry Drax of Saint Giles in the Fields, 20 Sept. 1682, National Archives, PROB 11/370/554.

[18] Baptism of Hannah Sophia Drax, 25 Oct. 1691, Baptized, Parish Register 1681–1692, St Martin in the Fields, 151. London Metropolitan Archives, London, England, STM/PR/6/32. Digitized copy of original consulted at <https://www.ancestry.co.uk> [accessed 1 April 2021].

[19] 'RUN away from Mr. William Bird … Anthony', *London Gazette*, 9 Aug. 1688.

Byrd inherited Stegge's estate. He married Mary Horsmanden in 1673, and all five of their children were sent back to England for their education under the watchful eye of Mary's family.[20]

In the spring of 1687 William Byrd I had sailed to England, where he succeeded in securing several major appointments, including deputy auditor and receiver general of revenues in Virginia. Presumably he also visited his children including his son William Byrd II, then about thirteen years old and in school but soon to begin working for the mercantile firm of Micajah Perry and Thomas Lane. Specialists in the Barbados and Virginia trade, Perry and Lane handled much of the Byrd family's business. William Byrd I left England for Virginia on 19 January 1688, some seven months before Anthony eloped. Had he left Anthony with family or business associates in London or as a personal servant for his son? The advertisement specified that if captured Anthony should be returned to Edward Bird in Durham Yard in the Strand, perhaps a member of the large extended family descended from John Bird.[21]

Anthony's birth in Barbados can easily be explained by the fact that William Byrd I – like other Virginians of this era – regularly purchased enslaved people from Barbados, and his correspondence with Perry and Lane (the merchants with whom his son would gain work experience) includes instructions to purchase enslaved people and goods from the island. On 30 December 1684, for example, William Byrd I asked the merchants to secure from Barbados '5 or 6 Negro's between 12 and 24 years old[,] about 1000 gallons of rum[,] 3 to 4000 pounds of sugar (muscovado) & abou[t] 200 pounds ginger'. A year later he wrote to another firm about his desire to purchase from Barbados '4 Negro's, 2 men 2 women not to exceed 25 years old & to bee likely', and he would later write that these 'Negro's proved well'.[22] Perhaps Anthony was one of these, and because Byrd was pleased

---

[20] The extensive family in London used both Bird and Byrd, and it was only later in life that William Byrd I began using only Byrd.

[21] While it is possible that Anthony belonged to a William Bird with no connection to the Byrds of Westover, there is no evidence of anyone with that surname in London having any kind of connection to the plantation colonies who might have owned an enslaved African. For the Byrd family in Virginia and London see *The Correspondence of the Three William Byrds of Westover, Virginia, 1684–1776*, ed. M. Tingling and L. B. Wright (Charlottesville, Va., 1987), i. 4; P. Marambaud, *William Byrd of Westover, 1674–1744* (Charlottesville, Va., 1971), pp. 15–17; *The Commonplace Book of William Byrd II of Westover*, ed. K. Berland, J. K. Gilliam, and K. A. Lockridge (Chapel Hill, N.C., 2001), pp. 7–9.

[22] W. Byrd I to M. Perry and T. Lane, 30 Dec. 1684, in *Correspondence of the Three William Byrds*, p. 29; W. Byrd I to Sadler and Thomas, merchants in Barbados, 10 Feb. 1686, pp. 50–1; Byrd to Sadler and Thomas, 18 Oct. 1686, p. 65.

with the young enslaved man's performance of his duties he had decided to take him to London, and then leave him there to serve his family.

It was not just colonial planters who used enslaved people to serve them during their visits to London. In late 1702, for example, the Barbados merchant Benjamin Quelch brought with him to London a young enslaved Black woman. Described in his advertisement as 'A Negro Maid, aged about 16 Years', she was 'much pitted with the Small-Pox, speaks English well, having a piece of her left Ear bit off by a Dog'. Only an unusual accident could have caused the latter injury, and it is possible that dogs had chased and bitten her during an earlier escape attempt in the colonies. She may have been serving both Quelch and his wife Elizabeth when she eloped on 8 December, and a first advertisement on 12 December was followed by a second on 2 January 1703, by which point the young woman had been at liberty for three weeks.[23] A year later Quelch and his wife would join the exodus from Barbados to South Carolina, taking enslaved people with him and buying land and establishing his business in the new colony. If she had been recaptured in London and brought back to Barbados, it is possible that this young woman would have been part of the human property Quelch transferred to South Carolina. But if she had eluded Quelch and had not been returned to him or to his representative 'Mr Lloyd, at his Coffee House', what might have happened to her? Well-dressed and experienced personal servants of colour were highly desirable appendages to the households of affluent Londoners and were beginning to appear in portraits of such people, human emblems of their wealth and success. With her experience and her proficiency in English, perhaps this young woman could have secured employment in such a household on her own terms rather than as the enslaved property of a man who would return her to Barbados and then South Carolina where her options would be far more limited and her situation far worse. Or perhaps she had found somebody with whom she might seek refuge. She might also have fallen prey to those who would not hesitate to seize her and sell her to a captain of a ship heading to West Africa or directly to the colonies where she might be sold at a handsome profit.[24]

---

[23] 'A Negro Maid', *The Flying Post: Or, The Post-Master*, 12 Dec. 1702; 'A Negro Maid', *The Post Man: And The Historical Account*, 2 Jan. 1703.

[24] J. P. Greene, 'Colonial South Carolina and the Caribbean connection', in *Imperatives, Behaviors, and Identities: Essays in Early American Cultural History*, ed. J. P. Greene (Charlottesville, Va., 1992), at p. 74; R. Waterhouse, 'England, the Caribbean, and the settlement of Carolina', *Journal of American Studies*, ix (1975), at p. 277; H. A. M. Smith, 'Georgetown: the original plan and the earliest settlers', *South Carolina Historical and Genealogical Magazine*, ix (1908), at p. 85.

Some colonists, like Henry Drax, made their fortunes and then returned permanently to England. One such was Captain Richard Pery, who had been born in London but then emigrated and made his fortune as a merchant ship captain and planter in Maryland. He returned to London in about 1672, retaining his Maryland plantation while establishing a trading business in London. This trade may have included enslaved people, for a decade later 'a Black Boy, aged about 10 years, born in Mary Land, [who] speaks only English' escaped from Pery.[25] Similarly, Samuel Tidcombe had returned from Barbados to take up residence in Little Chelsea, which lay a little over a mile south-west of Westminster. Tidcombe had married a wealthy Barbados heiress named Anna Kendall, and he had represented St Lucy parish in the Barbados Assembly (at the same time that Henry Drax was a member of the Bajan Governor's Council), and the 1680 census revealed him to own a 300-acre plantation and 135 enslaved people.[26] Perhaps one of these was John Mings, 'A Blackamore Foot-man' who escaped from Tidcombe in August 1683. Mings was 'three and thirty years of Age, middle sized, with the sign of the Small-Pox in his face', and he was dressed smartly in a 'dark coloured Livery lined with Crimson, and Brass Buttons'.[27]

Another migrant from Barbados was Sir Edwyn Stede. He had travelled to Barbados as a government official and had become the Royal African Company's agent on the island. Between 1685 and 1690 Stede served as governor of Barbados, after which he returned to London with at least one enslaved servant in tow. On 14 June 1694 Quomino (also known as Thomas Baker) eloped from Stede's house in Great Queen Street, just west of Lincoln's Inn Fields in the parish of St Giles in the Fields. This thirty-year-old freedom seeker's original name indicated that he had probably been born in West Africa, and his new name may have been acquired in London rather than Barbados. Stede reported that Quomino 'speaks

[25] 'ON Thursday the 11th … a Black Boy', *London Gazette*, 18 May 1682. See 'Perry (Pery), Richard', in *A Biographical Dictionary of the Maryland Legislature 1635–1789*, ed. E. C. Papenfuse, A. F. Day, D. W. Jordan and G. A. Stiverson (Baltimore, Md., 1985), ii. 644. There exist various documents relating to Pery's Maryland property: see R. Pery, letter of attorney, 12 Nov. 1674 in *Proceedings of the Provincial Court of Maryland 1670/1–1675, Court Series (10), Archives of Maryland LXV*, ed. E. Merritt (Baltimore, Md. 1952), p. 470; Petition of C. Rousby to manage the affairs of Captain R. Pery, in *Proceedings of the Council of Maryland, 1671–1681*, ed. W. H. Browne (Baltimore, Md., 1896), pp. 76–7.
[26] Barbados Census, p. 217. For Tidcombe's service as an assemblyman see 'Names of the Assembly', 1 April 1680, 'America and West Indies: April 1680', in *Calendar of State Papers Colonial, America and West Indies: x, 1677–1680*, ed. W. N. Sainsbury and J. W. Fortescue (London, 1896), pp. 507–21, *British History Online* <http://www.british-history.ac.uk/cal-state-papers/colonial/america-west-indies/vol10/pp507-521> [accessed 30 April 2020].
[27] 'A Blackamore Foot-man named John Mings', *London Gazette*, 13 Aug. 1683.

English very well', and this, together with years of experience of domestic service, equipped the man to seek freedom in London. Escape was a wise move, for when Stede died a year later his will ordered his executors to take possession of 'my Negro Servants both here and in Barbados and also my lands and Plantations and all my estate in Barbados' and 'sell the same as soon as may be conveniently [*sic*]', with the proceeds to be placed in trust for his son Dutton. Informed by decades of living in Barbados as racial slavery hardened, Edwyn Stede regarded Quomino and the other enslaved people he owned as property, whether they were in Barbados or in London. He did not hesitate to order the sale and probable transportation back to the plantation colonies of people who had served him in London. Little wonder, then, that Quomino sought freedom.[28]

That Barbados was the source of so many of the enslaved Africans brought to Restoration London is not surprising. Between 1627 and 1700 some 236,725 enslaved Africans were taken to Barbados, while during that same period as few as 16,152 enslaved Africans were transported to the Chesapeake colonies of Virginia and Maryland, and 119,208 to the newly acquired colony of Jamaica.[29] The 1680 Barbados census revealed that Colonel William Allambey owned a 101-acre plantation with thirty-seven enslaved people in St Thomas parish, and served as a member of the Governor's Council. When he returned from Barbados to England be brought with him Jemmy, a twenty-four-year-old 'very black Negro Man … woolley Hair'd, well set, middle Statured'. Allambey reported that Jemmy 'speaks good English, but [is] somewhat slow of Speech'. In a separate and longer advertisement Allambey listed the goods he believed the resourceful Jemmy had stolen when he escaped, including notes of debt, bonds and lottery tickets, twenty-seven guineas in gold, and three rings. This represented a significant theft: if Jemmy remained at liberty these items may well have helped him forge a new life, but if he were recaptured he would almost certainly have faced a significant punishment.[30]

[28] 'A Negro Servant run away from his Master … his Name was Quomino', *London Gazette*, 18 June 1694; Will of Sir Edwyn Stede, 7 Sept. 1695, National Archives, PROB 11/429/154. For further information about Stede in Barbados, see R. S. Dunn, *Sugar and Slaves: the Rise of the Planter Class in the English West Indies, 1624–1713* (Chapel Hill, N.C., 1972), pp. 101, 197.

[29] See S. P. Newman, *A New World of Labor: the Development of Plantation Slavery in the British Atlantic* (Philadelphia, Pa., 2013), p. 1.

[30] Barbados Census, p. 224; Note of Barbados Council membership in *Calendar of State Papers, Colonial Series, America and West Indies, 1689–1692*, ed. J. W. Fortescue (London, 1901), xiii. 636; 'Jemmy, alias James, a very black Negro Man', *London Gazette*, 3 June 1700; 'Stolen the 28th Instant out of Colonel William Allamby's Lodgings', *London Gazette*, 30 May 1700.

Among the White men who brought enslaved people to London on a more temporary basis were colonial ship captains, and one of these was a slave-ship captain from New England named Thomas Edwards. In 1676 Edwards had captained the *Society* on a slave-trading voyage to Madagascar, quite possibly the first such direct voyage from the American colonies to this island in the Indian Ocean. It was perhaps on this voyage that Edwards had acquired Joseph as a young teenager, and several years later the 'Answers from Massachusetts' to a series of questions posed by the Committee for Trade and Plantations recalled the arrival in the colony of Edwards's ship. Noting that 'No Company of blacks has been brought there [Massachusetts] for fifty years from the beginning of the plantation' the report then described the exception, 'one small vessel … after 20 months voyage from Madagascar with 40 or 50 negroes', a reference to Edwards's ship the *Society*.[31] Twelve years later in October 1688 'a Malegasco Negro Man, his Name … Joseph, aged about 25' eloped from Edwards in London.[32] If Joseph had been aboard the *Society*, this was an example of an enslaved person seeking liberty in London after a relatively long period of enslavement, probably spent in New England and on board Edwards's ships. Edwards continued his slave-trading voyages, and if this had been Joseph's background perhaps he no longer wanted to participate in these voyages. Alternatively, he may have preferred the possibilities open to him in London rather than the life he faced on board ship or back in Boston.

Whether freedom seekers who escaped in London were running from colonists who were either temporarily in the capital or who had moved back to their permanent residence in England, these people of colour may have felt particularly vulnerable to being trafficked back to the colonies. The men who commanded them were intimately connected with colonial societies and regularly travelled to or communicated with them. An enslaved servant who displeased their master might easily find themselves being transported back to the plantation colonies, or sold back to the colonies after their master's death. Whatever their motivations, a significant number of the bound servants of colonists in London did not hesitate to seek freedom.

---

[31] Voyage of the *Society*, Voyage 21510 in Slave Voyages: Trans-Atlantic Slave Trade database; 'Answers from Massachusetts to the 27 inquiries of the Committee for trade and Plantations', 18 May, Boston, 'America and West Indies: May 1680, 17–31', in *Calendar of State Papers Colonial, America and West Indies*: x, *1677–1680*, pp. 524–43, *British History Online* <http://www.british-history.ac.uk/cal-state-papers/colonial/america-west-indies/vol10/pp524-543> [accessed 30 April 2020]. See also L. Mosca, 'Slaving in Madagascar: English and colonial voyages in the second half of the 17th century AD', in *Tadia, the African Diaspora in Asia: Explorations on a Less Known Fact*, ed. K. K. Prasad and J. P. Angenot (Bangalore, 2008), pp. 595, 604–5. The voyage of the *Society* was also recorded in *Précis of the Archives of the Cape of Good Hope: Journal, 1671–1674 & 1676*, ed. H. C. V. Leibbrandt (Cape Town, 1902), pp. 249, 303.

[32] 'RUN away … Joseph', *London Gazette*, 8 Oct. 1688.

14. *Calib* and *'a Madagascar Negro'*: freedom seekers in the London suburbs and beyond

Run away from his Master, Charles Pope of Bristol, on Saturday the 17th past, an Indian Boy, about 14 years old, strait black hair, with a sandy coloured Coat, lined with straw coloured Crape, with a grey cloth Cap lined with red Serge, his name Calib. Whoever gives notice of him to Mr. Walter Masters in St. Martins-lane, London, or at the Royal Coffee House over against the Royal Exchange London, or to his aforesaid Master, shall have 20s. Reward.

The London Gazette, 12 November 1685

Run away the 13th instant from Mr. Nath. White, a Madagascar Negro, aged about 15, in an old grey Coat, Linnen flower'd Breeches, blue Stockings, without a Hat or Cap, and lately come from India. Whoever secures him, and gives Notice to Mr. Baker, an Apothecary in Cheapside, London, or to Mr. White at Ipswich in Suffolk, shall have a Guinea Reward and Charges.

London Gazette, 23 July 1691

Freedom seekers from outside London either escaped in their own localities and made their way to the capital or during visits there while accompanying those they served. Of the 174 runaway advertisements that include a clear indication of where the runaway had escaped from, twenty-five specified locations outside London. An unnamed 'Negro about 18 years old' escaped 'from Hogsden in Hertfordshire, and is about London'.[1] Neither the freedom seeker nor the person he escaped from are named in the advertisement, and it is unclear how the latter knew the former was in the capital, although London was a highly likely destination. This young man would have faced challenges in making the journey of perhaps twenty-five miles to London, for he 'speaks very little English', but a week after his escape he was still free. In early March 1691 'a Negro named Philip' escaped from 'Mr. William Alexander at Malden-Ash in Essex'. Alexander appears to have been a London merchant of that name with a family home in Ongar, the Essex parish in which the hamlet of

---

[1] 'A Negro about 18 years old', *London Gazette*, 8 Sept. 1684.

Marden Ash is situated.[2] Salvador, 'A Black about 25 years of Age', escaped in Gravesend in Kent in late May 1692. Despite being unable to speak English, he was still at liberty three weeks later because he had either disappeared into London some twenty miles to the west or had joined one of the many vessels moored by or passing Gravesend as they headed out to sea.[3] The identity of the person seeking and claiming Salvador is unclear, but he could be returned 'to Mr. Peter Hobland in Sice-lane' in Cheapside. This was Peter Houblon, a member of a well-established Huguenot family of London merchants, and the nephew of Sir John Houblon who served both as lord mayor of London and the first governor of the Bank of England. Several members of the Houblon family were shareholders in and directors of the East India Company.[4]

Other freedom seekers appear to have eloped while in London with enslavers whose permanent residence lay outside of the city. In July 1691 'a Madagascar Negro' eloped from Nathaniel White.[5] The unnamed freedom seeker was 'aged about 15, in an old grey Coat, Linnen flower'd Breeches, blue Stockings, without a Hat or Cap, and lately come from India'. He could be returned for the reward of one guinea and charges to an apothecary named Baker in Cheapside or to the man who claimed ownership of him, 'Mr. White at Ipswich in Suffolk', some eighty miles north-east of the capital. White was a surgeon in Ipswich, which may explain his connection with the London apothecary Baker.[6] It is unclear how or why Nathaniel White was in possession of a young and newly arrived enslaved person, but it is not surprising that this young man sought to escape. Ipswich was a sleepy Suffolk market town which probably contained few if any other people of colour.

---

[2] 'RUN away … a Negro named Philip', *London Gazette*, 19 March 1691. Marden Ash in the parish of Ongar may well be the Malden-Ash specified in the advertisement. It is about 30 miles north-east of the City of London. Will of William Alexander, Gentleman of Chipping Ongar, Essex, 1672, National Archives, PROB 11/340/11; Will of William Alexander, Merchant of London, 1726, National Archives, PROB 11/607/116.

[3] 'A Black … his Name Salvador', *London Gazette*, 16 June 1692.

[4] Peter Houblon, Junir, is listed as living in Sice Lane in S. Lee, *The Little London Directory of 1677: the Oldest Printed List of the Merchants and Bankers of London* (London, 1863). His will makes clear his relationship to other members of the family, including his uncle Sir John Houblon (Will of Peter Houblon, Merchant of London Saint Peter Westcheap, National Archives, PROB 11/483/240). For details of John Houblon's life see H. G. Roseveare, 'Sir John Houblon' (2004), *Oxford Dictionary of National Biography* <https://doi.org/10.1093/ref:odnb/13861> [accessed 1 May 2020].

[5] 'Run away … a Madagascar Negro', *London Gazette*, 23 July 1691.

[6] Nathaniel White was named as a surgeon in documents related to the case of R. Barnard innholder, of Ipswich, Suffolk v. N. White surgeon, of Ipswich, Suffolk, Court of Chancery (Six Clerks Office, Records of Equity, Records created, acquired, and inherited by Chancery, National Archives, C 6/360/16).

In July 1677 'A Negro Man, by name *Anthony*' escaped 'from Colonel *Cowper* of *Dickham* place, in the Counties of *Sussex* and *Hampshire*'.[7] It is not clear whether Anthony, who was about twenty-four years old, 'of a middle stature, very bushy hair, much pock-broken, and in old ragged Cloathes', escaped from Cowper's home on the Sussex and Hampshire border, or if he seized the opportunity of escaping during a visit with Cowper to the capital. Cowper advertised for Anthony six weeks after his escape, so the freedom seeker was at liberty for at least that length of time, probably in London. Cowper gave two contacts to whom Anthony might be returned, both in the capital: Thomas Vyle, a bookseller, printer and newspaper editor 'at the Office of the *City Mercury* at the Northwest corner of the *Royal Exchange*', and William Jeston, a smith at the sign of the Scythe and Frying Pan in Clerkenwell.[8]

Over a period of three years two people escaped from a Bristol merchant named Charles Pope. In mid-November 1685 Calib, 'an Indian Boy, about 14 years old', escaped from Pope, followed three years later by Gambo, a thirty-five-year old 'Negro man' (also known as John Gobe).[9] Both advertisements referred to 'Charles Pope of Bristol', so the two freedom seekers may have escaped from him there or about 115 miles to the east in London, for Pope's business regularly took him to the capital. Pope's father, Thomas, was also a Bristol merchant and had owned two plantations in Virginia, one of them near Pope's Creek in Westmoreland county.[10] A decade later Charles Pope was listed as one of the owners of the Bristol ship the *Maryland Merchant*, which was engaged in 'the Plantation-Trade'.[11] Clearly the Pope family were deeply invested in both the plantation trade and plantations themselves; these activities, together with their status as prominent Bristol merchants, made the ownership of enslaved people all too probable. To have two enslaved people attempt escape from Charles Pope within three years may suggest a particularly unhappy environment, although in the end we cannot know what inspired a fourteen-year-old South Asian boy and then a thirty-five-year-old African man to escape.

---

[7] 'A Negro Man, by name *Anthony*', *London Gazette*, 30 Aug. 1677.

[8] D. F. McKenzie and M. Bell, *A Chronology and Calendar of Documents relating to the London Book Trade, 1641–1700*: ii, *1671–1685* (Oxford, 2005), p. 351; A. W. C. Hallen, 'A family of Smiths', *Genealogical Magazine*, ii (1898), 45–8.

[9] 'Run away … an Indian Boy', *London Gazette*, 12 Nov. 1685; 'ON the 18th … a Negro man', *London Gazette*, 22 Oct. 1688.

[10] Will of Thomas Pope, Merchant, 1684, National Archives, PROB 11/381/273.

[11] Ship Maryland Merchant, 'House of Commons Journal Volume 12: 27 May 1698', in *Journal of the House of Commons: xii, 1697–1699* (London, 1803), pp. 287–9, *British History Online* <http://www.british-history.ac.uk/commons-jrnl/vol12/pp287-289> [accessed 23 Jan. 2019].

Furthest from London was an unnamed fourteen-year-old boy who 'was taken away … by a Person on Horse back, from Bangor near Wrexham', approximately 250 miles north-west of London. According to the newspaper advertisement, this boy belonged 'to my Lady Broughton of March whiel Hall'. He was marked by 'four figures upon his breast, likewise several marks on his hips', former perhaps West African country markings although they could have been brand marks.[12] It is unclear whether the person on horseback was helping to liberate this boy who was claimed as property by Lady Broughton or simply stealing him: an attractive enslaved boy could be sold to another person in England or to a merchant or ship captain for trafficking to the colonies. Lady Broughton's son Edward had become a planter in Jamaica, where he represented St George's parish in the island's assembly in 1682.[13] This is the most likely explanation for how the widowed Lady Mary Broughton came to hold this young boy as her property. The family were clearly wealthy, and when she died a decade later Lady Broughton left several properties in Westminster and London to her children, even though she had been resident in Marchwiel in Wales, and her status was confirmed by her subsequent burial alongside her late husband in Westminster Abbey.[14]

Even when freedom seekers eloped dozens or hundreds of miles from London, advertisements appeared for them in the capital's newspapers and listed contacts in the city to whom they might be returned. London clearly attracted people of colour who might disappear into the mass of people and find new opportunities for work, community or even escape from England. Moreover, the *London Gazette* and other newspapers were read not just in the capital but all over England, and so were an effective means of advertising for runaways more widely. In runaway advertisements English men and women were helping to develop racial slavery as a social construction and a lived reality, one that was becoming normalized for the many thousands of English men and women who casually perused these advertisements as they read the newspapers, gradually becoming accustomed to slaves and slavery in England.

[12] 'A Black Boy', *London Gazette*, 28 Oct. 1686.

[13] List of Assembly, Minutes of the Council of Jamaica, 21 Sept. 1682, 'America and West Indies: September 1682', in *Calendar of State Papers Colonial, America and West Indies*: xi, *1681–1685*, ed. J W. Fortescue (London, 1898), pp. 291–305, *British History Online* <http://www.british-history.ac.uk/cal-state-papers/colonial/america-west-indies/vol11/pp291-305> [accessed 1 May 2020].

[14] Will of Dame Mary Broughton, Widow of Marchwiel, Denbighshire, 1695, National Archives, PROB 11/429/84. For the Westminster Abbey graves of Lord and Lady Broughton see 'Sir Edward Broughton', Westminster Abbey <https://www.westminster-abbey.org/abbey-commemorations/commemorations/sir-edward-broughton> [accessed 1 May 2020].

15. *'Peter'*: London's connected community of slave-ownership

AN East-Indian Tawney-black boy, long haired and slender, a mark burnt in his forehead and brest, his name Peter, in a Purpel Suit and coat, ran away the 17 of this instant September; Whoever can bring him to Mr. Beasley at my Lady St. John's house neer the Globe Tavern in Long Acre, or to Mr. Thomas Joyce at his house in Bow-lane London, shall be well rewarded for his pains.

> *Mercurius Publicus, Comprising the Sum of all Affairs now in agitation in England, Scotland, and Ireland, Together with Forrain Intelligence; For Information of the People, and to prevent false News,* 25 September 1662

These few dozen words are all that we know of a young South Asian boy who eloped from a London house in 1662. Named Peter, he was described as 'AN East-Indian Tawney-black boy, long haired and slender', and was a well-dressed personal attendant 'in a Purpel Suit and Coat'. The 'mark burnt in his forehead and brest' were probably the result of brandings intended to mark him as property while identifying the person who owned him, although the one on his forehead may have been punishment for a prior escape attempt.[1] Thus what is probably the only surviving archival record of this person reproduces his bondage, his subjection and the erasure of his identity. The historical archive privileges enslavers over enslaved, and the limited and implicitly violent record is rendered all the more troubling by the fact that we can piece together various archival records to learn a great deal more about those who owned or sought out Peter, those who were, directly or indirectly, a party to the violence enacted upon his body. Perhaps the most striking feature of London's seventeenth-century runaway slave advertisements is that they reveal distinct networks of professionals and of elite English men and women, some of them well-known members of a community of men and women who were invested in the creation of colonies, empire and the racial subjection and slavery upon which they were built.

The advertisement for Peter promised a reward to anyone who would return him to 'Mr. *Beasley* at my Lady *St. John's* house neer the Globe Tavern

---

[1] 'AN East-Indian Tawney-black boy … *Peter*', *Mercurius Publicus,* 25 Sept. 1662.

Figure 33. Wenceslaus Hollar, 'Piazza in Covent Garden'
(c.1647). © The Trustees of the British Museum.

in Long Acre, or to Mr. *Thomas Joyce* at his house in Bow-lane *London*'.
Long Acre was a handsome street just north of Covent Garden in the parish
of St Martin in the Fields. Oliver Cromwell had resided there during the
early years of the Civil War, and in the 1660s it was home to such residents
as the earl of Peterborough, John Dryden and Lady Elizabeth St John, wife
of Sir Oliver St John. A leading lawyer and Parliamentarian, St John appears
to have had few if any direct colonial and mercantile interests.[2] However,
his third wife Elizabeth was the widow of the London merchant Caleb
Cockroft, who had been engaged in the East India Company's trade in
saltpetre and gunpowder.[3] Thomas Joyce, who may have been the father of
the man in Bow Lane to whom Peter might be returned, had spent years
in South Asia as an East India Company agent and commanding officer.[4]

---

[2] W. Palmer, 'Oliver St John' (2009), *Oxford Dictionary of National Biography* <https://
doi.org/10.1093/ref:odnb/24504> [accessed 15 May 2020].

[3] See 'Order of the same Commissioners on the petition of Caleb Cockroft, merchant',
in *Calendar of State Papers, Domestic Series, of the Reign of Charles I, April–Nov 1637, Preserved
in the State Paper Department of Her Majesty's Public Record Office*: xi, *April–Nov 1637*, ed.
J. Bruce (London, 1868), p. 187.

[4] Thomas Joyce appears in numerous East India Company records. See eg 'Commission
from President Wm. Methwold and Council to Capt. John Weddell', 21 April 1634, in *Calendar
of State Papers Colonial, East Indies and Persia*: viii, *1630–1634*, ed. W. N. Sainsbury (London,
1892), pp. 533–9, *British History Online* <http://www.british-history.ac.uk/cal-state-papers/

We do not know exactly how Peter came to belong to Lady Elizabeth St John, but it may have been through her first husband Caleb Cockroft or through his mercantile connections with the Joyce family, and Oliver St John's wealth and reputation in mid-seventeenth-century London made the family's ownership of a liveried and branded personal attendant possible. The London townhouse from which Peter ran away was probably a large and well-staffed household, but at about the time that the young South Asian made his bid for freedom, Sir Oliver St John – a Parliamentarian known as Oliver Cromwell's 'Dark Lantern' who had much to fear following the Restoration – went into exile on the Continent.[5] Perhaps Peter seized his opportunity during a time of familial chaos to escape not just from his mistress but also from a network of lawyers, merchants, politicians and others in London who embodied the metropolitan core of a fast-growing network of colonies built around bound labour.

In the wake of the Cromwellian era the restored royal family were at the head of England's rapidly expanding slave-trading operations. In December 1660 Charles II had granted a charter to the Royal Adventurers into Africa, which three years later was rechartered as the Company of Royal Adventurers of England Relating to Trade in Africa. The king and his brother, the duke of York, were major investors in both. Indeed, the king loaned ships to the company, including one named the *Blackamore* which in 1663 took a cargo of 373 enslaved Africans from the kingdom of Allada (or Ardra) on the Bight of Benin to Barbados. In this early voyage the mortality rate was a shocking 60 per cent, and only 150 enslaved people disembarked. Between 1663 and 1672 the Royal Adventurers organized ninety-six slave-trading voyages, carrying some 26,666 enslaved people from Africa and disembarking 20,088 survivors in the English colonies. Charles II dissolved the Royal Adventurers in 1662 and issued a new charter to the Royal African Company, and the duke of York became the new company's governor. Over the eighty years up to the company's dissolution

colonial/east-indies-china-japan/vol8/pp533-539> [accessed 4 March 2019]; 'East Indies: 15 February 1628', in *Calendar of State Papers Colonial, East Indies, China and Persia*: vi, *1625–1629*, ed. W. N. Sainsbury (London, 1884), pp. 458–72, *British History Online* <http://www.british-history.ac.uk/cal-state-papers/colonial/east-indies-china-japan/vol6/pp458-472> [accessed 4 March 2019]; 'Commission and Instructions from the President and Council at Surat to Thomas Joyce, Appointed Agent on the Coast of Coromandel, April 16, 1633', in *The English Factories in India, 1630–1633: a Calendar of Documents in the India Office, Bombay Record Office, Etc.*, ed. W. Foster (Oxford, 1910), p. 301.

  5 W. Palmer, 'Oliver St John'; 'Long Acre', in *Survey of London*: xx, *St Martin-in-The-Fields*: pt iii, *Trafalgar Square and Neighbourhood*, ed. G. H. Gater and F. R. Hiorns (London, 1940), pp. 125–7, *British History Online* <http://www.british-history.ac.uk/survey-london/vol20/pt3/pp125-127> [accessed 4 March 2019].

Figure 34. Unknown artist, *Elihu Yale; Dudley North; Lord James Cavendish; David Yale; and an Enslaved Servant* (*c.*1708), oil on canvas, Yale Center for British Art, Gift of Andrew Cavendish, 11th duke of Devonshire. The enslaved child stands in contrast to the White children playing in the background: he is looking towards the four men he is serving, and his clothing and turban mark him as an exoticized attendant. His collar marks him as the property of one of the men, quite possibly the duke of Devonshire.

in 1752 it 'shipped more enslaved African women, men, and children to the Americas than any other single institution during the entire period of the transatlantic slave trade'. Thus, from the moment Charles II was restored to the throne, the royal family were deeply invested in racial slavery, and many of the bodies of enslaved people were branded with the initials 'DoY' or 'DY' for the duke of York or 'RAC' for the Royal African Company. With the monarch's family chartering, investing in and profiting from slavery and imperial trade, it is hardly surprising that so many wealthier Londoners followed their lead, or that some of these people ended up owning enslaved people in the capital itself.[6]

---

[6] W. A. Pettigrew, *Freedom's Debt: the Royal African Company and the Politics of the Atlantic Slave Trade, 1672–1752* (Chapel Hill, N.C., 2013), at p. 11; K. G. Davies, *The Royal African*

In early March 1662 a 'Moor going by the name of *Anthony*' eloped from Henry Rowe in Shacklewell, Hackney.[7] Apart from noting that he was about sixteen or seventeen years old, the advertisement did not describe Anthony, focusing instead on his clothing. Wearing 'an olive coloured suite and coate lined through with yellow lace, in yellow stockins lac't with yellow', Anthony was well dressed, as befitted his position as servant to a well-respected and leading London mercantile family. Rowe's great-grandfather and great-great-grandfather had each served as lord mayor of London, and had built their home at Shacklewell into one of the significant landed estates within easy access of the City of London.[8] Susan Rowe, Henry's aunt, had married Sir Robert Rich, second earl of Warwick. Rich was deeply engaged in colonial endeavours as a founding member of both the Company of Adventurers and the Bermudas Company, and before the Civil War he had controlled the patent for Trinidad and Tobago.[9] Perhaps Anthony had come to the Rowe family's manor house at Shacklewell from one of Rich's colonial ventures, but whatever his route there he appears to have been determined to free himself. Three months later a second advertisement announced that the young man had 'RUnne away again'.[10] By the time this advertisement appeared, he had been free more than two weeks: perhaps he had learned from his first escape attempt and this second bid for freedom was successful.

The identities of those who sought to recapture freedom seekers in Restoration London, and the people they relied upon as contacts, illustrate how quickly racial slavery permeated and became embedded in respectable society. Slavery was not simply a new plantation labour system thousands of miles from England but instead was an institution that was both real

---

Company (London, [1957] 1999), pp. 41–5; G. F. Zook, 'The Company of Royal Adventurers of England trading into Africa, 1660–1672', *Journal of Negro History*, iv (1919), p. 146; Voyage of the *Blackamore*, Voyage 9552 in Slave Voyages: Trans-Atlantic Slave Trade – Database <https://www.slavevoyages.org/voyage/database> [accessed 14 March 2021]; Royal Adventurers statistics from Slave Voyages: Trans-Atlantic Slave Trade – Database. For the branding of enslaved Africans see W. St Clair, *The Grand Slave Emporium: Cape Coast Castle and the British Slave Trade* (London, 2006), pp. 211–12.

[7] 'RUnne away … *Anthony*', *Mercurius Publicus*, 13 March 1662.

[8] A. P. Beaven, 'Notes on the Aldermen, 1502–1700', in *The Aldermen of the City of London Temp. Henry III–1912* (London, 1908), pp. 168–95, *British History Online* <http://www.british-history.ac.uk/no-series/london-aldermen/hen3-1912/pp168-195> [accessed 18 May 2020]; 'Hackney: Manors', in *A History of the County of Middlesex: x, Hackney*, ed. T. F. T. Baker (London, 1995), pp. 75–91, *British History Online* <http://www.british-history.ac.uk/vch/middx/vol10/pp75-91> [accessed 1 March 2019].

[9] S. Kelsey, 'Robert Rich, second earl of Warwick' (2008), *ODNB* <https://doi.org/10.1093/ref:odnb/23494> [accessed 18 May 2020].

[10] 'RUnne away again … *Anthony*', *Mercurius Publicus*, 3 July 1662.

and present in London. Merchants, printers, goldsmiths, ship owners and captains, and members of the aristocracy were not only investing in and profiting from colonial ventures and the fast-growing slave trade, but some of them were also the owners of enslaved people in the capital itself. In January 1682 an unnamed 'tall Blackamore' escaped from Crambourn Lodge near Windsor, wearing 'a Green Doublet and Breeches, with a large Chairmans Coat of the same colour, Laced with Sir Robert Holmes, his Livery'.[11] Holmes, an admiral in the Restoration navy, had led naval squadrons defending Royal African Company ships and trading posts along the West African coast, and had captured several Dutch slave-trading vessels.[12] Perhaps this freedom seeker was an African who, rather than being liberated from a captured Dutch slave ship, had instead become a prize of war, human property displayed by Holmes to show his standing and even his martial success. Another unnamed enslaved man, described as 'a black Negro Man about 30 years of age' and also dressed in a smart livery, eloped from Spitalfields, just east of the City, four years later.[13] The only person named in this advertisement was the contact to whom information about the freedom seeker might be submitted, the merchant Paul Allestree. His premises were on St Martin's Lane, a street that was 'well built and inhabited by Merchants' in Langborne ward.[14] Allestree had become one of London's leading merchants in the Barbados trade and was all too aware of the increasing use of enslaved African servants in London.[15]

The royal family was deeply entrenched in the companies supervising and profiting from the transatlantic slave trade, and equally involved in the holding of enslaved people in London. On 16 February 1689 Charles Hector, 'a Negroe belonging to ye Duchess of Monmouth', was baptized

---

[11] 'Run away ... a tall Blackamore', *The London Gazette*, 5 Jan. 1682.

[12] J. D. Davies, 'Sir Robert Holmes' (2014), *ODNB* < https://www-oxforddnb-com. ezproxy.lib.gla.ac.uk/view/10.1093/ref:odnb/9780198614128.001.0001/odnb-9780198614128-e-13600?rskey=qcNOkw&result=2> [accessed 30 Sept. 2021]. See also R. Ollard, *Man of War: Sir Robert Holmes and the Restoration Navy* (London, 1969).

[13] 'Run away ... a black Negro Man', *London Gazette*, 30 Sept. 1686.

[14] J. Strype, *A Survey of the Cities of London and Westminster ... written at first in the year MDXCVIII by John Stow ...* (London, 1720), i. 190.

[15] N. Zahedieh, 'Making mercantilism work: London merchants and Atlantic trade in the seventeenth century', *Transactions of the Royal Historical Society*, ix (1999), 143–58, at p. 146; N. Zahedieh, 'Credit, risk and reputation in late seventeenth-century colonial trade', in *Merchant Organization and Maritime Trade in the North Atlantic, 1660–1815*, Research in Maritime History 15, ed. O. U. Janzen (St John's, Newfoundland, 1998), pp. 68–9; K. G. Davies, 'The origins of the commission system in the West India trade', *Transactions of the Royal Historical Society*, ii (1952), 89–107, at pp. 104–5.

at St Martin in the Fields.[16] A wealthy Scot in her own right (as the duchess of Buccleuch), Anne Scott was the widow of James Scott, the duke of Monmouth. As Charles II's illegitimate son, he had led the ill-fated Monmouth Rebellion against James II, for which he was executed in July 1685.[17] The duke of Monmouth justified his rebellion as vital for the liberties of Englishmen 'unless we could be willing to be Slaves as well as Papists, and forget the Example of our Noble and Generous Ancestors, who conveyed our Privileges to us at the Expence of their Blood and Treasure'.[18] We can only imagine how Charles Hector may have felt about the slavery that so concerned the late duke.

The contacts specified in runaway advertisements to whom freedom seekers or information on their whereabouts might be transmitted were as important as enslavers themselves in showing the spread of racial slavery through a network of London merchants, investors and their associates. When Stephen, a twenty-year-old 'Negro Man' who 'speaks good English, being a Native of the Leeward Islands', escaped in October 1701, an advertisement indicated that he might be returned to the merchant Joseph Martyn at his premises in Love Lane, just east of Tower Hill.[19] Martyn had spent time in Nevis and, on his return to London, had specialized in the Caribbean sugar trade, representing the Leeward Islands as their London agent. By the end of the seventeenth century he was one of only two private merchants who came close to competing with the Royal African Company in the volume of sugar he imported.[20] William Mead, who claimed ownership of Stephen, was a leading Quaker merchant best known for standing trial alongside William Penn in 1670.[21] Later, in the eighteenth century, Quakers would play a prominent role in early abolitionism, but during these early years Quaker merchants did not shy away from the transatlantic slave trade or even slave-ownership, and William Mead's brother Thomas was

---

[16] Baptism of Charles Hector, 16 Feb. 1689, Baptized, Parish Register, 1558–1612, St Martin in the Fields, p. 114. London Metropolitan Archives, London, England, STM/PR/6/32. Digitized copy of original consulted at <https://www.ancestry.co.uk> [accessed 1 April 2021].

[17] T. Harris, 'James Scott [formerly Crofts], duke of Monmouth and first duke of Buccleuch' (2009), *ODNB* <https://doi.org/10.1093/ref:odnb/24879> [accessed 22 Jan. 2021].

[18] 'The DECLARATION of James Duke of Monmouth', in D. Defoe, *An Account of the Proceedings against the Rebels, and Other Prisoners ...* (London, 1716), p. viii.

[19] 'A Negro Man named Stephen', *London Gazette*, 20 Oct. 1701.

[20] Pettigrew, *Freedom's Debt*, pp. 68, 72.

[21] William Penn and William Mead, *The People's Ancient and Just Liberties Asserted in the Trial of William Penn and William Mead, at the Sessions Held at the Old-Baily in London* (London, 1670). See also G. Skidmore, 'William Mead' (2004), *ODNB* <https://doi.org/10.1093/ref:odnb/18469> [accessed 18 May 2020].

co-owner of at least three slave-trading voyages between 1699 and 1705.[22] Perhaps Stephen's bid for freedom was successful, for a second advertisement published on 24 November, almost fifty days after his escape, indicated that he remained free.[23]

Merchants engaged in the North Atlantic trade regularly featured in advertisements as the contacts who would take custody of recaptured freedom seekers. Thus, for example, Rowland Tryon (a merchant and the brother of Thomas Tryon, London's sixth-largest importer of Caribbean and North American goods in 1686) was the contact named by Edward Archer in his advertisement for Quoshey; Paul Allestree, the eighth-largest importer in 1686, was the contact in an advertisement for the freedom seeker Tom Bay; Bartholomew Gracedieu, the twelfth-largest importer, was the contact named in an advertisement for Tony; Stephen Skinner, the fourteenth-largest importer, was the contact named by Edwin Stede in his advertisement for Quomino; and Richard Cary, the eighteenth-largest importer, was the contact nominated by James Yeames in an advertisement for an unnamed freedom seeker.[24] London's merchants did not simply participate in the trade in enslaved Africans and the crops they grew: from their homes and counting houses in London, they willingly participated in the attempts to recapture bound and enslaved servants who dared to escape.

The runaway advertisements published in London between the 1650s and the early 1700s reveal a network of investors, patrons and aristocrats, merchants, ship captains and military officials who either owned enslaved people or facilitated the capture of such people. Together they helped make racial slavery real in London, transforming a colonial abstraction into a local social reality. They were the people who crafted and populated the first runaway slave advertisements, helping to construct what would become a primary mechanism for the prevention and punishment of escape, the single most significant individual form of resistance to enslavement.

---

[22] Voyage of the *Donegal*, Voyage 21276; the *Gerrard*, Voyage 21295; and the *Olive Tree*, Voyage 21406 (1705) in Slave Voyages: Transatlantic Slave Trade database.

[23] 'A Negro Man, named Stephen', *London Gazette*, 24 Nov. 1701.

[24] 'A Negro, named Quoshey', *London Gazette*, 30 Dec. 1700; 'Run away the 22d Instant', *London Gazette*, 30 Sept. 1686, and 'THE Notice of the Negro Man (his Name Tom Bay)', *London Gazette*, 4 Oct. 1686; 'RUN away … a Black-Moor Fellow named Tony', *London Gazette*, 6 Aug. 1696; 'A Negro Servant … Quomino', *London Gazette*, 18 June 1694; 'An East-India Mallatto', *London Gazette*, 19 May 1684. The table of merchants and the value of their trade with the Caribbean and North American colonies is from N. Zahedieh, *The Capital and the Colonies: London and the Atlantic Economy, 1660–1700* (Cambridge, 2010), p. 61.

PART III

Freedom seekers in the colonies

16. Freedom seekers and the law in England's American and Caribbean colonies

The earliest surviving runaway advertisement to be printed in England's colonies was published as a broadside in Boston in 1697 (Figure 35). It was an ephemeral item and if other such notices were printed they have not survived. This broadside included descriptions to help identify the twenty-two-year-old freedom seeker, indicating that he spoke English well, was 'a well-set Fellow', and was wearing 'a new black Hat, a new light coloured cloth Coat with pewter Buttons, lin'd with yellow, canvas Breeches buttoned at the Knees with pewter buttons, yarn Stockings Tarred, Leather Heel'd Shoes'. As such it was similar to the runaway advertisements that had been appearing in London newspapers for almost half a century, but not in colonies without newspapers and – in the Caribbean and Chesapeake colonies – without printing presses. It was not until the early eighteenth century that the first newspapers appeared in the colonies, complete with the colonies' first runaway slave advertisements.

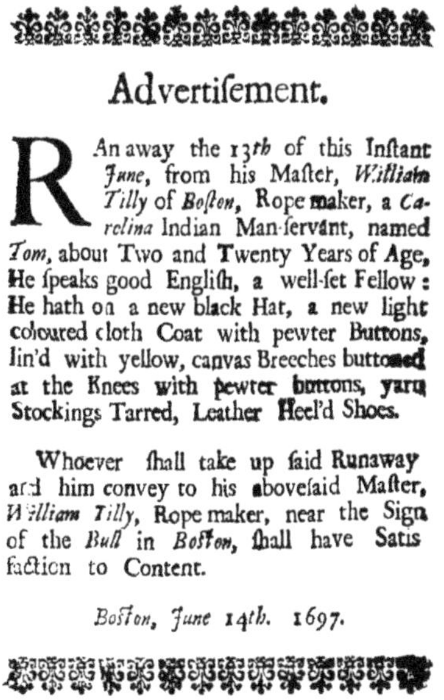

Advertisement.

Ran away the 13th of this Instant June, from his Master, *William Tilly* of *Boston*, Rope maker, a *Carolina* Indian Man-servant, named *Tom*, about Two and Twenty Years of Age, He speaks good English, a well-set Fellow : He hath on a new black Hat, a new light coloured cloth Coat with pewter Buttons, lin'd with yellow, canvas Breeches buttoned at the Knees with pewter buttons, yarn Stockings Tarred, Leather Heel'd Shoes.

Whoever shall take up said Runaway and him convey to his abovesaid Master, *William Tilly*, Rope maker, near the Sign of the *Bull* in *Boston*, shall have Satisfaction to Content.

Boston, June 14th. 1697.

Figure 35. William Tilly, 'Advertisement. Ran Away the 13th of this Instant June …' (Boston, 1697). Original held by Boston Public Library, reproduced by Readex in Early American Imprints, series 1. Image reproduced by permission of NewsBank.

Freedom-seeking enslaved people were, however, ubiquitous in the colonies. If freedom seekers challenged the authority of enslavers in late seventeenth-century London, enslaved people who attempted to escape represented a far greater threat to planters in the North American and Caribbean colonies. During the seventeenth century Londoners made use of newspaper advertisements in constructing the idea of the runaway slave and the practice of broadcasting information designed to secure freedom seekers, while English colonists responded to runaways in a more forceful and comprehensive manner by creating new laws and practices that were unprecedented in English law. Freedom-seeking bound labourers threatened the entire colonial enterprise, for the mid-seventeenth-century development of staple crop economies had rendered the plantation colonies almost wholly dependent on bound labour forces. In 1664 the Council of Foreign Plantations in London prefaced a series of recommendations with the observation: 'It being universally agreed that people art the foundation and Improvement of all Plantations and that peopl. art increased principally by Sending of Servants thither, It is necessary that a Settled course be taken for the furnishing them with servants.'[1] The Barbados planter Richard Ligon was well aware that, while sugar was the most valuable crop sent from the colonies back to England, the leading 'Commodities these Ships bring to the Island; are, *Servants* and *Slaves*'.[2] Securing the labour first of indentured servants and then of enslaved Africans and indigenous Americans was essential to colonial success.

At first it was impoverished White Britons who laboured on early Chesapeake and Caribbean plantations. The unhealthy environment and gender imbalance meant that for a century or longer mortality rates were substantially higher than birth rates, necessitating a constant influx of new workers. The high costs involved in obtaining these workers meant that the year-long terms of service common for agricultural and urban servants in England were replaced by far longer terms of four to seven years for indentured White servants from the British Isles. During the seventeenth century perhaps 90,000 servants travelled from the British Isles to the Chesapeake colonies of Virginia and Maryland, and as many as 75,000 to England's Caribbean colonies. Some travelled voluntarily, desperate for a new start after completing their term of service, while others were vagrants, convicts and prisoners of war from England, Scotland and Ireland who were

---

[1] 'Certaine Propositions for the better accommodating ye Foreigne Plantations with Servants reported from the Committee to the Councell of Foreign Plantations' (1664), Papers relating to English Colonies in America and the West Indies, 1627–1699, British Library, Egerton MS 2395, fo. 277.

[2] R. Ligon, *A True & Exact History of the Island of Barbados* (London, 1657), p. 40.

transported to the colonies and whose labour was sold without their consent. However, as more servants survived their terms of service, a declining number were able to acquire good land and a viable foothold in the colonies, leading to social unrest and even armed conflict, most famously in Bacon's Rebellion of 1676–7 in Virginia. From the 1650s onwards the declining cost and increased availability of enslaved African labourers led planters to shift from bound White servants to enslaved Africans who would not be freed. This began on a large scale in Barbados, then spread to Jamaica and to the southern mainland colonies. By the end of the seventeenth century racial slavery was ubiquitous throughout England's New World colonies.[3]

Indentured servants and then enslaved Africans and indigenous Americans routinely resisted their subordination. Men, women and children defied those who commanded them by feigning sickness, temporarily absenting themselves, working slowly, engaging in sabotage, escaping and even plotting and occasionally engaging in violent rebellion. This routine resistance was dramatically different in both scale and nature from any that had occurred among servants in husbandry and domestic servants in medieval and early modern England. The need to find gainful employment and to save for marriage and the creation of their own households encouraged many English youths to voluntarily contract for a year at a time, often changing employers at the end of that term – a useful safety valve for any labourers unhappy with their employer. The self-interest of these labourers, along with occasional laws and the actions of local courts, generally proved sufficient to control most members of England's vast servant population.[4] But in the colonies the existence of a qualitatively different subordinate population of long-term involuntary indentured servants, and then permanently enslaved people, required new systems and practices for regulation and control of a large, potentially rebellious workforce that enjoyed fewer and then eventually none of the rights and expectations of servants in England.

Furthermore, as neither parliament nor the English courts addressed the issue of colonial bound servants, and most especially enslaved people who challenged their subordination, it was left to colonial legislatures and courts and to the private actions of enslavers to create a system for controlling plantation labourers. Colonial legislative assemblies were able to develop these systems with little imperial oversight and beyond the pale of English common law, not least because many of these laws and codes were developed and honed during a period of minimal imperial oversight.

[3] S. P. Newman, *A New World of Labor: the Development of Plantation Slavery in the British Atlantic* (Philadelphia, Pa., 2013), pp. 71–107.
[4] Newman, *A New World of Labor*, pp. 17–35.

Between the 1620s and the 1660s England's government was engulfed by the political and military strife of the Personal Rule of Charles I, the English Civil War and the ensuing Wars of the Three Kingdoms, the execution of the monarch, the revolutionary Protectorate of Oliver Cromwell and the Restoration of Charles II.[5]

The regulation and policing of bound labourers in England's frontier colonial societies developed in a piecemeal fashion during the seventeenth century. Individual enslavers regulated their own workers and punished those who resisted, including those who attempted to escape. Over time, courts and legislative assemblies began to institute policies and practices that suited their environment and labour force and the needs of wealthy landowners, slowly constructing a corpus of law and practice within each colony. The details of these first tentative steps have not survived for some of the colonies, especially Barbados. The early seventeenth-century records are better for the northern mainland colonies, although during the seventeenth century these laws were primarily focused on regulating the White servants who dominated the region's bound labour force.

The earliest surviving colonial legislation dealing with freedom-seeking White servants and enslaved Black people was passed in the northern colonies, but the most significant legal innovations were in the plantation colonies to the south on the mainland and in the Caribbean colonies that were dependent on large numbers of bound or enslaved workers.[6] This process began in the Chesapeake colonies of Virginia and Maryland, where

---

[5] For recent discussions of the development of colonial laws about servants and the enslaved, see H. Brewer, 'Slavery, sovereignty, and "inheritable blood": reconsidering John Locke and the origins of American slavery', *American Historical Review*, cxxii (2017), 1048–71; A. Watson, *Slave Law in the Americas* (Athens, Ga., 1989), pp. 63–4; E. B. Rugemer, *Slave Law and the Politics of Resistance in the Early Atlantic World* (Cambridge, Mass., 2018), pp. 25–74; J. A. Bush, 'Free to enslave: the foundations of colonial American slave law', *Yale Journal of Law and Humanities*, v (1993), 417–70.

[6] See eg 'They will not take from the service …', 7 June 1629, and 'Whereas many Servants daily run away …', 9 Aug. 1640, in E. B. O'Callaghan, *The Laws and Ordinances of New Netherland, 1638–1674* (Albany, N.Y., 1868), pp. 7, 24; 'Acts respecting masters, servants and labourers', ch. lxviii (1630), in *The Charters and General Laws of the Colony and Province of Massachusetts Bay* (Boston, 1814), pp. 155–6; 'June the 3, 1644', in *The Public Records of the Colony of Connecticut, Prior to the Union with New Haven, Conn. Colony, May 1665* (Hartford, Conn., 1850), i. 105; and 'Breach of covenant' (1647), in *Records of the Colony of Rhode Island and Providence Plantations, In New England …: i, 1636 to 1663*, ed. J. R. Bartlett (Providence, R.I., 1856), p. 182. For a discussion of freedom-seeking runaway servants in Massachusetts see L. W. Towner, *A Good Master Well Served: Masters and Servants in Colonial Massachusetts, 1620–1750* (New York, 1998), pp. 195–217. For a discussion of laws relating to enslaved African Americans in the colonial middle colonies, see O. Williams, *African Americans and Colonial Legislation in the Middle Colonies* (New York, 1998).

the attempts of labourers to escape threatened the ability of Chesapeake planters to successfully oversee the planting, cultivation, harvesting and processing of a tobacco crop that could quickly and easily spoil.[7] All of the earliest legislation in the Chesapeake colonies dealing with runaways was focused on bound White servants from the British Isles, who at that time dominated the workforce. The Maryland Assembly moved first, legislating against any servants who 'depart away Secretly from his or her Master or dame', as well as those who knowingly aided and abetted such runaways. A year later the Virginia Assembly acted against those who encouraged or employed runaway servants, prefacing their action with the observation that 'complaints are at every quarter court exhibited against divers persons who entertain and enter into covenants with runaway servants'.[8] In Virginia the penalties were greater for a second attempted escape, and such 'incorrigible rogues' were to 'be branded in the cheek with the letter R'.[9] In 1658 Virginia's earlier statutes were consolidated into a single law entitled 'Against Runaway Servants', while in April 1662 Maryland passed a comprehensive 'Acte touching Runawayes', designed to address the 'great prejudices, Losses and Damages' sustained by planters 'by reason of their Servants running Away or absenting themselves'.[10]

Virginia and Maryland were essentially frontier colonies with no major urban centres and with a limited transportation and communication infrastructure, an underdeveloped policing system and only occasional court sessions. Consequently, policing the bound workforce and pursuing runaways presented a logistical challenge to planters and the rudimentary legal system. With this in mind, the Virginia Assembly built on English precedents by mandating a formalized system of 'huie[*sic*] and cries after

[7] See W. M. Billings, 'The law of servants and slaves in seventeenth-century Virginia', *Virginia Magazine of History and Biography*, xcix (1991), 45–62; L. Working, '"The savages of Virginia our project": the Powhatans in Jacobean political thought', in *Virginia 1619: Slavery and Freedom in the Making of English America*, ed. P. Musselwhite, P. C. Mancall, and J. Horn (Chapel Hill, N.C.: 2019), pp. 42–59.

[8] 'An Act against Fugitives', 26 March 1642, in *Archives of Maryland: Proceedings and Acts of the General Assembly of Maryland, January 1647/8–September 1664*, ed. W. H. Browne (Baltimore, Md., 1883), i. 124; 'An Act against ffugitives', 2–21 April 1649, in *Archives of Maryland*, i. 249–50; Act XXI, March 1643, in *The Statutes at Large: a Collection of the Laws of Virginia, from the First Session of the Legislature, in the Year 1619 …*, ed. W. W. Hening (New York, 1823), i. 253.

[9] 'An Act against Fugitives', 26 March 1642, in *Archives of Maryland*, i. 124; 'An Act against ffugitives', 2–21 April 1649, in *Archives of Maryland*, i. 249–50; Act XXI, March 1643, in *The Statutes at Large: a Collection of the Laws of Virginia*, p. 253; Act XXII, March 1643, *The Statutes at Large: a Collection of the Laws of Virginia*, i. 254–5.

[10] Act XVI, March 1658, 'Against Runaway Servants', in *The Statutes at Large: a Collection of the Laws of Virginia*, i. 440; 'An Acte touching Runawyes', in *Archives of Maryland*, i. 451–2.

runaway servants'. Once endorsed by the governor or a member of the Governor's Council, these handwritten documents detailing runaways were distributed to local commissioners, who then required heads of household to attest that they had no knowledge of the runaways.[11] These were probably the first runaway advertisements produced in the mainland American colonies, although, not surprisingly, none have survived. It was by no means easy to tell who was a legitimately bound servant, who was a freeman and who was a runaway. In an attempt to ease identification of repeat runaways, a law in 1659 entitled 'How to Know a Runaway Servant' mandated that enslavers crop the hair of all recaptured runaways 'close above the ears, whereby they may be with more ease discovered and apprehended' should they again attempt to escape.[12] Other laws were designed to mobilize the entire free White community against runaways, and a law simply entitled 'Against Runawayes' sought to enlist all free White men by promising anyone who caught a runaway a reward of 1,000 pounds of tobacco: this was to be paid by the legal owner of a runaway, who in turn would be reimbursed by the enforced additional service of the runaway. In the eyes of Virginia's legislators, the escape of bound labourers was an offence against not just individual enslavers but also the entire community, and all free men were required to police the bound workforce and would be rewarded for this work.[13]

Entire laws designed to prevent escape and to punish runaways and those who assisted or harboured them represented both a departure from and a revealing addition to broader English laws addressing servants. Emanating from a labour-poor colonial environment, these legal innovations demonstrate the absolute dependence of planters on their bound workforce. But it was in their attention to freedom-seeking enslaved runaways that colonial assemblies proved most innovative. In 1672 the Virginia Assembly passed 'An act for the apprehension and suppression of runaways, negros and slaves', the first such law to focus more on escaped enslaved Africans than on White servants from the British Isles. For the first time freedom-seeking enslaved people were identified as being 'in rebellion', and not only White settlers but also 'neighbouring Indians' were 'Required and enjoyned' to apprehend runaways. Just four years before the outbreak of violence on the Virginia frontier that ignited Bacon's Rebellion, members

---

[11] Act CXIII, March 1658, 'Concerning Huie and Cries', in *The Statutes at Large: a Collection of the Laws of Virginia*, i. 483.

[12] Act III, March 1659, 'How to Know a Runaway Servant', in *The Statutes at Large: a Collection of the Laws of Virginia*, i. 517–18.

[13] Act VIII, Sept. 1668–Oct. 1669, 'Against Runawayes', in *The Statutes at Large: a Collection of the Laws of Virginia*, ii. 273–4.

of the assembly had been clearly concerned about the 'many mischiefs of dangerous consequence' that might occur should these freedom-seeking rebels escape to the Virginia frontier. The law absolved from criminal responsibility any person killing an escaped enslaved person who resisted recapture, while promising financial restitution to the person who claimed ownership of the runaway. Clearly and definitively, enslaved people were to be treated as property, and their attempts at resistance by escape were defined as rebellion.[14]

It was not until 1705 that Virginia's legislation relating to indentured servants and enslaved people was consolidated into a single comprehensive law, and the prevention of and punishment for escape was a central theme of 'An act concerning Servants and Slaves'. By this time the Chesapeake colonies of Virginia and Maryland contained approximately 20,000 enslaved Africans and a little over 3,000 White servants, and thus most of this comprehensive law was focused on the enslaved.[15] Ten years later Maryland followed suit with 'An ACT relating to Servants and Slaves'.[16] The violence towards enslaved freedom seekers permitted and indeed mandated by Chesapeake laws stood in stark contrast to English laws delineating the relationship between masters and any of their servants who absconded.

But it was in the Caribbean that large-scale plantation agriculture had first appeared with very large populations of enslaved people. Consequently, it was in those colonies where innovative legal and social mechanisms for the subordination of bound workforces and the prevention and punishment of escape were first created, and eventually spread to South Carolina on the mainland, whence it informed laws throughout the lower South. Large-scale plantation slavery developed initially in Barbados, where a clear differentiation between enslaved people and bound White servants was already appearing by the mid seventeenth century. In mainland North America racial slavery advanced fastest in the Chesapeake colonies of Virginia and Maryland, a region in which an estimated 16,151 enslaved Africans in total arrived during the seventeenth century. During the same period the small island of Barbados received approximately 236,724

---

[14] Act VIII, Sept. 1672, 'An act for the apprehension and suppression of runaways, negros and slaves', in *The Statutes at Large: a Collection of the Laws of Virginia*, ii. 299–300. Maryland passed a similarly comprehensive law four years later, although this piece of legislation gave relatively equal attention to indentured servants and enslaved people: 'An Act Relateing to Servants and Slaves', May–June 1676, in *Archives of Maryland*, ii. 523–8.

[15] Ch. XLIX, Oct. 1705, 'An act concerning Servants and Slaves', in *The Statues at Large …*, ii. 447–62. See also C. Tomlins, *Freedom Bound: Law, Labor, and Civic Identity in Colonizing English America, 1580–1865* (Cambridge, 2010), p. 271.

[16] 'An ACT relating to Servants and Slaves', in *Laws of Maryland at Large, with Proper Indexes …*, ed. T. Bacon (Annapolis, Md., 1765), pp. 262–9.

enslaved Africans, a huge forced migration unparalleled in seventeenth-century England's colonies.[17] During the seventeenth century almost 84 per cent of the estimated total of enslaved Africans brought to all of England's Caribbean and North American colonies were landed in Barbados, Jamaica and South Carolina. In these plantation societies, enslavers and their legislative assemblies developed and honed the laws of slavery and their mechanisms for the prevention and punishment of rebellion and escape out of necessity, for it was here that escape and rebellion represented the greatest threat.

As in the mainland colonies, plantation agriculture in Barbados began with bound White servants from the British Isles, but within a generation these workers were being replaced by enslaved labourers. Relations between planters and their servants were defined less by English law than by the localized and developing 'custom of the country', which illuminated both planters' attitudes to their servants and the harsh working conditions and low life expectancy of these men and women. During the crucial period between the 1630s and the early 1660s, with English authorities overwhelmed by the strife of the mid seventeenth century, the Barbadian planter elite were able to fashion labour and agriculture as they saw fit. Few of the earliest laws and policies constructed by Barbados planters survive: one of the earliest is an 'Act to restrain the wandering of Servants and Negro's', a 1653 measure directed less against escape than against 'the wandring of Servants and Slaves, on Sundayes, Saturdayes in the afternoon, and other days wherein the said Servants, or Slaves do not work'. This law required servants and enslaved people to carry a 'Ticket' created by enslavers and overseers permitting absence from the plantation, and mandating punishment of those caught without such permission.[18]

In the 1653 law the penalties were identical for White servants and enslaved Africans, with this one law covering runaways from both groups. However, well in advance of enslavers on the North American mainland, Barbados planters soon recognized and sought to address what they saw

---

[17] Statistics generated by the estimates tool of the Slave Voyages: Trans-Atlantic Slave Trade database <https://www.slavevoyages.org/assessment/estimates> [accessed 7 Nov. 2019]. For the development of bound White and enslaved Black labour systems in Barbados and beyond, see S. P. Newman, *A New World of Labor: the Development of Plantation Slavery in the British Atlantic* (Philadelphia, Pa., 2013). According to the estimates function of the Slave Voyages: Trans-Atlantic Slave Trade database, between 1600 and 1700 some 425,073 enslaved Africans arrived in England's New World colonies, 355,933 of them (83.73%) in Barbados, Jamaica and the Carolinas.

[18] 'An Act to restrain the wandring of Servants and Negro's', 4 June 1652, in *Acts and Statutes of the Island of Barbados: Made and Enacted since the Reducement of the Same, unto the Authority of the Commonwealth of England* ... (London, 1654), pp. 81–3.

as fundamental differences between the two groups of bound labourers, and a separate law passed a year earlier was focused exclusively on 'Runaway Negroes', the first English colonial law directed specifically at enslaved African runaways. Clearly, freedom seekers were a significant problem, as both the penalties for harbouring them and the rewards for reporting them were higher than those for White bound servants.[19]

These laws, all passed during the 1650s, marked the years in which sugar production exploded in Barbados and enslaved workers began outnumbering the dwindling number of bound White servants. The transition was swift. In 1643, with relatively few Africans on the island and most planters still growing tobacco, cotton or indigo, James Holdip had twenty-nine bound White labourers working his 200-acre plantation. Three years later Sir Anthony Ashley Cooper's similarly sized plantation was worked by twenty-one bound Whites and nine enslaved Africans. But by 1654 Robert Hooper's 200 acres were worked by thirty-five White servants and sixty-six enslaved people, and by 1656 George Martin had no White servants and sixty enslaved people at work on his 259 acres.[20]

During the two decades of the English Civil War and the Cromwellian Protectorate, Barbados planters spent approximately £1 million purchasing Africans, a vast sum indicative of the profits to be made from sugar. The status of these enslaved labourers was defined by 'An ACT declaring the Negro-slaves of this Island to be Real Estates', a law that began with the observation that 'a very considerable part of the wealth of this Island consists in our Negro-slaves, without whose labor we should be utterly unable to manage our Plantations'.[21] Building on that fundamental legal foundation, the Barbados Assembly then passed the transformative law entitled 'An act for the better ordering and governing of Negroes'.[22] No known copy of

---

[19] '[T]o prevent the injurious keeping of Run-away Negroes', 7 Oct. 1652, in *Acts and Statutes of the Island of Barbados*, pp. 43–5.

[20] R. S. Dunn, *Sugar and Slaves: the Rise of the Planter Class in the English West Indies, 1624–1713* (Chapel Hill, N.C., 1972), p. 68.

[21] 'An ACT declaring the Negro-slaves of this Island to be Real Estates', 29 April 1668, in *The Laws of Barbados, Collected in One Volume, by William Rawlin* (London, 1699), pp. 72–3.

[22] See 'An Act for the better ordering and Governing of Negroes', 27 Sept. 1661, National Archives, Lists of Acts Barbados 1682, CO 30/2/16-26. A second copy of the law can be found in the William Blathwayt Papers, 1657–1770, Box 1, BL 369, Huntington Library. I am grateful to Holly Brewer for sharing her transcription of the former, and to Justin Roberts for sharing his transcription of the latter. There is no known surviving copy of the original 1661 law, and the version in the National Archives appears to be the 1667 revision, including at least two amendments. The Huntington Library version also appears to be a slightly later and somewhat revised version of the 1661 original law. All references are to the manuscript in the National Archives unless otherwise specified.

the 1661 Barbados Slave Code survives, but a slightly revised 1667 version that has survived appears to have differed little from the original. Most of the laws passed by the Barbados Assembly at this time were relatively short, often consisting of no more than about 200 words of text designed to adapt English law and precedents to the local situation.[23] Far longer were the laws designed to deal with bound White servants (4,814 words of text), but longest of all was this new Slave Code (4,968 words). The unique nature and significance of bound White and enslaved Black labour as they existed and functioned in Barbados necessitated significant legal innovation and the creation of entire legal codes rather than short and simple laws. Indeed, the introductory paragraph of the Barbados Slave Code noted that English law contained 'no tract to guide us where to walk nor any Rule set us how to Governe such Slaves', and then set out the reasons why a long and detailed legal code was required to 'renew and revive' useful elements of existing laws while creating significant legal innovations.[24]

By 1661, when the first Barbados Slave Code went into effect, there were almost certainly more enslaved Africans and indigenous Americans on Barbados than White labourers, and the enslaved may have already outnumbered the island's entire White population. By 1675 an estimated 58,000 enslaved Africans had been brought to Barbados, supplemented by an unknown number of enslaved indigenous Americans from as far away as New England. In 1680 the first reliable census revealed that 38,352 enslaved people massively outnumbered a rapidly dwindling population of only 2,193 White servants and 3,311 planters and heads of household.[25]

One of the most striking things about the Barbados Slave Code is that more than one third of the 1667 revision of the 1661 original, some 1,762 words, was focused on the dangers posed by freedom seekers and how best to deal with them.[26] Much of this new law revolved around a series of

---

[23] The following laws are good examples of relatively short statutes passed by the Barbados Assembly in 1661: 'An Act appointing a Special Court for the speedy deciding of Controversies between Merchant and Merchant', 4 July 1661 (205 words); 'An Act for the Certain and constant appointment of all Officers Fees within this Island', 8 Aug. 1661 (181 words); 'An Act for the Encouragement of such as shall plant or raise Provisions to sell', 13 March 1661 (164 words). See *The Laws of Barbados*, pp. 15–16, 52, 54.

[24] 'An Act for the better ordering and Governing of Negroes', p. 16.

[25] 'An Act for the better ordering and Governing of Negroes', pp. 25–6. For population statistics, the estimates function of the Slave Voyages Transatlantic database extrapolates a total of 58,327 African arrivals between 1626 and 1675. See also Barbados Census, 1680, American and West Indies, Colonial Papers, Jan.–May 1680, National Archives, CO 1/44, pp. 242–3.

[26] 'An Act for the better ordering and Governing of Negroes'. The manuscript copy of this law in the National Archives is quite difficult to read, and there is disagreement about the transcription of one phrase. E. Rugemer reads this as 'an uncertain and dangerous pride of

measures designed to prevent, proscribe and punish illegal absence and escape. The substance of the law actually began with a first clause focused on enslaved people who were absent from plantations without permission, and White men were enjoined to apprehend and whip any person found absent from home without a ticket.[27] The fourth and the sixth to tenth clauses dealt explicitly with 'Runaway or fugitive Negro[s]'. The fourth was addressed to White people who were harbouring or holding enslaved people, giving them six days from the publication of the Slave Code to return the runaways to their legal owners or face a fine, up to thirty lashes or a seven-year period of servitude. The sixth required Whites to take into custody 'any Runaway Negro' and surrender the freedom seeker to the authorities within forty-eight hours, and the seventh clause specified the rewards to be paid for such action. The eighth clause required owners to pay the authorities and set fees for the recovery of enslaved runaways who had been incarcerated at the public expense, while the ninth provided for compensation to be paid to the owners of enslaved people who died while in public custody.[28]

The tenth clause went into greater detail about processes, specifying that those who handed fugitives over to the authorities needed to submit their own names and addresses as well as information about 'where hee apprehended such fugitive Negro', and that the treasurer or other officials were

> required to take and enter in a Book the intent that all Owners of such Negroes may come to the right knowledge and understanding when their Negroes were apprehended and by whom and whether they might be wrongfully taken up or not, and that the keeper of the Prison at the delivery of any Negro do take a Receipt of the person to whom delivered and therein incert the mark or description of the Negro delivered, any usage or Custome to the Contrary heretofore had in any wise notwithstanding.[29]

Barbados lawmakers clearly saw the value in creating a system of public recording of as much information as possible about freedom seekers, including physical descriptions and information about where, when and by whom they were apprehended. But at this time the distribution of such

---

people', suggesting an early instance of identification of enslaved Africans as more animal than human ('The development of mastery and race in the comprehensive slave codes of the greater Caribbean during the seventeenth century', *William and Mary Quarterly*, 3rd series, lxx (2013), 429–58, at pp. 438–9). However, using the Huntington Library version, J. Roberts has suggested that the relevant word is 'kind' rather than 'pride', and H. Brewer's reading of the National Archives version likewise identifies the key word as 'kind'. I have elected to use 'kind' as it appears to better fit within the sentence structure.

[27] 'An Act for the better ordering and Governing of Negroes', p. 17.
[28] 'An Act for the better ordering and Governing of Negroes', pp. 18–20.
[29] 'An Act for the better ordering and Governing of Negroes', p. 20.

information was not easy: Barbados had no printing press or newspaper and these records were all handwritten.

The twelfth clause of the 1667 Slave Code continued the discussion on freedom seekers, this time focusing on long-term escapees who had remained at liberty for more than one year. Significant rewards were offered to any who apprehended such long-term runaways, including other enslaved people who would enjoy both a cash reward and 'a Badge of a Red cross on his right Arm whereby he might be known and cherished by all good people for his good service to the Country'.[30] The thirteenth clause then dealt with those who 'attempted to steal away Negroes by spurious pretences of promising them freedom in another Country', recognizing that the escape of the enslaved might be triggered by White people who 'tempt or persuade any Negro to leave their Master or Mistress' service to whom they are Slaves'.[31]

The seventeenth to twenty-first clauses addressed enslaved people who rebelled through armed uprising or by individual escape. Individuals who undertook either form of resistance were considered by lawmakers to be 'out in rebellion', and the punishment for rebellion could be 'death or other pain as their Crimes shall deserve'.[32] The subsequent clauses focusing on runaways were far longer than the paragraph on rebellion, for, while slave uprisings posed the greatest threat to the White population, running away was a far more common and a costly problem.[33]

The first of its kind in England's New World colonies, the comprehensive Barbados Slave Code of 1661 was amended several times before a significant redrafting in 1688 that remained in use with only occasional modifications for more than a century.[34] The 1688 code was almost 10 per cent longer than the 1661 original, but there were few substantive differences. What had changed most was the tone, for by this time racial slavery was well established and institutionalized in Barbados, and planters and their legislative assembly were far more confident in their articulation of what was required for the successful operation of a system of racial slavery.

Barbados is a relatively small island of under 200 square miles with no mountains, and by the late seventeenth century the island's remaining forested areas were rapidly dwindling. The island's size meant that neither plantations nor the enslaved population would grow beyond a certain level and, as all land that was fit for cultivation had been settled, there were

---

[30] 'An Act for the better ordering and Governing of Negroes', p. 21.
[31] 'An Act for the better ordering and Governing of Negroes', pp. 21–2.
[32] 'An Act for the better ordering and Governing of Negroes', pp. 25, 24.
[33] 'An Act for the better ordering and Governing of Negroes', pp. 24–5.
[34] 'An ACT for the Governing of Negroes', 8 Aug. 1688, in *The Laws of Barbados*, pp. 156–64.

few places where rebels and runaways might hide. Jamaica, captured from the Spanish in 1655, was an altogether different proposition. An island of more than 4,200 square miles, Jamaica is a great deal larger than Barbados, and the island's heavily forested mountainous heart would prove a tempting destination for freedom seekers and a secure base for the Maroon communities they formed there. A decade later, in 1663, Charles II awarded territory south of the Chesapeake colonies to the lords proprietors of the Carolinas, and this land grant covered an area that was as much as 500 times larger than Barbados. Like Jamaica, this region featured heavily forested and initially inaccessible interior areas. First Jamaica and later South Carolina would develop plantation complexes and enslaved populations far larger than those of Barbados. It was not just the large size of a potentially rebellious enslaved population that frightened White planters in these colonies, but also the mountains, forests and unsettled frontier regions of these new colonies, which could provide refuge for runaways and bases for rebels. In both colonies but especially in Jamaica, the existence of Maroon communities of escaped enslaved people constituted a major threat to the survival and the success of planters.[35]

In 1684 Jamaica developed a Slave Code modelled on the Barbados code. Six years later South Carolina's Slave Code was in turn based on the new Jamaican law. Thus the legal systems of these three key English plantation slave systems had much in common. The process began early, and the governor of Jamaica in 1664, Thomas Modyford, a recent arrival from Barbados, signed into law a slave code that was an almost word-for-word copy of the Barbados code.[36] Jamaica's 1684 Slave Code echoed the Barbados code's provisions relating to runaways, amending them only slightly to suit the local situation. For example, Jamaica's larger size led the island's assembly to limit the mileage fees that the captors could charge enslavers for returning their runaways.[37]

---

[35] Charles II's 1663 grant to the lords proprietors gave them control of what would later become North Carolina, South Carolina and part of Georgia. See D. W. Fagg Jr, 'Sleeping not with the king's grant: a rereading of some proprietary documents, 1663–1667', *North Carolina Historical Review*, xlviii (1971), 171–85. For the English conquest of Jamaica see Dunn, *Sugar and Slaves*, pp. 149–87.

[36] 'For the Better Ordering and Governing of Negro Slaves', 2 Nov. 1664, Acts Passed by the Governor, Council and Assembly of Jamaican Colonial Office and Predecessors', Jamaica, Acts, National Archives, CO 139/1, fol. 66–9. I am grateful to Prof. Vincent Brown for sharing his copy of this law.

[37] 'Act for the Better Ordering of Slaves', in *The Laws of Jamaica, Passed by the Assembly, and Confirmed by His Majesty in Council, April 17, 1684* (London, 1684), p. 141. For a discussion of the transmission of the Barbados law to Jamaica see Rugemer, 'The development of mastery and race', pp. 444–9.

But, as Jamaica and South Carolina grew into far larger slave societies than Barbados, their assemblies went beyond Barbadian precedents. Jamaica's revised Slave Code of 1696 began with an acknowledgement that the rebellion of runaways who joined large and dangerous Maroon communities 'hath proved the ruin and destruction' of many Whites, and the newly revised code was aimed against their 'bloody and inhuman Practices'. Savage violence against runaways was sanctioned by Jamaican lawmakers who offered a reward of £5 to any White man and 40 shillings and a badge of honour to any enslaved person who 'shall kill or take any rebellious Slave or Slaves'.[38] Whites and those who served them were not just exempted from punishment for murdering freedom seekers, but were now lauded and rewarded for their actions. Local White officials were empowered to raise hunting parties to locate the 'Haunt, Residence, or hiding Place of any Runaway Slaves', and the law required the owners of any runaways captured to pay 40 shillings for anyone captured alive and 20 shillings 'for every Slave killed'. Whites who harboured or concealed runaways faced a very large fine of £100, a sum that was possibly more than the cost of an enslaved person. A number of the law's provisions dealt with the owners of small boats and the captains of larger vessels, recognizing that, unlike Barbados, Jamaica was relatively close to other islands and attracted more mercantile and naval vessels, making escape by sea more likely.[39]

The South Carolina Assembly first addressed freedom seekers in 'An Act Inhibiting the Trading with Servants or Slaves' (1686), which ended with a provision addressing White indentured servants who absconded, before declaring it illegal for 'any negroe or negroes, or other slave, upon any pretence whatsoever, to travel or go abroad, from his or their masters or mistresses house … without a note'. Any White person who took into custody an enslaved person absent from their home without proper authorization was empowered 'to chastise and correct' the freedom seeker before returning them.[40] Then, in 1690 the South Carolina Assembly passed its own 'Act for the Better Ordering of Slaves', a Slave Code modelled on Jamaica's. Although this law replicated a good deal of the earlier Barbados and Jamaica statutes, there were some differences, including the recognition that runaways – and the enslaved population at large – included both 'negro

---

[38] 'An Act for the Better Order and Government of Slaves' (passed 1696, confirmed 1699), in *The Laws of Jamaica, Pass'd by the Governour's, Council and Assembly in that Island, and confirm'd by the Crown* (London, 1716) pp. 225, 235.

[39] 'An Act for the Better Order and Government of Slaves', pp. 244, 238–9, 243.

[40] 'An Act Inhibiting the Trading with Servants or Slaves' (1686), in *The Statutes at Large of South Carolina; edited, under the Authority of the Legislature, by Thomas Cooper.* ii, *Containing the Acts from 1682 to 1716, Inclusive* (Columbia, S.C., 1837), p. 23.

or Indian' people. Freedom seekers who resisted recapture were ordered by the assembly to be 'severely whipped', to have their noses slit and their faces branded and potentially even to suffer 'death, or any other punishment'.[41] In an attempt to ensure that recaptured runaways could be identified and returned, the law required local officials who held runaways in custody to 'give an account in writing' to each meeting of the assembly 'of what negroes he hath in prison, with their marks and names, and the time they have been in his custody, and as near as he can learn, how long each hath been from his respective owners'.[42]

By the end of the seventeenth century, England's New World colonies had created the entirely new legal category of the runaway slave. Where London masters had made racial slavery real and present in the English capital, using newspapers and networks of those engaged in trade and empire to pursue and capture freedom-seeking enslaved runaways, escaping slavery became a crime in the plantation colonies, and the violent intimidation and punishment of the enslaved who risked escape was legitimated. The very bodies of the enslaved were treated both by enslavers and by colonial authorities as property. While the elopement of enslaved Black and free White servants in England was an annoying inconvenience for masters, the escape of the enslaved in the colonies represented a potentially calamitous theft of one of plantation society's most valuable forms of property. Thus colonial laws and social practices had evolved quickly to safeguard planters against the loss of their property in bound labourers and to punish any who sought to escape and those who might harbour them.

---

[41] 'An Act for the Better Ordering of Slaves' (1690), in *The Statutes at Large of South Carolina; edited under Authority of the Legislature, David J. McCord*: vii, *Containing the Acts relating to Charleston, Courts, Slaves, and Rivers* (Columbia, S.C., 1840), p. 343.

[42] 'An Act for the Better Ordering of Slaves', p. 346.

17. London precedents in New World contexts: the runaway advertisement in the colonies

While it is possible to trace the development of colonial laws against runaways, it is far harder to ascertain how escape from bound labour and the reactions that it prompted played out on a day-to-day basis. How did planters in the seventeenth-century southern and Caribbean colonies enforce local laws against escape? In the absence of printing presses and before the first colonial newspapers appeared, how was information about a runaway from one plantation conveyed to other plantations and communities, and how was information about the taking up of suspected runaways spread? It was one thing for the South Carolina Assembly to mandate the reporting and description of all incarcerated runaways, but in a sparsely settled frontier colony without good roads and easy communication it would not have been easy to enforce this law. It was not until 1732 that South Carolina gained its first printing press and newspaper, and the ability to distribute printed material around the colony. The same was true in the other plantation colonies: large planters would have attended meetings of the assembly or perhaps the Governor's Council, and many planters would have served on local courts and as militia officers, and presumably information about freedom seekers may have been spread on these occasions and through social interactions. But it was not until the first colonial newspapers in the early eighteenth century that published information about freedom-seeking enslaved runaways could be distributed widely in a standardized and recognizable format.[1] As we have seen, it was in seventeenth-century London, not the colonies, that newspaper advertisements and the existence of a network of merchants, ship captains and others invested in the colonial enterprise enabled slave-holders to create a system for the identification and recapture of enslaved freedom seekers.

The first newspaper in England's American and Caribbean colonies was the *New England Courant*, which appeared briefly in Boston in 1697, and the single surviving issue contains no advertisements. This was soon followed by the *Boston News-Letter*, first published in 1704. The *American Weekly Mercury* was Philadelphia's first newspaper, published from 1719, and in the same year the *Weekly Jamaica Courant* became the first newspaper in

---

[1] A. S. Salley, 'The first presses of South Carolina', *Proceedings and Papers of the Bibliographic Society of America*, ii (1907), 29–33.

the British Caribbean. Just over a decade later, in 1731, the *Barbados Gazette* appeared, followed one year later by the *South Carolina Gazette* and in 1736 by the *Virginia Gazette*.[2]

The earliest surviving runaway slave newspaper advertisement appeared in the *Boston News-Letter* on 26 June 1704:

> Ran-away from Capt. Nathanael Cary, of Charlston, on Saturday the 17th Currant, a well set middle sized Maddagascar Negro Woman, called Penelope, about 35 years of Age: With several Sorts of Apparel; one whereof is a flowered damask Gown; she speaks English well. Whoever shall take up said Negro Servant, and her convey to her above-said Master, shall have sufficient Reward.

Cary did not specifically identify Penelope as enslaved, although that was probably her status. The newspaper's first advertisement to identify freedom seekers as enslaved was published one year later. William Pepperil of Maine advertised for 'a Negro Man-Slave named Peter, aged about 20, speaks good English, of a pretty brown Complexion, [and a] middle stature'.[3] Colonial advertisements like these were virtually indistinguishable from the English newspaper advertisements published in London over the previous half-century. As each new colonial newspaper appeared, so too did runaway advertisements like these.

The correlation and connections between London and the earliest newspapers in the plantation colonies of the lower South and the Caribbean are clear. A case in point is Robert Baldwin, who commenced publication of the *Weekly Jamaica Courant* in 1718. The earliest surviving issue from July of that year contained six runaway slave advertisements for seven men and boys and four women and girls. Above Baldwin's name at the foot of the newspaper's final page were advertisements including one for 'a lusty Ebroe [*sic*] Negroe-Man named Jack, or a pale Black complexion, part of his Nose cut off', perhaps evidence that he had already endured mutilation as a punishment for absconding. Jack had eloped from the estate of William Pusey in Vere, perhaps taking advantage of the death of his owner, for the advertisement noted that 'a lean Calamante Negroe-Boy named Darby' had escaped too. This was not the first escape by Darby, who 'used to conceal himself about the Town', but he could be identified by his late owner's initials WP branded onto his body. Daniel Plowman advertised for an unnamed 'Negroe Girl' who had eloped from his pen in St Catherine parish

[2] C. S. Brigham, *History and Bibliography of American Newspapers, 1690–1820* (Worcester, Mass., 1947), i. 322–3, 327–9, 890–1, 1037–8, 1158–9; H. S. Pactor, *Colonial British Caribbean Newspapers: a Bibliography and Directory*, Bibliographies and Indexes in World History 19 (New York, 1990), pp. ix, 57, 18.

[3] 'Ran-away from his Master … Peter', *Boston News-Letter*, 10 Dec. 1705.

three months earlier and who was identified by his brand on her breast marking her with a 'D. a hart and P'.[4]

Although the earlier details of his life are uncertain, it appears that Robert Baldwin had been a Stationers' Company apprentice in London who completed his apprenticeship in 1716, and he may well have been a member of the Baldwin family, who were well-known London printers and book publishers. One member of this family, Richard Baldwin, had published the *Post Boy and Historical Account* and then the *Post Man and The Historical Account* near the Oxford Arms in Warwick Lane, London. The former newspaper had published at least one runaway slave advertisement, for a '*Negro Man* or *Blackamore*' named Caesar who had spent time in Barbados but then eloped in London in July 1695.[5] When Baldwin began publishing Jamaica's first newspaper he would have been very familiar with London's half-century of runaway slave advertisements.

It was not until 1731 that Samuel Keimer began working the first printing press in Barbados, and in that year the *Barbados Gazette* became the colony's first newspaper. Very few of the earlier issues of this newspaper survive: one exception is the fifth issue, dated 6 November 1731, which contained two advertisements. Neither of these was for freedom seekers, although runaway advertisements were soon evident in subsequent issues.[6] Keimer had been born in Southwark in London in 1689. He was apprenticed and then worked as a printer in London, and founded the *London Post* which he published in 1715–16 from King's Arms Court on Ludgate Hill. After moving to Philadelphia, Keimer established the *Pennsylvania Gazette*, in which he published numerous advertisements for indentured servants who had eloped: at this time bound White servants outnumbered enslaved

---

[4] 'RUN away from the Estate of William Pusey' and 'RUN away from Mr. Daniel Plowman', *Weekly Jamaica Courant*, 30 July 1718. This is the tenth issue of the *Weekly Jamaica Courant* (Kingston), and is the oldest surviving edition. It is held in the Burney Collection, British Library: all of the advertisements cited in this paragraph are from this issue. See also F. Cundall, 'The press and printers of Jamaica prior to 1820', *Proceedings of the American Antiquarian Society*, xxvi (1916), 290–354, at pp. 292–3; W. S. Reese, 'The first hundred years of printing in British North America: printers and collectors' (1990) <https://www.abaa.org/member-articles/the-first-hundred-years-of-printing-in-british-north-america-printers-and-c> [accessed 19 Dec. 2019]; Pactor, *Colonial British Caribbean Newspapers*, p. 57.

[5] 'Run away from *James Thomas* … Caesar', *Post Boy and Historical Account*, 13 Aug. 1695; R. Cave, 'Early printing and the book trade in the West Indies', *Library Quarterly*, xlviii (1978), 163–92, at p. 171; A. M. Fraas, 'The Calve's Head and early printing in Jamaica', *University of Pennsylvania Scholarly Commons*, June 2012 <https://repository.upenn.edu/cgi/viewcontent.cgi?article=1002&context=uniqueatpenn> [accessed 20 Dec. 2019].

[6] Issue 5 of the *Barbados Gazette* (Bridgetown) is held in the British Library's Burney Collection. See also Reese, 'The first hundred years of printing in British North America'; Pactor, *Colonial British Caribbean Newspapers*, p. 18.

workers and were the essential labour force for the young colony. Keimer then sold the newspaper to a young Benjamin Franklin and moved on to Barbados, where he published the *Barbados Gazette* between 1731 and 1738. In this newspaper Keimer introduced runaway slave advertisements to Barbados, such as one for 'a young Barbadian Negro-man named Tom'.[7]

Thomas Whitmarsh published the first newspaper and earliest runaway slave advertisements in South Carolina. He had known Benjamin Franklin in London and was taken on by Franklin as a journeyman printer in Philadelphia in the spring of 1730. A year later Franklin and Whitmarsh decided to take advantage of the financial incentives offered by the South Carolina Assembly to induce a printer to begin operating in Charleston. Whitmarsh travelled south and established the *South Carolina Gazette*.[8] One of the earliest issues of the *South Carolina Gazette*, published on 5 February 1732, contained several advertisements including one for the sale of 'Forty-two choice Negroes' and other chattel from the estate of John Godfrey.[9] Two weeks later the newspaper published South Carolina's first runaway slave advertisement:

> RUN away from her Master's Service, since Christmas last, a Pawpaw Negro Woman named Jenny, formerly belonging to the Estate of Mr. Giles Cooke, Deceased, being a lusty Woman about 30 years of Age, having blue Bays Clothes. Whoever brings the said Negro to her Master, in order for Sale, shall have 40s. Reward, and reasonable Charges paid, by John Mortimer in Christ Church Parish.[10]

Colonists with or without enslaved servants travelled regularly to London and England during the second half of the seventeenth century, and London's newspapers were shipped to North America and the Caribbean, where they were read and exchanged by colonists When newspapers

---

[7] 'A likely Young Negro Man', *Pennsylvania Gazette*, 2 Jan. 1729; *Barbados Gazette*, 3 May 1735. See also S. Keimer, *A Brand Pluck'd from the Burning; Exemplify'd in the Unparalleled Case of Samuel Keimer ...* (London, 1718), pp. 3, 75–7, 85, 88; C. Winton, 'Samuel Keimer' (2004), *Oxford Dictionary of National Biography* <https://doi.org/10.1093/ref:odnb/15258> [accessed 19 Dec. 2019]; and J. A. Harris, 'Order, disorder, and reorder: the paradox of creole representations in *Caribbeana*', in *Literary Histories of the Early Anglophone Caribbean*, ed. N. N. Aljoe, B. Carey and T. W. Krise (London, 2018), pp. 81–106.

[8] L. Lemay, *The Life of Benjamin Franklin*: ii, *Publisher, 1730–1747* (Philadelphia, Pa., 2006), pp. 26–8.

[9] 'On Wednesday the First of March ensuing, will be exposed to sale', *South Carolina Gazette*, 5 Feb. 1732. The *South Carolina Gazette* (Charleston) was South Carolina's first newspaper, printed from 1732 by Thomas Whitmarsh, the colony's first printer. See Salley, 'The first presses of South Carolina', pp. 28–32.

[10] 'RUN away from her Master's Service ... Jenny', *South Carolina Gazette*, 19 Feb. 1732.

finally appeared in the colonies many were printed by men who had lived and trained in London. Runaway slave advertisements would develop a distinctive form in the Caribbean and mainland North American colonies, but it is abundantly clear that a half-century of enslaved and bound people of colour who had sought freedom in London had initiated the creation in that city of the first runaway slave advertisements. It is not just that the London advertisements provided the templates for the first runaway notices in the earliest colonial newspapers. Rather, it is that London's runaway advertisements were essential for the regularization of ideas and practices that turned bound and enslaved people of colour into criminal fugitives and property. Where colonial slave laws had codified measures for the prevention and punishment of resistance by escape, the bids for freedom by enslaved people in London, many of them little more than children, had prompted the creation of the runaway slave advertisement and all that it represented. London's runaway advertisements had regularized the treatment of enslaved people as property to be taken up when they dared to challenge their status by escaping, creating a public discourse of slavery, escape and capture within the pages of the city's newspapers.

Epilogue: *King*

ABSENTED from his Master's Service, a likely BLACK BOY, named KING, but sometimes calls himself JOHN KING, about sixteen Years of Age, and is somewhat paler than the generality of Negroes. Took with him a good Hat with a Silver Button and Loop, an old blue Frock and Waistcoat much worn and dirtied, Leather Breeches, and spotted Worsted Stockings. He left a new Livery behind him, probably that he might the better pass for a free Negroe; but it is not unlikely that he may change his Cloaths. It is supposed that he has an intention of going on board some Privateer or Letter of Marque. All Captains of Vessels or others, to whom he may apply, are requested to stop him, and send Information thereof to Mrs. Stevenson near Charing-Cross. Whoever apprehends and secures the said Negroe, or informs where he is, so that his Master may have him again, shall have One Guinea for their Trouble, and all reasonable Charges.

N.B. Whoever harbours or conceals him will be prosecuted.

The Public Advertiser, 13 April 1762

It is perhaps not surprising that Benjamin Franklin helped introduce both newspapers and runaway slave advertisements to some of England's plantation colonies. Between 1724 and 1726 Franklin had completed his apprenticeship as a printer in London, and once back in Philadelphia he began editing the *Pennsylvania Gazette*. Notices for runaways comprised about one quarter of the advertisements published by Franklin and as such represented a significant source of his income.[1] By the time that Franklin returned to London in 1757 his publishing business had helped to make him a wealthy man, and he and his son William were accompanied by two enslaved servants named Peter and King. On at least two occasions King escaped, and both of these attempts prompted the Franklins to place newspaper advertisements in London's *Public Advertiser*.[2]

---

[1] D. Waldstreicher, 'Reading the runaways: self-fashioning, print culture and confidence in slavery in the eighteenth-century mid-Atlantic', *William and Mary Quarterly*, 3rd series, lvi (1999), 243–71, at p. 250.

[2] 'ABSENTED from his Master's Service, a likely BLACK BOY, named KING', *Public Advertiser*, 13 April 1762. An earlier advertisement had appeared two months earlier: see 'ABSENTED from his Master's Service, a likely black BOY, named King', *Public Advertiser*, 16 Feb. 1762.

The runaway slave advertisement had come full circle. This mechanism for the recovery of enslaved people who had escaped would eventually create the largest and richest resource for the study of resistance by escape in England's colonies and then in the United States. But it had been invented in London, where it was used for half a century before the first colonial newspapers began printing runaway advertisements. More than a century after London's first such notices appeared, the most famous of all colonial newspaper editors and printers did not hesitate to write and publish his own runaway slave advertisement in a London newspaper. A year earlier Benjamin had written to his wife, Deborah, that King had been 'of little Use, and often in Mischief', but what was an annoyance to the Franklins may have been 'good trouble' for King. The Franklins' advertisement noted that the young man had already rejected the single name imposed upon him, and he 'calls himself JOHN KING'. Only sixteen years old, John King walked in the footsteps of the many enslaved people who been brought to London since the mid seventeenth century and had asserted their independence and sought freedom by escaping.[3] Although Peter returned to Philadelphia with Franklin, there is no further mention of John King. We do not know whether he secured his freedom, but we do know that he was one of the many bound and enslaved Black Londoners who, for more than a century, had asserted their freedom in London.

[3] B. Franklin to D. Franklin, London, 27 June 1760, in *The Papers of Benjamin Franklin*: ix, *January 1, 1760 through December 31, 1761*, ed. L. W. Labaree (New Haven, Conn., 1966), pp. 174–5. For more on King's escape see S. P. Newman, 'Freedom-seeking slaves in England and Scotland, 1700–1780', *English Historical Review*, cxxxiv (2019), 1136–68, at pp. 1140–1.

Index

Printed in the USA
CPSIA information can be obtained
at www.ICGtesting.com
JSHW071128220324
59632JS00004B/4